CM

Church Plate

of the

Diocese of Chester

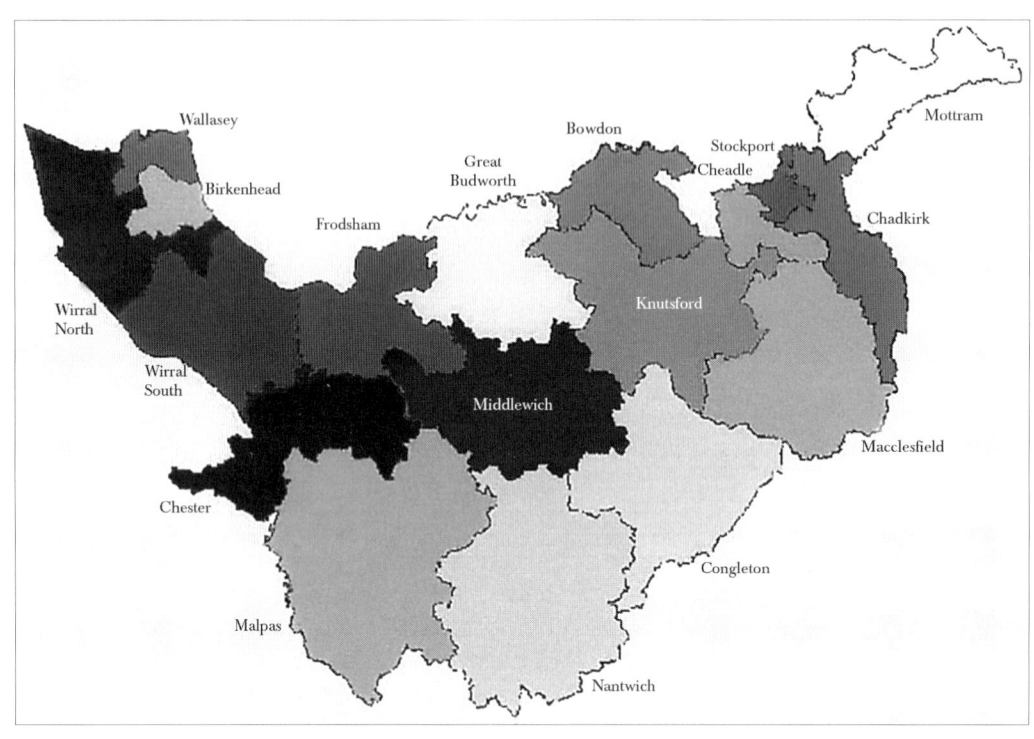

Map of the Diocese of Chester showing the deaneries.
Reproduced by kind permission of the Chester Diocesan Board of Finance

CHURCH PLATE
OF THE
DIOCESE OF CHESTER
(to 1837)

Maurice H. Ridgway
B.A., F.S.A.

edited by
Michael Sherratt

Phillimore

2008

Published by
PHILLIMORE & CO. LTD
Chichester, West Sussex, England
www.phillimore.co.uk

© Maurice H. Ridgway, 2008

ISBN 978-1-86077-476-8

Printed and bound in Great Britain

Principal books on silver by Maurice H. Ridgway
Chester Goldsmiths from early times to 1726
Chester Silver 1727-1837
Chester Silver 1837-1962 with special reference
to the Chester Plate Duty Books 1784-1840
Church Plate of the St Asaph Diocese

With Philip T. Priestley
The Compendium of Chester Gold & Silver Marks 1570-1962

Dedication

Dedicated to Sandy Campbell and Michael Sherratt
for their hard work in bringing this book to publication

and to

the Clergy of the Diocese, past and present,
in which Maurice and his father served their entire ministries

Contents

Preface	ix
Foreword by the Bishop of Chester	xi
A note from the Editor	xiii
List of Plates	xv
Introduction	xvii
I The Survey	1
II The Plates	104/05

Appendices
1 – Abbreviations	181
2 – Makers' Marks 1697-1837 from Grimwade	182
3 – Makers' Marks 1570-1962 from The Compendium	188
4 – Makers' Marks, Provincial, Unascribed, Foreign and Indistinct	192
5 – List of Plate in Parishes	199
6 – Pieces on Permanent Display in the Ridgway Gallery in the Grosvenor Museum, Chester	212
7 – List of Parishes and their Plate	214
Bibliography	231

Preface

The initial plan was to arrange the Diocese into Rural Deaneries, but this was frustrated by the frequent transfer of parishes to new Rural Deaneries and it was decided to arrange the parishes in alphabetical order, making it far easier for the wider public, with the hope that a parish would not be transferred to another Diocese as has happened in other areas in the past.

No accurate or authentic record has been done with the exception of the churches of the City of Chester by T. Stanley Ball, published in 1907, but since his time a great many changes have taken place. Many of these City churches have been made redundant and some have been demolished, their plate distributed and in a few cases lost or sold. The task of tracing this has been quite difficult.

This survey covers the plate remaining until 1837 and has taken over fifty years to complete. This has been possible with the help, almost without exception, of the clergy and wardens, and by many friends. I have been able to see almost all the silver described. The loan of photographs has helped to illustrate the book, but most have been taken by the author, often under difficult conditions – especially when kept in a bank.

Lastly I would like to put on record the great help given me in preparing the manuscript by Beryl Richards of Rhydycroesau.

Maurice H. Ridgway

Foreword

by the Bishop of Chester
the Rt Revd Dr Peter Forster

Maurice Ridgway's ministry as a priest was served wholly in the Diocese of Chester, in four of its historic parishes, most particularly in Bunbury (1949-62) and Bowdon (1962-83). He was also an Honorary Canon of Chester Cathedral. He is recalled as a faithful pastor, a true friend, and a most distinguished man of learning. Each of the parishes in which he served thrives today, both honouring their rich traditions and heritage yet also adapting to the needs of a new century.

Canon Ridgway loved old silver, sacred and secular, but he took a particular delight in working on this authoritative account of the silver in the Diocese of Chester. Some years before his death I was able to discuss the project with him, and his childlike enthusiasm sat easily with a measured judgement.

Church silver has a practical as well as an aesthetic purpose. At the heart of Christian worship is a sacramental meal, which is traced back to Jesus' final meal with his disciples. It involves eating and drinking, from a common loaf and a common cup. The use of precious metal discourages the transmission of infection, and allows for easy cleaning. It also encourages a worshipper to glimpse the precious gift which is received in a humble form. How appropriate that over the centuries the finest gifts of the silversmith have been demonstrated in the Church's plate. It witnesses to the beauty of holiness.

This comprehensive book will be a great blessing to all who wish to know about the historic church plate of the Diocese which nurtured him, and in which he served such a distinguished ministry. It is a fitting tribute to a very fine Priest and Scholar.

+ Peter Cestr.
Bishop of Chester

A note from the Editor

The reader will have noted in the Preface that Maurice had been working on this survey for over fifty years. This takes us back to an entirely different world, where a survey like this would have been undertaken as an academic and antiquarian enterprise, with only passing acknowledgement to the monetary value of the pieces being researched. This is not to say that security of plate was ignored, but it was of a much lower priority than it was to become, with the value of much church plate now posing many problems on the incumbents and wardens of all parishes. Maurice acknowledges this and the help given by so many of the clergy.

My first contact with this work was late in the year 2000, when Maurice sent me a batch of the typescript for checking, and over the next twelve months batches of copy came and went. There then followed a pause while Maurice turned his energies to completing *The Compendium of Chester Gold & Silver Marks 1570 to 1962*, his joint enterprise with Philip Priestley, which he saw through the proofing stage before he died.

In the latter part of 2004 the typescript, by now completely retyped and much modified from its original state, came back to me, along with some of Maurice's files, to be prepared for publication.

With some minor alterations the work is as Maurice wrote it, except for the section on the Chester City Churches, which has been slightly modified to make it a little more narrative and to avoid repetition of some of the history surrounding the movement of parishes and plate. All measurements are as Maurice recorded them, in eighths, quarters, fifths and tenths of inches, and the weights of pieces, unless recorded as scratch weights, have been left as written, some in Troy, some in avoirdupois, but in all probability the majority in the latter. The numbering scheme for Chester makers' marks as set out in The Compendium has been adopted in this work.

A number of parishes and chapels have been omitted from the survey. From Maurice's notes it is evident that the pieces concerned had been examined and recorded, but the relevant copy was clearly marked 'not to be published', and a trawl through Maurice's notes threw no light on this instruction. I feel that little will be gained from speculating on it.

Maurice has already acknowledged the assistance of clergy, wardens and friends, and my role in the work could not have been completed without help from a number of people whom I would like to thank:

Lord Leverhulme's Charitable Trust and The Goldsmiths' Company for generous financial support; Faber & Faber Ltd, London, for permission to use the Grimwade numbers from *London Goldsmiths 1697-1837, their marks and lives* by Arthur G. Grimwade; Antique Collectors' Club, Woodbridge, for permission to use the Compendium numbers from *The Compendium of Chester Gold & Silver Marks 1570 to 1962* by Maurice H. Ridgway and Philip T. Priestley; Chester Diocesan Board of Finance for permission to reproduce the map of the diocese; Peter Boughton of the Grosvenor Museum, Chester for information about church plate in the Ridgway Gallery; Peter Bamford of Cheshire Record Office and Derek Nuttall of Chester Archaeological Society for help with bibliographical references; Simon Davidson for helping with the Richardsons and for making the arrangements with the publishers; Nicholas Shaw of Petworth whose work on the date letters at York mirrors that done by Maurice in series 4 of the Chester date letters; Sandy Campbell for advice, the loan of records, friendship and hospitality; Philip Priestley for reading the proofs and for all the work he did to simplify the appendices and make them into a valuable archive; Candice Reeves, my daughter Sarah Wilson, and my son John Sherratt who all came to my rescue when computer problems seemed insurmountable; and my wife Julia, who has put up with my long absences in the office over a long time.

I regard my work on this book as my personal tribute to Maurice Ridgway. He was my parish priest and became a good friend. He assisted at our wedding in the neighbouring parish of St Mary, Rostherne, and over the years we enjoyed many discussions teasing out information about Chester silver.

I am very grateful for the opportunity to help bring this book to fruition.

Michael Sherratt

List of Plates

between pp.104 and 105

Frontispiece: Map of the Diocese of Chester showing the deaneries

1. Chester Cathedral: Chalice, London 1496/97
2. Chester Cathedral: Marks on chalice, London 1496/97
3. Chester Cathedral: Communion cup
4. Chester Cathedral: Maker's mark TD on communion cup and on paten covers
5. Chester Cathedral: Two paten covers
6. Chester Cathedral: The arms of Bridgman on front of paten cover
7. Chester Cathedral: Two stand patens, London 1662/63
8. Chester Cathedral: Pair of flagons, London 1662/63
9. Chester Cathedral: Maker's mark on one of flagons
10. Chester Cathedral: Alms dish, London 1673/74
11. Chester Cathedral: Maker's mark on alms dish
12. Chester Cathedral: Pair of candlesticks, London 1678/79
13. Chester Cathedral: Pair of alms plates, Chester 1737/38 with mark of Richard Richardson II
14. Chester Cathedral: Communion cup, London 1685/86
15. Chester Cathedral: Engraving on foot of communion cup
16. Chester Cathedral: Dean's verge; Canon's verge
17. Chester Cathedral: Engraving on top of Dean's verge
18. Chester Cathedral: Engraving on top of Canon's verge
19. Chester Cathedral: Head of mitred mace, London 1787/88
20. Chester Cathedral: Strainer spoon, London 1691/92
21. Chester Cathedral: Communion cup, possibly Swiss
22. Chester Cathedral: Chalice and cover, possibly Dutch
23. Chester Cathedral: Coat of arms engraved underneath chalice
24. Chester Cathedral: Communion cup and cover, London 1678
25. Chester Cathedral: Alms box, London 1677/78
26. Astbury: Mark of possibly William Faudrey on communion cup
27. Astbury: One of pair of flagons, London 1716/17
28. Aston: Medieval chalice
29. Aston: Engraving of St John on foot of medieval chalice
30. Bowdon: Alms dish, London 1775/76
31. Bowdon: One of pair of flagons, London 1775/76
32. Bowdon: Pair of communion cups and salver, London 1775/76
33. Bunbury: Pair of flagons, London 1735/36; pair of alms plates, London 1747/48; stand paten, London 1716/17; communion cup, London 1632/33; paten, Chester late 16th/17th century
34. Bunbury: Mark of Griffith Edwardes I on paten
35. Carrington: Flagon, London 1688/89

36. Carrington: Mark of Magdalen Feline on communion cup, London 1759/60
37. Chester: Bishop of Chester's private chapel: Communion cup possibly by Richard Richardson I, Chester
38. Chester St Bridget: Flagon, London 1697
39. Chester St Bridget: Mark of Hugh Roberts, London 1697, on pair of plate patens
40. Chester St Michael: Communion cup, Chester *c.*1570, by William Mutton
41. Chester St Michael: Communion cup by Edward South, London 1635/36
42. Chester St Peter: Flagon, London 1719/20; stand paten, London 1708/09; communion cup, Chester 1762/63
43. Church Minshull: Mark of John Bingley of Chester on communion cup
44. Daresbury: Stand paten, London 1654/55
45. Daresbury: Flagon, London 1731/32
46. Daresbury: Mark of Richard Richardson II of Chester, and inscription under stand paten
47. Daresbury: Communion cup, London 1773/74
48. Daresbury: Mark of Richard Morson and Benjamin Stephenson on communion cup
49. Eccleston: Communion cup, late 17th century
50. Eccleston: Flagon, London 1746/47
51. Great Barrow: Communion cup and paten cover
52. Great Barrow: Flagon, London 1718/19
53. Hargrave: Maker's mark on beaker, possibly Dutch
54. Hargrave: Beaker, *c.*1700, possibly Dutch
55. Hargrave: Paten, *c.*1700, possibly Dutch
56. Malpas: Communion cup and paten cover, York 1674/75
57. Malpas: One of pair of flagons, London 1795/96
58, 59. Malpas: Details of handle of flagon
60. Malpas: One of pair of candlesticks, Sheffield 1809/10
61. Middlewich: Communion cup, London 1608/09
62. Middlewich: Flagon, London 1732/33; communion cup, London 1667/68; flagon, London 1739/40
63. Mobberley: Communion cup, London 1571/72
64. Nantwich: Maker's mark on one of pair of flagons, London 1659/60
65. Nantwich: Communion cup and paten cover, London 1604/05
66. Overchurch: Communion cup, London 1618/19
67. Pott Shrigley: Flagon, London 1711/12
68. Stockport St Mary: Communion cup and paten cover, London 1580/81
69. Swettenham: Communion cup, Chester 1704/05; stand paten, London 1713/14
70. Tarporley: Communion cup, London 1711/12
71. Tarporley: Flagon, London 1711/12
72. Tarporley: Chalice, possibly Italian
73. Tarporley: Detail of stem of chalice
74. Tarvin: Flagon, London 1776/77
75. Wincle: Communion cup, London 1645/46

Introduction

The magnificent 13th-century chalice found near Dolgellau in 1890 along with a paten (now in the National Museum of Wales) is an example of the form of chalice used before the Church in this country withheld the chalice from the laity at the administration of the Sacrament. It dates from when Edward I and his court were stationed at Chester preparing for the invasion of Wales. A Latin inscription under the foot of the chalice shows that 'Nicholas de Herefordie' made it. At about the same time there was at Chester a goldsmith referred to as Nicholas 'dictus magnus' – Nicholas 'called great' – who worked in the city near Eastgate Street.

Shortly after the time of Edward I, small 'massing chalices' were introduced which held enough wine for the priest alone. These smaller chalices continued to be used until the Reformation and the reign of Edward VI, when 'massing chalices' gave way to communion cups.

Numerous early wills mention these smaller chalices, given at a time when a priest was paid to pray for the donor, his good estate if still alive, and for the welfare of his soul if dead. Often, when a priest died, a funeral chalice and paten in pewter were placed in his grave, as can be seen at St Asaph Cathedral.

Richard Starkey of Oulton (1527) wrote in his will: 'I bequeath towards the maynteyning of devyne service at the chapell or orratorye of St Savoyr off Stretton a chalice gilt with these words graven in the upper part of the said chalice on the owt side Ex Rici Starky.' Late in 1559 Robert Booth of Dunham bequeathed a 'silver chalice to Bowdon with a pattern to be contynually prayed for their', but it is not known whether his wishes were allowed.

The Diocese of Chester had been established in 1541, separated from the Diocese of Lichfield and Coventry. The Benedictines had been turned out of their church at Chester and the abbey had become a cathedral, and elsewhere in the diocese similar changes had taken place. The last warden of the Collegiate Church of Secular Canons at Bunbury had become the first vicar.

In February 1548 the Sheriffs listed all the church plate, jewels, bells and lead, and had issued certificates to parishes to prevent them from selling any of these valuables within a year of their commission. This did not stop Sir Piers Leigh at Disley claiming the chalice and bells there as 'his own and not His Majesty's'. At Brereton the broken bell was sold for the necessary repairs to the church in order to lead the roof and 'cover the aisle, glaze the windows and deck the church with stories', but this still left the church with a chalice and a paten and three bells. Rondall Myshall of Holgrave took the chalice from Minshall without the permission of the parish and refused to return it and, at Malpas, Kathlyn Edge removed the chalice presented by the curate, and refused to give it back.

Although throughout the ancient Hundreds of Northwich, Macclesfield, Bucklow, Eddisbury, Wich Malbank and Wirral at the time of the Reformation the Sheriffs listed 117 chalices (and accompanying patens), only one medieval chalice and paten have survived in the diocese – at Aston near Runcorn, unmarked, but 14th century. There is a medieval chalice at the cathedral, but it was given by the family of Dean Darby in 1955. The foot bears the London hallmark for 1496/97, the leopard's head crowned and a maker's mark as yet unidentified.

In 1553 the covetous hands of the Royal Commissioners removed and sold a large quantity of cathedral goods, leaving only two gilt chalices with patens, weighing 37 ounces (for the continuing use of the cathedral). No one knows what happened to the rest after it was sold by the Commissioners to prop up the State's finances.

What is believed to be one of the oldest post-Reformation cups, and which might belong to the reign of Edward VI, is an unmarked cup at Gawsworth, 6½ inches high; the accompanying plate paten, also unmarked, is 4½ inches in diameter. The cup has a gilded band of inscription which is continued on the paten. The words are in Latin, and Charles Oman pointed out that they follow the Vulgate rather than the later version of Beza which had come to this country and was greatly influenced by Calvin. The maker might have been William Mutton of Chester, as it is very like the cup and plate paten recorded in the churchwardens' accounts of 1570 at Chester (Holy and Undivided Trinity) and now removed to the new church at Blacon.

A cup dated 1567 is to be found at Thornton in Wirral. Runcorn and Handley both have unmarked cups, although the date was usually inscribed on the extended foot. A number of Elizabethan cups have lost their paten covers, but there is a group of cups and patens in the St Asaph Diocese which seem to have been made in Chester, and is shown in *Church Plate of the St Asaph Diocese* as belonging to Group B. These are at Bodfari, Bryneglwys, Cilcain, Denbigh, Gwaenysgor, Llandrillo, Llangwm Dinmael, Llannefydd and possibly Trelawnyd.

The Chester goldsmiths John Lingley and Griffith Edwardes I provided silver for Baddiley and Bunbury respectively, where only plate patens have survived. There is a very similar plate paten at Alderley Edge, but the mark cannot be deciphered. At Woodchurch there is a communion cup with the mark of J. Lingley, but an inscription and the date 1625 were added to the side of the bowl some years after both John Lingleys had died.

At Pott Shrigley there is a paten cover with the date 1576 and the incised mark PC, once thought to be the maker's mark of Peter Conway of Chester, but now believed to stand for Pott Chapel (by which it is sometimes known).

Cups of this period made in London can be seen at Mobberley (1571/72), Davenham (1570/71) and Stockport St Mary (1580/81). There was a cup and paten at Siddington dated 1597 on the cover paten, but it was stolen in 1792 and never recovered. At the neighbouring parish of Marton, theft perhaps encouraged the parish to purchase a new cup in 1597; it is still there. An Elizabethan cup at Cotebrooke, a Victorian church linked with Tarporley, was given to the church along with other silver from a church in Dorset.

Theft from and desecration of churches is an age-old problem. As early as 1439/40, at Daresbury, Richard Bannister was accused of coining at Nantwich and of entering Daresbury Church and robbing it of 'a booke called a masse book worth ten marks and thrown a chalice with the body of Christ exhibited thereon to the ground and taken a spoon value 2s'. Theft of plate continued throughout the diocese as elsewhere.

The relative absence of plate in the diocese dating from the start of the 17th century is probably due to the fact that the churches already had enough to meet their needs. There were still places which required larger communion cups, especially in those areas where the trend towards puritanism was strong, but they remained within the Established Church. Examples of this can be seen at Nantwich where the church received a large cup with a bucket-shaped bowl made in London in 1604/05 and a paten cover to match. At Macclesfield there are two cups with paten covers (1624/25); at Bunbury a communion cup of 1632/33; at Acton (once the parish church of Nantwich) a communion cup of 1633/34; at Audlem nearby a cup of 1635/36; at Cheadle an early 17th-century cup by the Manchester goldsmith RW, perhaps Robert Welshman, and at Wincle there is a Commonwealth cup of 1645/46.

The churchwardens' accounts at Prestbury record that in 1572 they paid 11s 2d for a communion cup, that it was made in Manchester and that in 1573 they received 2s 8d from the goldsmith for 'overweight' of the communion cup, showing that it was replacing an earlier cup. The cup no longer exists, but a new communion cup and cover were bought in 1628 at a cost of £7 5s.

The mid-17th century saw the outbreak of the Civil War. At Nantwich Alice Wilbraham bequeathed a communion cup of 1633/34, and in 1639 Elizabeth Davenport and Margaret Woodnoth left £26 for 'two flagons and a silver paten', but these were not provided until the end of the Commonwealth and are dated 1659/60. It would seem that, for a paten, trustees at the time provided a secular dish commonly referred to as a sweetmeat dish, a provision made in a number of churches which seems to have been caused by losses during the Civil War. When dated they appear to be earlier than the time of provision. At nearby Whittington, just across the border in the Diocese of Lichfield, a similar dish of 1631/32 was given by John Thurston in 1660. Two others in the Diocese of St Asaph, at Llannefydd (1639/40) and at Efnechtyd (1629/30); one in the Diocese of Bangor, at Llandudwen (1636/37) and one, undated, at Wrenbury in the Diocese of Chester.

The few cups of Commonwealth date that survive are of wine cup shape – a small bowl standing on a tall baluster stem. In many cases they appear to have been used as domestic wine cups before being given to the church, probably as a memorial to one who had used them. The cup at Chelford is of this form, date 1652/53, but it was given by Mrs Elizabeth Baskerville in 1677. It could have been her husband's favourite wine cup, and probably came to the church to supply a need, as well as a memorial of him.

At Brereton there is a similar, large, cup, 9½ inches high, given by William Smithwick. At Marple there is a tall wine cup 9¾ inches high, with the name of the donor accompanied by a fine coat of arms and an inscription: 'Huic Templo Alicia Johannis Pimlott de Marple Armigeri Relictae Dono Dedit 1762', but this inscription is misleading, for the cup was made in 1629/30. There is another similar cup at Pott Shrigley dated 1622/23.

The city of Chester, which suffered considerably in the Civil War, gave a large quantity of silver (much of it drawn by Randle Holme before it was handed over) to pay for the disliked Irish troops and for the Chester-minted coinage. Although the city fathers (and perhaps the cathedral) contributed to this sacrifice, several city churches – among them St Michael's and Holy and Undivided Trinity – seem to have retained their Elizabethan silver made by William Mutton, the Chester goldsmith. At Pott Shrigley a wine cup similar to those mentioned above to renew or supplement what they already had, is dated 1622/23, but at St John without the Northgate the wine cup of 1641/42 was given in 1777 by Alderman Thompson, and St John the Baptist Church has one of 1633/34. The fashion for using these wine cups of domestic origin was short-lived in the diocese.

The Goldsmiths' Company at Chester managed to survive the Civil War and the siege, through the vision of Gerrard Jones and his young apprentice Peter Edwardes. By the time of the restoration of the King and the Church of England, there had emerged a strong Company who later produced some excellent silver for both Church and country, with an extended trade into North Wales and throughout the county. Little silver was provided during the Commonwealth, though some made in the latter years in London was supplied after the Restoration – at Sandbach a communion cup of 1656/57 and at Brereton a cup of 1653/54.

What happened to most of the silver at Chester Cathedral remains a mystery. If it was not confiscated it could have given rise to a firmly held belief that it had been hidden, a view held when the cathedral was drastically restored in the 19th century, and still held by some. It is hard to believe that the cathedral was without plate until 1662, when Dean Bridgman provided a new suite of silver, including two cups with plate patens. The cups survived until 1836 when Dean Anson sold them to Barnard's of London who supplied two other cups of a different pattern. The earlier patens remain, bearing the mark TD which presumably the cups would also have had. This view is strengthened by the survival of a cup with a bucket-shaped bowl and marked TD given by Dean Bridgman to Great Barrow where he had been rector. Although the two baluster flagons at the cathedral are of the ewer form, the cups with bucket-type bowls introduced at this time seem to have set a pattern for the Chester goldsmiths to follow until the end of the 17th century. This form is found throughout North Wales, at Dyserth, Llanarmon yn Ial and St

George (Ceygiddog) on cups by Nathaniel Bullen who also made a paten for Chester St Mary in 1638 and by Peter Pemberton who produced a cup for Shotwick about 1685.

This older form, bucket-shaped, was also used by other goldsmiths throughout the country, doubtless being asked for by incumbents or parishioners as being more convenient for larger congregations. Thomas Mangy of York produced a fine communion cup for Malpas (1674/75) and there are London-made cups at Barthomley (1669/70 and 1676/77). At Lymm (1691/92) a narrow knop separates the bowl and stem, whilst at Prestbury the bottom of the bowl is treated with a band of ropework decoration.

The Diocese of Chester is rich in late 17th-century communion cups. The style began to change at the beginning of the 18th century when in 1711/12 Nathaniel Bullen introduced a bell-shaped bowl on a knopped stem for Waverton.

The vessels used for the Sacrament – the communion cup and paten – were generally of silver, but the flagons, which were usually of pewter, may owe their survival to a reluctance to change to silver or to a lack of donors willing to give a silver flagon in someone's memory. The oldest surviving flagons in the diocese are at the cathedral, part of the refurbishing by Dean Bridgman in 1662. They are of ewer form (without lids) and one is unmarked, but this style was not taken up by other churches where either a plain tankard or an enlarged tankard (which became a flagon) was used.

There used to be a tankard (1677/78) at Wybunbury, given to the church by Thomas and Rhoda Delves, but it was sold in 1977 and passed into private ownership. Prestbury has a traditional flagon (1668/69) of extended tankard form; there are others at Lower Peover (1685/86), Carrington (1688/89) (once at Bowdon and now removed to Partington), and two 1701/02 once at Chester St Michael and now owned by the Grosvenor Museum, Chester.

There are two ewer-type jugs (1719/20) at Great Budworth and another, at Wrenbury, dated 1719 and made by John Lingard, was given to the church in Queen Victoria's Jubilee year. At Coddington there is a lidded jug by Richard Richardson I dated 1727/28 and at Eccleston a large beer jug made by John Berthelott in 1746/47, which serves as a flagon, was given in 1746. Similar jugs are at Harthill (1774/75), and Handley (1734/35) given in 1747. A little later, in 1763/64, Boulton and Fothergill of Birmingham provided Frodsham with two classical lidded ewers, and among the interesting suite of silver at Disley are two identical lidded ewers which are unmarked. A similar suite at Burleydam is referred to in the diaries of Dr Samuel Johnson and Mrs Thrale when they visited the church in July 1774. The flagon was made in 1769/70 by Augustin Le Sage, a Huguenot goldsmith. His mark includes the gold cup, which was the shop sign he had used with his father in Suffolk Street, London. As little is known of his work, these pieces are of especial interest. A ewer, given to Stoak Parish Church by John Grace of Whitby in 1772 was made by John Dare in 1771/72, but was sold to the Grosvenor Museum, Chester in 1995. A ewer at Burton (1809) was stolen in 1991.

Stand patens came into use either as patens or as credence patens on which the bread could be placed and cut before being transferred to the paten for consecration. In certain parts of North Wales the flagon was consecrated and the wine transferred to the communion cup, which may have happened to the bread when still on the stand paten. A knife remains, of later date, at Rug (see Ridgway, *Church Plate of the St Asaph Diocese*, p.242). One of the earliest stand patens is at Brereton (1660/61), but they are also to be found at Aston near Runcorn (1675/76), Barthomley (1681/82), Carrington (from Bowdon, now at Partington) (1688/89), Birkenhead Priory (1698/99), Congleton (1699/1700), Church Hulme (1700/01), Wybunbury (1702/03), Bebington (1704/05), a pair at Acton (1706/07) and one at Astbury (1707/08).

Large numbers of stand patens were provided in the diocese during the first half of the 18th century, whereas only eight have been recorded in the latter half.

A few salvers were introduced to serve the same purpose, as at Great Budworth (1766), Delamere (a late gift) (1768/69), Tattenhall (1767/68) and two at Bowdon (1775/76).

Distinguishing between alms dishes and plates has always been difficult. Generally speaking they denote vessels associated with money. *The Book of Common Prayer* of 1662 refers to the offertory as consisting of 'alms and oblations' as well as the prayers of the faithful, which are offered in the prayer for 'the Church militant here on earth'. The oblations here are the bread and wine, and the alms the collection which has been brought up to the altar and offered by the priest.

What would appear to be the earliest alms dish is at Prestbury, inscribed 'Prestbury alms Basyn 1586', but it is in fact Victorian (1883/84), though it may have been modelled from an older one; at Christleton a plain dish-like alms basin was given in Victorian times, but the date is 1595/96. At Chester St John the Baptist there is an alms dish made by Ralph Walley of Chester with the names of the wardens and the date 1683 inscribed on it. Stockport St Mary has a large dish dated 1674/75, 11½ inches in diameter, given by the son of a former rector of Stockport; at Bowdon there is an alms dish 18 inches in diameter of 1705/06. All these dishes seem to have been used for presenting the alms when they had been collected in smaller plates from the congregation. At other times they were placed upright in the centre of the altar where a cross is now placed. There were usually two of the smaller plates, many of them hardly distinguishable from domestic dinner plates: at Chester St Michael (1724/25) and Chester St John the Baptist (1735/36), Bunbury (1747/48), Tarporley (1737/38), Malpas (1742/43), Macclesfield (1758/59), Nantwich (*c.*1740), Grappenhall (1797). There are single examples at Chester St Peter (1736/37), Sandbach (*c.*1737), Warmingham (1786/87), Whitewell (1819/20) and Chester St Mary (1822). At Christleton a dish like an alms dish (1763/64) by Richard Richardson II is inscribed 'a gift to the altar'.

At Chester Cathedral the alms dish was stolen and replaced by another (diameter 18¾ inches) in 1673/74 and there are two plates with silver handles made by Richard Richardson I (1737/38). A little under 8 inches in diameter, they seem to be very small for a cathedral congregation but, in the absence of any other vessel for that purpose, the suggestion that they may have been used for collecting briefs at the end of the service is not ruled out.

The splendid suite of silver at Burleydam was given by Sir Lynch Cotton when the new church was opened in 1769. It consists of a communion cup, paten, a stand paten and a flagon, all made by Augustin Le Sage in 1769/70.

A suite of silver at Bowdon was provided by a Mr Oliver Bellefontaine from Dunham Massey Hall in 1759. It consisted of two silver cups and two salvers, one large, the other smaller, and two flagons. It was all stolen in 1774 and, not being recovered, was replaced by a similar suite in 1775 by John Carter II.

At Disley the interesting suite of silver was given to the church at the time when 'the old plate was exchanged for two ewers, a chalice and cover, and two oval plates, all nobly gilt' in 1769. These six pieces remain. One of the ewers is inscribed 'Morson & Stephenson, No. 98 Fleet Street Fect', but there are no other marks except EV in a rectangle, which is probably that of Edmund Vincent.

At Alsager there is a suite of a communion cup, plate paten, stand paten and a flagon given when the church was built in 1789. A smaller suite was provided by Sir John Chesshire at Halton, near Runcorn, who also donated a library there. This suite comprised a communion cup, a paten and a flagon, made by Thomas Tearle in 1731. A long inscription on the side of the flagon makes it abundantly clear who was the donor. A communion cup with paten cover, a flagon and an alms dish were given to Haslington near Crewe in 1811/12.

There are few examples of early candlesticks in the diocese, but those at the cathedral, dated 1678/79, are of particular interest. They were bought to replace those stolen which had formed part of the Dean Bridgman provision. At Malpas there is a pair of Sheffield-made candlesticks by Nathaniel Smith & Co. (1809/10).

Chester St Mary has an unusual flagon stand or ring. It was made by the Chester goldsmith Thomas Robinson in 1711/12 to accompany the new flagon made by Nathaniel Lock, and is recorded in the churchwardens' accounts.

Later gifts which came to the cathedral include a strainer spoon of 1691/92 given in 1869 by Bishop Jacobson. At Great Barrow a list of silver given to the church in 1888 by Mr Hugh Lyle Smyth of Barrowmore included a strainer spoon which has since disappeared. At the same time he also gave other pieces of silver which were antique, and one must assume that the spoon was also old. Unfortunately there are no descriptions of it. Chester St Mary was given an 18th-century mote spoon by Mrs Tarvin when the church was dedicated in 1887, and at Malpas there is a very small (though now broken) 'salt' spoon which may have been used for the same purpose. At the time of its dedication Mr Lowe, the Chester goldsmith, gave to Chester St Mary without the Walls, often referred to as Chester St Mary, Handbridge, some silver book corners which were put on the altar books, and might be listed as church silver.

Very little foreign silver is recorded in the Diocese of Chester and most of it seems to have come from gifts at a date much later than its manufacture, but at Hargrave there is an exception. A small beaker 3⅜ inches high (accompanied by a plate) has a single mark AT and an inscription in Latin taken from the Vulgate of Matthew v.6. The plate, with the AT mark struck twice, has an inscription also in Latin, offering the gift of vessels that they may be a fit commemoration of the love of Christ. The date on the beaker is 1700. The maker has not been traced, but it has been suggested that the pieces may be Dutch.

At the cathedral a communion cup given in 1903 is of Swiss origin, probably Payerne, and a ciborium given by Bishop Paget in 1919 is possibly Dutch. At Audlem there is a cup or ciborium and a wafer box which began life associated with the 18th-century German army, and most of the silver at Cholmondeley (private) chapel are late gifts and of foreign origin. At Nantwich a form of Apostle spoon given in 1883 bears the mark of Basle in Switzerland.

I
The Survey

CHESTER CATHEDRAL
CHRIST AND THE BLESSED VIRGIN MARY

1   CHALICE
A gilt chalice given to the Cathedral by the Darby family in 1955. It had been owned by Dean Darby who had purchased it from Lowe's of Chester. Its origin is unknown. Oman states that it belongs to his Group VIII and lists two others, one at Clifford Chambers in Gloucestershire and the other at West Drayton in Middlesex which are hallmarked like the Chester example, and 19 others in the same group which are not hallmarked.

The chalice is 6½ inches high with a small bowl and weighs 4 oz. The six-sided stem is divided by an ornate knop with six projecting facets. Below the stem are six panels, one of which has the figure of Christ crucified. There are six protruding flat feet. There are three marks: (i) Date letter T (cycle I), 1496/97, London; (ii) Leopard's head crowned; (iii) Maker's mark believed to be a grasshopper by Oman, a jug by Jackson, or perhaps a priest's hand in blessing by this author! (Plates 1, 2.)

References:
PSA, vol.XI, New Series, pp.207-08.
Jackson 1921, p.92.
Oman, p.301.

2   COMMUNION CUP
One of two communion cups, part of the Restoration silver of 1662 which were exchanged in 1839 for two contemporary communion cups (no. 26). In 1936 a Mr E.A. Ebblewhite of Epsom claimed to have found one of the original cups, and it was restored to the Cathedral by an anonymous donor. The maker's mark, TD, similar to that upon the paten covers which were retained (nos. 3 and 4), supports the cup's origin. The communion cup is gilt, 8½ inches high, with a plain almost bucket-shaped bowl, rim diameter 5¼ inches. The bowl is 5 inches deep with slightly sloping sides and everted moulded lip. The sides turn to a wide trumpet-shaped stem, curving sharply to a wide flange, diameter 5¼ inches. There is only one mark, that of the maker, punched immediately below the rim: TD, with five point mullet above and below, with tiny rings on either side of each pellet, within a square frame with clipped corners (compare no. 4, where the same mark is used in 1662/63). (See also Great Barrow no. 1 and Wybunbury no. 1.) (Plates 3, 4.)

3   PATEN COVER

Although the two gilt patens supplied in 1662/63 are not identical (see no. 4) they are by the same maker, TD.

A gilt paten cover diameter 6⅘ inches and 1½ inches high, weight 8 oz. The edge moulded ¾ inches and the depression so caused is abrupt and deep. It stands upon a spool-shaped stem. The foot is blocked and bears the arms of the Diocese of Chester and Bridgman surrounded by a wreath. On the edge is inscribed: 'Ecclesia Christi et beatiae Mariae Cestriae DDD'.

There are four marks: (i) Date letter Gothic E (cycle X), 1662/63, London; (ii) Lion passant guardant; (iii) Leopard's head crowned; (iv) Maker's mark TD (as on 2 and 4). (Plate 5.)

Reference:
Ball 1907, p.21. (Ball's description is not accurate in some details.)

4   PATEN COVER

A gilt paten cover, slightly under 5½ inches diameter with a border 9/10 inches wide, forms a shallow depression. It stands 1 1/10 inches high overall and rests on a compressed spool and foot which is blocked and carries an engraving of the arms of Bridgman. Weight 7 oz. (Plates 5, 6.)

5 & 6   STAND PATENS

A matching pair of gilt stand patens each weighing 19 oz.

Diameter 9⅕ inches with a 2-inch wide border with a single scribed line following the rim, forming a shallow depression. The paten stands 3 inches high and the stand is spool shaped. There is a scribed line at the top and bottom of the spool stem. The base, diameter 3 9/10 inches, is blocked and plain. Although part of the Restoration plate there is neither inscription nor coat of arms.

In a clear reference to one of the patens, the Barnard Day Book of 1839 records: 'Setting to rights 4 Patines, taking off one of the feet and replenishing as new'.

There are four marks on the border: (i) Date letter Gothic E (cycle X), 1662/63, London; (ii) Lion passant guardant; (iii) Leopard's head crowned; (iv) Maker's mark RN with a pellet between above a five-point star within a shaped shield. (Plate 7.)

7 & 8   FLAGONS

A matching pair of silver gilt flagons, from the original Restoration plate supplied by Bishop Hall, differing only in that one is slightly heavier than the other. The weights are inscribed on the base of each, 41.10 and 41.70 respectively.

Of ewer form with bulbous sides, each flagon is 12¼ inches high. The circular domed foot is separated from the body by a short stem in the form of a flattened ball. The neck is engraved with a winged cherub's head. The rim is shaped and moulded and the moulding continues round the lip rim. Beneath the lip are engraved the arms of Bishop Hall, who held office from 1662 to 1668 (argent three talbot heads couped gules, their tongues hanging out), impaling those of the Diocese (gules three mitres two and one or). Below the arms is the inscription: 'Georgius Hall Cestriae Ep [iscop] us Sacro Usui dedit dicavit'. The scroll handle is decorated at the thumb piece with an applied cherub and scrolls.

The flagons were sent to Barnard's for repair in 1839, and the firm's account books record that this included the engraving on the jugs. They also appear to have been gilded at the same time, as was the other plate.

One of the flagons is unmarked, but the other has four marks: (i) Lion passant guardant; (ii) Leopard's head crowned; (iii) Date letter Gothic E (cycle X), 1662/63, London; (iv) Maker's mark IN above a five-point star within a heart-shaped frame. (Plates 8, 9.)

References:
Ball 1907, p.20.
Richards, p.97.
Brocklehurst, no. 21, and plate VII.
Ridgway 1980, pp.95ff.

9 ALMS DISH

A large gilt alms dish provided to replace the one stolen and irreparably damaged by thieves who were apprehended in York in 1672.

The alms dish, 18¾ inches diameter, is formed with a single depression and a border 3½ inches wide with a moulded rim. On the centre of the plate is a representation of the sacred symbols in rays, probably engraved upon it in 1839 by Barnard's, who were paid for 'Setting to right a large round Dish'.

There are four marks: (i) Maker's mark TC, a motif (probably a fish) above and a fleur-de-lis below, in an ornamental shield; (ii) Leopard's head crowned; (iii) Lion passant guardant; (iv) Date letter Gothic Q (cycle X), 1673/74, London. (Plates 10, 11.)

References:
Cheshire Sheaf, 3rd series, vol. 32, 1937, p.13, no. 7043.
Burne, p.138.

10 & 11 CANDLESTICKS

Once believed to be part of the Restoration plate of 1662, but now firmly established as of 1678/79. Purchased to replace those stolen from the Cathedral in 1672.

A matching pair of altar candlesticks, each 12 inches high, with plain and flat socket top, 4 inches across, to hold a candle, diameter 1⅖ inches. Beneath this is a simple moulded support above a fluted stem which rests upon a wide sweeping base, each segment being subdivided by a double concave step, in all 5¹⁄₁₀ inches across. This in turn is supported by a short round stem resting upon a repeat octagonal foot, the upper two thirds repeating the subdivision of each section, but repeated twice.

On the stem are four very worn marks: (i) Date letter Gothic T (cycle X), 1678/79, London; (ii) Leopard's head crowned; (iii) Lion passant guardant; (iv) Maker's mark (indecipherable). (Plate 12.)

Reference:
Burne, p.134.

12 & 13   ALMS PLATES

An identical pair of collecting plates of plain circular form, each with a single depression 9/10 inch deep, diameter 7 4/5 inches and a rim a little over 1 inch wide with simple mouldings. Attached to this by scrolls is a plain pear-shaped handle, 3½ inches in length. The rim on one plate has been moulded near the handle. Weight of each is 15 oz. There is an inscription on the surface, 'The Gift of the pious Mrs Sarah Buckley to the Cathedral Church of Chester 1737'.

There are five marks: (i) Maker's mark RR adorsed within a shaped shield, Richard Richardson II Type 1 (also Richard Richardson I Type 6) (Compendium 7376); (ii) Lion passant guardant; (iii) Leopard's head crowned; (iv) Chester City coat; (v) Date letter script M (series 3), 1737/38, Chester. (Plate 13.)

References:
Brocklehurst, no. 49 and plate X.
Ridgway 1985, p.141.

14   COMMUNION CUP

A parcel gilt communion cup 8¼ inches high, weight 6 oz., with a 3¼-inch deep bell-shaped bowl, diameter 3½ inches. Engraved on the side is the sacred monogram IHS surrounded by rays. The stem is divided by a narrow band of large beads or pellets (strangely reminiscent of the treatment found in Roman silver of the first century A.D.). These pellets are repeated at the bottom of the stem above a plain moulded shoulder on which is inscribed: 'Exchang'd 1687'. Although it is not known what this refers to, it may have had some link with the damage done to the Cathedral at the time of the Duke of Monmouth's visit to Chester in 1683 or the visit of James II in 1687, after which the Bishop ordered the suspension of the Dean.

This cup is not mentioned by Ball, in the valuation of the plate by Lowe & Sons in 1967, nor in the current Cathedral inventory.

The four marks are on the side of the bowl: (i) Maker's mark (indecipherable); (ii) Leopard's head crowned; (iii) Lion passant guardant (repeated under the base); (iv) Date letter apparently B (cycle XI), 1685/86, London. (Plates 14, 15.)

15 & 16   THE CATHEDRAL VERGES

The Statutes of the Cathedral in 1544 state that a verge should be carried before the cross whenever the Bishop or Dean should go to and return from the Cathedral. The author believes that these verges, previously thought to have dated from the Restoration, are in fact the verges referred to in the

16th-century Cathedral accounts. They probably survived in the keeping of the person accustomed to carry them, to be reinstated when Dean Bridgman came into office, when they were repaired and engraved with a contemporary inscription.

Ball commented 'Both are heavily weighted and bear the hallmarks of the year 1662 and the same maker's mark as on the large patens'. The author believes Ball was mistaken – there are no traces of hallmarks on either mace. Ball also stated that a third mace, with a mitred head, had been used at the Cathedral but was missing at the time of his survey of the Cathedral plate and goods. It has since reappeared (no. 17). (Plate 16.)

Reference:
Ball 1907, p.25.

15 THE DEAN'S VERGE

The verge was usually carried before the Dean by the Head Verger.

It is 26 inches in length, with a substantial, circular and blocked foot, having now lost its plate base. The plain tapered shaft is divided by three knops, the centre one lower than the others, having in each case collars above and below. A further collar is placed beneath the bowl or head, which consists of a half sphere with cresting and a series of ten plain lobes on the side. Its diameter is 3 inches and it is 2¼ inches deep, having been compressed by damage from its original 2½-inch depth. The cresting of the serrated top is composed of semicircular perforations. There is a depressed flat plate on the top on which is engraved the arms of Bridgman and an inscription: 'Virga Ecclesia Cathedralis Christi et beata Mari a Verginis Cestria Henrius Bridgman D. Decanus Cestria'.

The cross pieces of the engraving, compared with the very worn state of the inscription on the Canon's verge (no. 16), suggests that at some time after 1907 when Ball saw the base, the inscription was re-engraved without regard for the original spelling, or that Ball's record is inaccurate. The plate is held in position by four quatrefoil studs, one of which is now missing.

Although Ball stated that there were hallmarks of 1662 and a maker's mark, as on the patens, no trace of these can be seen today, and the author suggests that this is in fact one of the 16th-century maces. It compares favourably with the civic mace at Holt a few miles away across the border in Wales, which was made by John Lingley, the Chester goldsmith, and bears only his mark and an inscription date of 1606. (Plate 17.)

Reference:
Ridgway 1968, p.48 and plates 23-26.

16 THE CANON'S VERGE

By tradition carried before the residential Canon, the verge is similar to, but not identical with, the Dean's verge, and is slightly longer, at 28¼ inches. The shaft is divided by three bands of approximately equal depth and terminates in a substantial circular foot, finishing in a silver plate. The head,

3¼ inches in diameter, is slightly deeper than that of the Dean's verge. The cresting is similar.

There is a depressed flat plate at the top, which was held together by four studs, but three are now missing. The plate is very worn and the inscription on it is now almost obliterated. There had been rays around the periphery surrounding the Latin inscription. The plate is now off-centre, suggesting that this verge has been extensively repaired.

Ball states that it bore London hallmarks for 1662 and the maker's mark TD, but these are not apparent. The author believes that this is the 1591 verge referred to in the Cathedral accounts which was reinstated after the Civil War. (Plate 18.)

17   Mitred Mace

Ball records that according to an account of the enthronement of Dr Blomfield as Bishop in 1824, his Lordship was attended at the west door by the apparitor of the Consistory Court 'bearing a massive silver mace surmounted with a mitre'. Later in the procession from the Chapter House the Minor Canons were followed by two vergers with their silver maces, then by the apparitor with the large mitred mace, and then by Bishop Blomfield.

When Ball made his survey of the Cathedral plate in 1907 he stated that this mace was no longer in existence. It is not known when it reappeared, but it is listed in a recent inventory as 'Modern Bishop's mace with rubbed Georgian marks', which is clearly incorrect. It is in frequent use.

The mitred head is silver, 4½ inches deep. The shaft, 31 inches in length with a halfway knop band, is plated, not silver, and is not tapered. On the upper section of the shaft is an ornamental shield, apparently silver but unmarked, with an inscription now obliterated.

There are five marks on the head: (i) Maker's mark partly rubbed out but for two initials one of which is H, within a rectangular frame; (ii) Lion passant guardant; (iii) Leopard's head crowned; (iv) Date letter m (cycle XVI), for 1787/88, London; (v) Duty mark. (Plate 19.)

18   Strainer Spoon

A gilt strainer spoon (not a chalice spoon) to remove impurities from the wine. It was given to the Cathedral in 1869 by Bishop Jacobson. The spoon is 5½ inches in length, having an oval rat tail bowl 2½ inches long and 2 inches wide, pierced with arabesque. The slender handle terminates in three lobes. Weight 2 oz.

The spoon is bottom marked with four worn marks: (i) Maker's mark IS with a crown above within a shaped frame – John Singleton; (ii) Lion passant guardant; (iii) Leopard's head crowned; (iv) Date letter O (cycle XI), 1691/92, London. (Plate 20.)

Reference:
Chester Cathedral.

19 COMMUNION CUP

A gilt communion cup 8½ inches high with a bell-shaped bowl, rim 3¾ inches diameter and 3½ inches deep with slightly everted lip. It stands on a six sided stem with a bold knop with diamond facets each containing four-petal conventional flowers. Below the knop is an ornamental skirt of conventional leaves and from this the stem ends on a moulded base, diameter 5¹/10 inches, round which has been pricked the later inscription '1903'.

The cup has been made with screw fittings so that it can be taken apart. This feature and other points of design give it a close resemblance to recusant chalices of *c.*1630.

There are possibly four marks between the lobes of the base: (i) A town mark, possibly Payerne, Switzerland; (ii) M(?) within an ornamental shield; (iii) A plainer ornamental shield with motif resembling M; (iv) Indecipherable.

It was presented to the Cathedral in 1903. (Plate 21.)

References:
Ball 1907, p.26.
Oman, p.257.

20 & 21 CHALICE AND COVER (or CIBORIUM)

A slightly ornate gilt communion chalice or ciborium with a corresponding cover given by Bishop Paget at the time of his enthronement in 1919. The height of the chalice is 8¾ inches and the rim diameter 4¼ inches. The goblet-type bowl has three panels on the sides depicting symbols of the Passion and nestles within a highly ornate casting of fruit and swags which covers the lower part, and stands on a rococo-style stem with ornate knop leading to a similarly ornamented shoulder and short moulded flange, diameter 4¼ inches. There is a much later inscription on the base: 'J.L.D. Decano H.L.C. Episcopo Sept. XXIV MCMXIX'. On the underside of the chalice is a coat of arms dividing the date figures 1661.

The domed cover has a serrated rim, and continues the elaborate decorative theme. There was originally a cross finial, but this has been lost. Weight of chalice 16¼ oz; of cover 5¾ oz.

Only the cover is marked: (i) An unidentified mark, possibly a Dutch town mark; (ii) The initials FA within an oval. (Plates 22, 23.)

THE LEYCESTER WARREN BEQUEST (nos 22-25)

In his will Lt.-Col. J.L.B. Leycester Warren of Tabley Hall near Knutsford left to the Cathedral the following four pieces of plate, all made by the same maker:

References:
Country Life, 18 July 1923.
Brocklehurst, no. 28 and plate VIII.

22 COMMUNION CUP (see no. 23)

A gold communion cup 4¾ inches high with a tumbler-cup-shaped bowl, rim diameter 3½ inches. It stands on a trumpet-shaped stem on which is engraved a crucifix and the date 1678. (Plate 24.)

There is one mark: TC a fish above and a fleur-de-lis below in a shaped frame (Jackson, p.133).

23   PATEN (see no. 22)
A gold paten on a low inverted trumpet-shaped foot, one inch high and 5½ inches diameter. It has a slightly raised rim. Engraved in the centre is a crucifix and the date 1678.

There is one mark only, as on the cup.

The communion cup and paten were made for Sir Robert Leycester, 2nd Bart as a present to his father, Sir Peter Leycester, 1st Bart, for the use of St Peter's Chapel, Nether Tabley. Both pieces are kept in a wooden case covered in crimson velvet bound with braid, with metal clasps and drop ring handles, which is in need of repair. (Plate 24.)

24   ALMS BOX
A cylindrical alms box – height 4 inches and diameter 3¾ inches. It stands on a moulded base, the body engraved with the sacred monogram in a wreath of foliage and the date 1678. The detachable flat-topped cover is decorated with a large rosette of cut card work, in the centre of which is a slot for coins.

There are four marks: (i) Maker's mark TC a fish above and a fleur-de-lis below in a shaped frame (Jackson, p.133); (ii) Lion passant guardant; (iii) Leopard's head crowned; (iv) Date letter U (cycle X), 1677/78, London. (Plate 25.)

Reference:
Brocklehurst, no. 29 and plate IX.

25   FLAGON
A silver flagon, overall height 10 inches with a bun-shaped lid and moulded rim attached to the top of an S-shaped handle with a thumb. The body is marked by a reeded band and below this the foot splays outwards to a base diameter of 7 inches.

There are four marks on the cover, which are repeated below the rim on the body of the flagon: (i) Maker's mark TC a fish above and a fleur-de-lis below in a shaped frame (Jackson, p.133); (ii) Date letter U (cycle X), 1677/78, London; (iii) Lion passant guardant; (iv) Leopard's head crowned.

---

26   COMMUNION CUPS
Although outside the present survey, these two communion cups are replicas made by Edward Barnard and Sons in 1838/39 – when they took the two Restoration cups in exchange (see no. 2). The cups are referred to in Barnard's

Day Book in 1839: '2 Upright Communion Chalices full pint on large Collet feet instead of 2 old ones 35oz 17 dwts at 6s 9d. Engraving 36s gilding £8.10.0 … £30'. In 1968 these cups were fitted with inner liners to make them shallower and easier for administration.

ACTON
ST MARY
Deanery of Nantwich

1   PLATE PATEN

What appears to be the earliest surviving silver at Acton is a heavy plate paten, diameter 6½ inches, having a sloping 1-inch border with two scribed lines close to the semi bead rim. The surface of the plate is now slightly concave. Although it has neither assay marks nor maker's mark, it appears to be of the 17th century and could belong to a communion cup of considerable proportions.

2   COMMUNION CUP

A communion cup 7½ inches high having a bell-shaped bowl 4½ inches deep, the rim slightly everted, diameter 3¾ inches. The stem is finely moulded, having a plain rounded knop ½ inch deep and concave stepped mouldings divided by a shoulder, and a flange. Diameter of base 3½ inches. On the side of the bowl an inscription in one line, punctuated by small flowers, each of which contains a numeral making up the date, 1633: (five-petal flower 1) Ex Dono (eight-petal flower 6) Aliciae (five-petal flower 3) Wilbraham (seven-petal flower 3) De Dorfould.

There are four marks on the side of the bowl: (i) Maker's mark imperfect, but appears to be one of a pair of letters … S above a fleur-de-lis within a plain shield. (Alice Wilbraham gave a similar cup to Nantwich in 1622 on which the missing letter is a V – (Jackson, p.115, Valerius Sutton); (ii) Leopard's head crowned; (iii) Lion passant guardant; (iv) Date letter q (cycle VIII), 1633/34, London.

3   FLAGON

A flagon 13 inches high with tapering sides. Rim diameter 4½ inches. The bottom of the flagon coincides with a reeded band above a splayed and moulded foot, diameter 7 inches. The lid is domed and has an acorn finial and S-scroll handle with simple ornamental hinge and an ornamental shield terminal. The corkscrew thumb is moulded on the inside and plain on the outside. The flagon is fully hallmarked on the flange of the lid and on the body – slightly below the rim. On the side of the flagon is an inscription: 'The Gift of the Hon[le] the Lady Wilbraham of Weston in Staffordsheir To the Church of Acton in Cheshire'.

There are four marks: (i) Maker's mark ANe (conjoined) Anthony Nelme (Grimwade 68) (repeated on the scroll handle); (ii) Britannia; (iii) Lion's head erased; (iv) Date letter K (cycle XII), 1705/06, London.

4   STAND PATEN (see no. 5)
A stand paten 7$^{1}/_{10}$ inches diameter and 2½ inches high with a ⅜-inch simple moulded border. There are three faint scribed lines on the face of the plate. The stem is tapered to a 1½-inch waist and the foot is moulded, diameter 2⅞ inches. The plate is inscribed in three lines: 'The gift of ye Honble Lady Wilbraham of Weston in Staffordsheir To the Church of Acton in Chessheir'.

There are four marks: (i) Maker's mark ANe (conjoined) Anthony Nelme (Grimwade 68); (ii) Britannia; (iii) Lion's head erased (repeated on the underside of the foot); (iv) Date letter L (cycle XII), 1706/07, London.

5   STAND PATEN (see no. 4)
A stand paten of like dimensions and character as no. 4 but with foot mouldings so damaged that they must be conjectures from the other member of the pair.

6   COMMUNION CUP
A bell-shaped communion cup, total height 7¾ inches with slightly tapered sides and everted rim with edge band, diameter 3½ inches. Depth of bowl 4¾ inches. The stem is compressed, with a ½-inch deep round knop. The foot is well moulded, diameter 3⅝ inches. Engraved on the side is an elaborate coat of arms and an inscription in three lines:

> 1st May 1765. The Gift
> of Mrs Tomkinson of Dorfold
> To the Parish Church of Acton

and engraved on the other side a sunburst enclosing IHS cross and nails.

There are four marks: (i) Maker's mark TW with C above and W below, within two concentric circles, Thomas Whipham II and Charles Wright (Grimwade 2976); (ii) Lion passant guardant; (iii) Leopard's head crowned; (iv) Date letter Gothic J (cycle XV), 1764/65, London.

There is an almost exact copy of the Anthony Nelme flagon (no. 3) but in Sheffield plate. The finial appears to be detachable and of a different material. On the side is an inscription: 'Thos Skarrett/John Pratchit/Church Wardens 1789'.

Note: Plate 21 in Richards is actually plate at Wrenbury, not Acton.

ALDERLEY EDGE
St Mary – formerly St Lawrence
Deanery of Knutsford

Earwaker gives a copy of an inventory of plate drawn up in 1548:

> A Challis with a paten parcell gilt
>
> Two crosses, the one of copper, and ye other plated with copper and a current (cruet) of pewter...
>
> (There follows a report on the future of the cross of silver within 'the sayd pish which was given by Roger Bostock decd to ye pishners of Alderley ...')

The plate mentioned in the inventory has not survived, but since that date the church has gained a small early plate paten, a communion cup of 1696, a small communion cup and paten for use when visiting the sick, undated but by the London maker Anthony Nelme, given in 1850, a stand paten of 1713 and a flagon of 1752/53.

Reference:
Earwaker, vol 2, p.627.

1 Plate Paten
A plate paten diameter 4⅞ inches, with a plain ⅝-inch rim giving a comparatively slight depression. It is in poor condition, bent and showing numerous knife marks. It carries only the maker's mark, which might be Le within a circle, perhaps provincial. It is not easy to date this kind of plate paten, but it closely resembles those at Bunbury (Griffith Edwardes) and at Baddiley (John Lingley) which belong to the last half of the 16th century.

2 Communion Cup
A communion cup 7⅛ inches high with a 4-inch deep bell-shaped bowl with everted rim, diameter 4½ inches. At the junction of the splayed stem and the bowl is a simple moulding, slightly concave, above a protruding downward sloping flange. The stem splays out to simple compressed mouldings and a foot, diameter 4¼ inches. The foot mouldings may have been repaired.

There are four marks on the side of the bowl: (i) Maker's mark JB above a crescent within a lozenge frame; (ii) Leopard's head crowned; (iii) Lion passant guardant; (iv) Date letter A (cycle XII), 1696/97, London.

Beneath the foot a single mark of the lion passant guardant, an example of the new series of date letters used on the eve of the introduction of the compulsory Britannia mark and used with the sterling mark. The Britannia mark was introduced on 27 March 1697.

3   COMMUNION CUP (for use when visiting the sick) (see no. 4)
A small communion cup, having bell-shaped bowl and strengthened rim, 4½ inches high. Rim diameter 2⅜ inches, depth of bowl 2¼ inches. The bowl curves to the stem, joining it with a simple moulding. The stem is divided by a rounded ½ inch-knop having a central girdle. The foot, diameter 1¼ inches, has simple mouldings. The bowl is engraved with a sunburst, IHS, cross and nails, and has been engraved at a later date:

D.D/Wm C Cruttenden M.A Rector/1850

The conjoined mark of the maker ANe, Anthony Nelme (Grimwade 68) is struck four times under the foot. This mark was entered at London 1697.

4   PLATE PATEN (see no. 3)
A small plate paten to accompany the communion cup (no. 3) for use when visiting sick communicants. The diameter is 5⅛ inches and it has a narrow reeded edge ⅜ inches wide. Like the cup, the surface is engraved with rays and the sacred symbols and a similar inscription. There are no marks and it appears to be later than the cup.

5   STAND PATEN
A stand paten diameter 9 inches with narrow moulded rim forming a slight depression. The stem is plain and the well moulded foot is 2¾ inches high and 3½ inches in diameter. An elaborate coat of arms is engraved on the surface of the plate, and underneath is the inscription: 'The gift of Thomas Hollinshead of Haywood to the Church of Alderley in the County of Chester, gent. 1714'.

On the surface of the plate are four marks: (i) Maker's mark Ne within two conjoined circles, Jonathan Newton (Grimwade 2087); (ii) Britannia; (iii) Lion's head erased; (iv) Date letter S (cycle XII), 1713/14, London.

6   FLAGON
A flagon 13½ inches high with high domed lid engraved with a sunburst. It has an open harp-shaped thumb. The double scroll handle terminates in a plain shield. There is a reeded girdle at the base of the tapered sides below which the base curves outwards to a moulded foot, diameter, 7¾ inches. A weight record is inscribed beneath the base – 53 oz 16.

On the side of the flagon is the inscription: 'The gift of the Revd & Mrs Croft, Rector, to the Parish of Alderley. AD 1753'.

On the side of the flagon are four marks: (i) Maker's mark script WG within a rectangular frame, William Grundy (Grimwade 3146 or 3147); (ii) Leopard's head crowned; (iii) Lion passant guardant; (iv) Date letter r (cycle XIV), 1752/53, London.

ALSAGER
CHRIST CHURCH
Deanery of Congleton

This suite of plate was provided when the church was built in 1789. Each piece is inscribed with the same inscription 'Christ Church Alsager 1789' and coat of arms within an ornamental shield. Each piece bears the same marks.

1 COMMUNION CUP

A communion cup with bell shaped bowl 8 inches high, diameter of rim 4 inches. The stem splays outwards to the foot, which has a simple mould and is 4 inches in diameter. On the side of the bowl are rays within a circle embracing an IHS with cross and nails, and below this the inscription. On the splay of the foot is the coat of arms within an ornamental shield.

There are five marks on the bowl: (i) Maker's mark IR with midway pellet within a rectangle, John Rowe (?Grimwade 1616); (ii) Lion passant guardant; (iii) Leopard's head crowned; (iv) Date letter O (cycle XVI), 1789/90, London; (v) Duty mark.

2 PLATE PATEN

A large plate paten, diameter $9\frac{3}{4}$ inches with a $1\frac{1}{2}$ inch-wide edge on which the coat of arms and inscription are engraved. The rays and sacred symbols are engraved on the centre of the plate paten. Marks as on nos 1, 3 and 4.

3 STAND PATEN

A small stand paten $5\frac{1}{8}$ inches diameter with a $\frac{3}{8}$-inch border and foot, diameter of 2 inches, blocked with a disc engraved with the rays and sacred symbols. The coat of arms and inscription are on the surface. Marks as on nos 1, 2 and 4.

4 FLAGON

A flagon 13 inches high and rim diameter $3\frac{1}{2}$ inches. The sides taper with a girdle to mark the bottom of the walls of the flagon. From this the foot splays out to a diameter of $6\frac{5}{8}$ inches and ends with a plain moulding. The flagon has a scroll handle with a capping running towards a curved thumbpiece. The inscription, rays and sacred symbols, and the coat of arms, are on the splayed base. The inside of the domed lid and the base bear the marks as on nos 1, 2 and 3.

ALTRINCHAM
St George
Deanery of Bowdon

The church was erected in 1799 as a daughter church to Bowdon and became a separate parish in 1868.
    The plate is of base metal, heavy and without character, but probably coeval with the building.
    There are two communion cups only, bell-shaped bowls with stems divided by knops and with blocked bases.

ASHTON UPON MERSEY
St Martin
Deanery of Bowdon

The silver was stolen in 1840 and not recovered. There appears to be no detailed list of the lost pieces.

ASTBURY
St Mary
Deanery of Congleton

The earliest known reference to the plate of Astbury in the Sheriff of Cheshire's Certificate of 1548 is in respect of the bells and plate, and the result of the injunctions of the previous year, when there were two chalices and four bells. At that time the Higher Chapel (see Congleton St Peter) and the Lower Chapel (now demolished) were also in Astbury parish and each had a chalice. We may also assume they would have patens as well.
    The next surviving inventory appeared nearly two centuries later, in 1727, when the church plate was handed over to the new churchwardens on 18 July. This reads:

> Two silver flagons weighing two hundred and
> thirty four ounces and ten pennyweights.
> Two silver salvers
> Two challices and two covers
> Two old pewter flagons

In 1871 this list is repeated, but with the addition of a spoon, about which nothing can be traced. This list remains intact for the rest of the older plate.

Reference:
Cartlidge, p.93ff.

1   COMMUNION CUP (see nos 2 & 3)
A communion cup, 8¾ inches high, with a bell-shaped bowl 3 inches deep, and rim diameter 4¼ inches. The sides curve into a stem which is divided by a narrow knop ¼ inch wide and sweeps down to a moulded foot, diameter 4⅛ inches which has been slightly crushed. Weight 51½ oz (avdp). On the bowl, arranged in a circle around the word 'Astbury' is the inscription: 'Ex dono Ricardi Henshall Anno Dom 1634', recording that it was given in 1634 by Richard Henshall, perhaps to commemorate his silver wedding to Elizabeth Hollinshead whom he had married clandestinely in 1609. It is, in fact, a replacement cup, given by Josiah Henshall, a schoolmaster from Congleton, who died in 1709.

There are four marks on the side of the bowl: (i) Maker's mark FA, a pellet between, within a circle, possibly William Fawdery who entered his mark in 1697 (Grimwade 664); (ii) Britannia; (iii) Lion's head erased (repeated under the foot); (iv) Date letter M (cycle XII), 1707/08, London. (Plate 26.)

2   COMMUNION CUP (see no. 1)
A communion cup similar to no. 1 but slightly more slender. Height 8¾ inches, rim diameter 4¼ inches, base diameter 4⅛ inches, knop diameter 1¾ inches. The word 'Astbury' is engraved on the side of the bowl.

Four marks as on nos 1 and 3.

3   STAND PATEN (see nos 1 & 2)
A stand paten made to accompany the two cups (nos 1 and 2); diameter 9⅞ inches with a narrow reeded border ⅓-inch wide. In the centre of the paten is the word 'Astbury' with three faint scribed lines as though intended for an additional inscription. The stand joins the stem with a simple mould and sweeps down to a moulded base, diameter 4¼ inches. Total height 3⅛ inches.

There are four marks on the paten surface – the same as on nos 1 and 2.

4   TAZZA
A tazza dish, diameter 9¾ inches, with plain sweeping sides almost 1½ inches in depth, on a curved stand with a waist slightly over 1½ inches which sweeps down to a moulded foot which has been crushed. Diameter 4¹⁄₁₆ inches. Total height 3⅜ inches. Weight 1 lb 9 oz (avdp). There is a two-line inscription on the underside of the dish: 'The Gift of Tho: Higginbothem Gent/to the Parish Church of: Asbury [sic]'.

There are four marks: (i) Maker's mark YO with pellet above and below within a shaped frame, Edward Yorke (Grimwade 3381); (ii) Britannia; (iii) Lion's head erased; (iv) Date letter O (cycle XII), (1709/10), London.

5 & 6   PATEN COVERS (see nos 7 & 8)
Two identical paten covers, diameter 5 inches, each with a narrow cut-back rim to accommodate the rim of the cup. The stand is curved with a waist and the base is blocked and carries the rays and sacred symbols. The foot is not moulded but has three scribed lines encircling at 1⅓ inches diameter.

There are four marks on the surface of each plate: (i) Maker's mark BA with pellet above and below, within a shaped frame, Richard Bayley (Grimwade 116); (ii) Britannia; (iii) Lion's head erased; (iv) Date letter R (cycle XII), 1712/13, London.

7 & 8   FLAGONS (see nos 5 & 6)
Two massive almost identical flagons, one slightly heavier than the other, 7 lb 2 oz and 8 lb, and different in a few details in the spelling of the inscription.

Each flagon is 18½ inches high. Rim diameters 5¹³⁄₁₆ inches with flattened domed lid – the lower moulding incurving. The sides batten only lightly and there is a girdle reeding before the splay of the foot to mark the bottom of the cylinder body. The moulded feet have a shoulder and step with narrow flange, and are 9⅜ inches in diameter. The flagons have an S-scroll handle with oval collars. The thumbs, of acanthus form, are identical with that on the Congleton St Peter flagon. Spouts have been added at a later date. Each has a long inscription on the side of the flagon: 'This flagon and such another were given for the use of the Communion Service in this Church by Peter Shakerley of Somerford in this Parish of Astbury Esq. Eldest Son of Sir Geoffrey Shakerley Knight by Kathleen his first wife Daughter of Wm Pennington of Muncaster in the County of Cumberland Esq 1716.'

The marks, inside the lid and on the body, are as follows: (i) Britannia; (ii) Date letter A (cycle XIII), 1716/17, London; (iii) Lion's head erased; (iv) Maker's mark (omitted on one flagon) – BA with pellet above and below within a shaped frame, Richard Bayley (Grimwade 116), (repeated on the handles of both flagons). (Plate 27.)

(See inscription on the flagon no. 5 at Congleton.)

ASTON
ST PETER
Deanery of Great Budworth

A Terrier contains the following extract on 3 May 1789:

> Item in the Chancel A Communion Table with a crimson woollen Carpet and for the time of Administration the Lord's Supper, a Decent Linen Cloth one of French plate Guilt with Gold Chalice,

one small paten of French Plate guilt, one large Silver paten, on quart flagon, Two small boxes to receive the alms of the communicants. The above plate, carpet and linen provided by the Aston family, and the plate and linen kept at the Hall.

The rest of the plate at Aston, a flagon, communion cup, paten and larger paten, are by Garrard, London, 1863/64.

References:
Brocklehurst, no. 1 and plate I.
Oman, p.43 and plate 10.

1   CHALICE (see no. 2)
Charles Oman places this medieval silver gilt chalice in Group 6, along with two other chalices of similar form and construction, one at Hanstall Ridware, Staffordshire and the other at Goathland, Yorkshire. This chalice is 5½ inches high with foot diameter 5¼ inches, rim diameter 3¾ inches. The hexagonal stem merges into the knop and base and has incurved sides decorated with a double row of quatrefoils, a feature uniform with the other two chalices. The foot is engraved on one facet with the crucifixion and on adjacent facets with the attendant figures. On the facet opposite the crucifixion is a coat of arms (on a cross, five lions rampant. Perhaps Belyn, Co. Chester).

There are no marks, but it is perhaps late 14th century. (Plates 28, 29.)

2   PLATE PATEN (see no. 1)
A silver-gilt paten to accompany the chalice (no. 1). Diameter 5 inches. The wide rim slopes to a depression. In the centre of the plate is a circular engraved representation of the Manus Dei on a saltire of small crosses within a wreath of lobes and scrolls. There are no marks but, as no. 1, is probably late 14th century.

3   STAND PATEN
A stand paten, overall height 2 inches, diameter 12½ inches with a 1¾-inch rim and shallow moulding around the edge. There is a pronounced depression, and in the centre of the plate a coat of arms of a small lion passant in the centre of a cross fleury. The coat is surrounded with plumes which are tied beneath the coat. The stand is attached to the bottom of the plate with a plain disc, and the stem, 1½ inches, sweeps towards a flat foot, diameter 3⅞ inches, which is blocked. There are shallow mouldings around the rim, and a single scribed line on the stem slightly above the junction with the foot plate.

There are four marks on the plate's edge: (i) Maker's mark RL above a fleur-de-lis within a plain shield; (ii) Leopard's head crowned; (iii) Lion passant guardant; (iv) Date letter S (cycle IX), 1675/76, London.

AUDLEM
St James
Deanery of Nantwich

Audlem parish church is rich in early plate. There are six pieces, four of English workmanship and two German. Both Richards and later Pevsner and Hubbard mention a paten cover. Richards stated that it was 'fitted to the chalice, possibly a little later in date, and often used as a paten', but this piece was not known to the Vicar in 1976. Pevsner and Hubbard report its existence, but query the date, and suggest 1635, the date of the communion cup referred to by Richards which is still the earliest plate to survive here.

1   COMMUNION CUP
A large gilt communion cup 9⅜ inches high with a bell-shaped bowl with an everted rim, diameter 4¾ inches. The bowl is divided from the stem by a tucked-in moulding, the top of the stem, where it overhangs, having a simple scribed line before coming to a waist 1 inch in diameter and a substantial knop ⅝ inch deep with top and bottom mouldings. The foot, diameter 4⅝ inches, is well moulded and the base has an enrichment of ovolos. Three quarters of an inch within the foot the base is blocked and inscribed with the weight '26..6..0'. Inside the foot is an inscription: 'Humbly dedicated to the service of God in the Parish Church of Audlem by RB 1635 +'.

There are four marks on the side of the bowl just below the rim: (i) Lion passant guardant; (ii) Leopard's head crowned; (iii) Maker's mark (inverted) P and another letter with pellets above and a crescent below within a shaped frame; (iv) Date letter indistinct but probably S (cycle VIII), 1635/36, London.

2   STAND PATEN OR ALMS DISH
A large credence, stand paten, or alms dish, diameter 13⅛ inches, with a trumpet-shaped stand, making a total height of 3½ inches. The foot has a diameter of 5½ inches and has an engraved inscription beneath the flange which reads, in script lettering: 'The gift of Thomas Lord, Viscount Killmorey to the Parish Church of Audlem, 1685'.

There are four marks on the surface of the plate: (i) Maker's mark RL above a fleur-de-lis within a plain shield, ?Robert Leake; (ii) Leopard's head crowned; (iii) Lion passant guardant (repeated under the foot); (iv) Date letter F (cycle XI), 1683/84, London.

Reference:
Brocklehurst, no. 32.

3   ALMS DISH (see no. 2)
An alms dish, diameter 14¾ inches, with a border 2⅓ inches wide sloping inwards, the rim moulded for ⅚ inch. The dish is 1 inch deep and has a single depression. There are four worn marks which can be reconstructed from those on the stand paten (no. 2) and are the same.

AUDLEM

4 BAPTISMAL BASIN

The gift of this baptismal basin to the parish church of Audlem is recorded on the Benefactors' Board in the church. Part of this reads:

> Benefactors to the Parish of Audlem by William Evans MA
> late Master of the Free School there and by Ann his widow
> both deceased.
> He gave a pew or seat in ye gallery of the church
> for the use of the school which cost him   3.0.0.
> She gave the Altar piece that cost her   14.10.0.
> Also the Silver Bason for the font value   10.0.0.

The basin has a diameter of 10 inches and is 3¾ inches high.

The fluted body stands on a circular foot with stepped mouldings ⅓ inch deep and 2¾ inches in diameter. The rim is everted and scalloped. Along with the inscribed weight record 24.4 there is a long inscription which has not obscured the assay marks:

> For the more decent Celebration of the Holy Sacrament of Baptism
> in the Parish Church of Audlem This Bason is Humbly dedicated to
> the font there by Ann Evans Widow of Wm Evans MA XXXV Years
> Master of the Free School of the Said Parish, out of her regard to her
> said late husband's intention tho' not requir'd by his Will 1744

There are four marks: (i) Date letter i (cycle XIV), 1744/45, London; (ii) Leopard's head crowned; (iii) Maker's mark EG with pellet above and below, within a lozenge frame, Elizabeth Godfrey (Grimwade 591); (iv) Lion passant guardant.

Reference:
Brocklehurst, no. 42.

5 CHALICE (see no. 6)

A German-made chalice 8½ inches high with a wide tapering bowl 3 inches deep, and rim diameter 4¼ inches. The stem is octagonal baluster inverted pear shape in section between two sets of circular mouldings. The uppermost ⅜ inches of the bowl is gilt and the interior parcel gilt. Immediately below the band of gilding on the bowl is an inscription in German:

MACHT UNS KEIN VON ALLEN
SUNDEN 1 JOH 1. v. 7
DAS BLUT JESU CHRISTI DES
SOHNES GOTTES
———

OBLATEN DOSE VON DENEN

<pre>
         HRN OFFICIEREN DES
           HRN OBRISTEN V
           SOMERFELDTS ZU
        GOTTES ERHEN NEBST
            DEN SILBERN
</pre>

<pre>
        REGIMENT GESCHENCKT
</pre>

<pre>
           DEN 21 XBR 1725
</pre>

The latter part of the inscription after the text may be loosely translated as follows: 'The wafer box from the Officers of Colonel Somerfeldt in honour of God together with the silver Presented to the Regiment 21 December 1725'.

The stem is attached to the octagonal foot by means of a screw and nut. It sweeps down to a series of simple bold mouldings to an octagonal foot diameter 5 inches.

Under which are two marks: (i) Very worn but perhaps an animal or bird head within an ornamental shield; (ii) The initials CI within an oval.

On the main moulding of the foot is a later inscription: 'To the glory of God and in loving and grateful memory of Annie Mary Baker died 9 September 1954' which continues under the foot: 'The gift of her husband William Mangnall Baker'. The chalice is kept in a leather case which appears to be contemporary.

Little is known of the history of this chalice or of the wafer box (no. 6). A note found with the wafer box states that it came from a sale some 50 years before the chalice was presented to the church. The German inscription is a little confusing, and appears to link the two pieces, but the marks are not the same.

6   WAFER BOX

An oval wafer box, $3^{3}/_{8}$ inches by $2^{7}/_{16}$ inches, of German origin, with a hinged, slightly domed, lid. The inside of the box and the outside of the lid are gilt as also the side of the lid, which is $5/16$ inches and the bottom of the side also $5/16$ inches. The total height of the box is $1^{1}/_{2}$ inches. Within a gilt oval on the top of the lid is a three line inscription:

<pre>
          MEIN FLEISCH XST
          DIE RECHTE SPEISE
             JON 6 v.55
</pre>

There are two marks on the side of the box: (i) Indistinct but probably some form of animal head in an irregular frame; (ii) Indistinct letters within a rectangular frame.

A loose paper kept inside the wafer box reads: 'Maker Carolus Unger Hanover/Eitstat', and a second paper states that the wafer box came from the Duke of Cambridge's sale in June 1907.

BACKFORD
St Oswald
Deanery of Wirral, South

Although a very old foundation, partly rebuilt in 1878, no early plate remains.

BADDILEY
St Michael
Deanery of Nantwich

Reference:
Ridgway 1968, pp.42-44, 46-47.

1   Plate Paten

The earliest surviving plate at Baddiley, an isolated part-timber-framed church now linked with Wrenbury, is a small plate paten, diameter 3⅞ inches, very plain, with only a slight depression and rim on which is a single incised line. It bears the single mark IL within an ornamental shield, of John Lingley the Chester goldsmith (Compendium 4195 or 4196), first mentioned in the Company Book in 1576 but listed as a freeman in 1565/66. He died in 1615 shortly after his son, also John.

This plate paten resembles that by Griffith Edwardes I at Bunbury and can be dated to the last quarter of the 16th century. In neither case has the contemporary communion cup survived.

2   Communion Cup

A communion cup with a goblet type bowl and slender baluster stem which spreads out to form the foot. Overall height 8¾ inches.

There are four marks on the side of the bowl: (i) Maker's mark IH above a five-point star within an ornamental shield; (ii) Leopard's head crowned; (iii) Lion passant guardant; (iv) Date letter g (cycle VIII), 1624/25, London.

BARNSTON
(see **BIRKENHEAD** St Mary)
Deanery of Wirral, North

BARROW
(see **GREAT BARROW**)
Deanery of Chester

BARTHOMLEY
St Bertoline
Deanery of Congleton

1   Communion Cup
A communion cup 6⅛ inches high with a straight-sided bucket-shaped bowl 4 inches deep, with the sides placed at a fifteen degrees splay, rim diameter 3½ inches. The bowl, which joins the stem with a cable moulding, has concentric incised lines on the underside. The stem is divided by a knop. The foot splays out trumpet fashion, diameter 3⅛ inches. Under the foot are the initials Z E above C (the initials of the donors, Zachery and Ellen Caudrey) and a repeat of the lion passant guardant mark. On the side of the bowl is the inscription in script lettering: 'The gift of Zachery Caudrey Rector, to the Parish of Bartholmley'.

   On the side of the bowl are four marks: (i) Maker's mark S.H above a fleur-de-lis within a heart-shaped frame; (ii) Leopard's head crowned; (iii) Lion passant guardant; (iv) Date letter M (cycle X), 1669/70, London.

2   Communion Cup (see no. 3)
A communion cup 6¼ inches high with bell-shaped bowl engraved 'The parish of Barthomly', having steep sides and slightly everted rim, diameter 4 inches. The bottom of the bowl turns sharply at an angle towards the stem which is trumpet shaped with a simple moulded base, diameter 4¼ inches. The weight record is inscribed beneath 09.18.00 where the lion passant guardant mark has been struck twice.

   There are four marks on the side of the bowl: (i) Maker's mark TC with a small fish above and a five-point star below, within a deckled shield; (ii) Leopard's head crowned; (iii) Lion passant guardant; (iv) Date letter T (cycle IX), 1676/77, London.

3   Paten Cover (see no. 2)
A stand paten, diameter 4½ inches, used as a paten cover to accompany Communion Cup no. 2. The plate has a single depression with a slightly rising border. The depression fits over the mouth of the communion cup. The plain stem splays outwards to an open flat foot ring. Its total height is 1 inch. The

edge of the paten is inscribed as on the communion cup no. 2: 'The parish of Barthomly'.

Although it is not marked, one can safely assume that it was made to accompany the cup of 1676/77 (no. 2).

4   STAND PATEN

A dish-like stand paten 8½ inches diameter, with a shallow curving bowl resting on an open trumpet stand, base diameter 4½ inches. Total height 2 inches. The foot shows pronounced hammer marks on the inside where the weight is also recorded – 12.11. Inscribed on the surface of the bowl is the sacred monogram IHS with cross and nails within rays, where are also the four marks.

There are four marks: (i) Maker's mark RL above a fleur-de-lis within a shaped shield; (ii) Leopard's head crowned; (iii) Lion passant guardant; (iv) Date letter d (cycle XI), 1681/82, London.

5 & 6   FLAGONS

A pair of flagons, identical except for the weights, 62.12 and 63.4, inscribed on the base of each. Each flagon is 13½ inches high with a domed lid and open scroll thumb above a broken scroll handle terminating in a plain shield. The cylindrical sides are tapered and moulded at the rim with a girdle to mark the junction of the body and base, which is splayed, with simple mouldings ending in a ribbed step under which is inscribed: 'The gift of Mrs Crewe'. There is a coat of arms on the side of each flagon – Crewe and Offrey quarterly impaling a variant of Maddox. The arms are within a lozenge frame surrounded by rococo scrolls and flowers.

There are four marks: (i) Maker's mark DP within lobed and shaped frame with a pellet above the initials, Daniel Piers (Grimwade 493) (repeated on the handle); (ii) Lion passant guardant; (iii) Leopard's head crowned; (iv) Date letter O (cycle XIV), 1749/50, London.

BEBINGTON
ST ANDREW
Deanery of Wirral, North

In *Old Cheshire Churches* Richards states that there was here a 'fine silver paten embossed with the hallmark of the Chester Silversmiths of 1697'. This is incorrect, and no such paten has been known at Bebington. The earliest stand paten is of London make, dated 1704/05 (see no. 1), but the two communion cups here (nos 2 and 3) are by Richard Richardson II of Chester.

1   STAND PATEN

A stand paten, diameter 8 inches, with a narrow moulded border forming a depression. On the centre of the plate is a later inscription:

Bebington Church Plate
JOHN OXTON ⎱ Ch. Wardens
WILL^m STANLEY ⎰ 1737

The plate rests on a plain stand with moulded foot, and is 2¼ inches high.

There are four very worn marks: (i) Maker's mark (indecipherable); (ii) Britannia; (iii) Lion's head erased; (iv) Date letter (perhaps) I (series XII), 1704/05, London.

2   COMMUNION CUP

A communion cup 5¼ inches high, having a bell-shaped bowl with slightly everted rim, diameter 2¼ inches. The bowl curves round to a wide stem divided by a narrow moulded band and the base mouldings have a shoulder and flange, diameter 2¼ inches. On the side of the bowl is an inscription: 'BEBINGTON PARISH', and on the opposite side the sacred monogram IHS, nails and cross, within rays in a circle.

There are five marks on the bowl: (i) Maker's mark RR adorsed within a shaped shield, Richard Richardson II Type 1 (also Richard Richardson I Type 6) (Compendium 7376); (ii) Lion passant guardant; (iii) Leopard's head crowned; (iv) Chester City coat (inverted); (v) Date letter script L (series 3), 1736/37, Chester.

3   COMMUNION CUP

A communion cup 7½ inches high with a bell-shaped bowl with everted lip. The bowl curves round to a broad stem divided by a narrow moulded band and the foot has a step, shoulder and flange. On the side of the bowl is an inscription:

Bebington Church Plate
JOHN OXTON ⎱ Ch. Wardens
WILL^m STANLEY ⎰ 1737

On the side of the bowl are five marks: (i) Maker's mark RR with a deckled frame, Richard Richardson II Type 6 (also used by the Richardsons until 1779) (Compendium 7403); (ii) Lion passant guardant; (iii) Leopard's head crowned; (iv) Chester City coat; (v) Date letter T (series 4), 1769/70, Chester.

BIDSTON
ST OSWALD
Deanery of Birkenhead

The plate disappeared before the end of the 19th century. There appears to be no record of what had disappeared, nor when.

BIRKENHEAD
St Mary (demolished)
and Priory Chapter House Chapel
Deanery of Birkenhead

The suite of silver plate consists of two communion cups, a plate paten and a flagon, nos 2 to 5, given by Francis Richard Price Esq. in 1828. The stand paten (no. 1) inscribed 'Birkenhead Chappel 1736', is on loan to Birkenhead Art Gallery. In 1984 one of the cups (no. 2 or 3) and a plate paten (no. 4), were lent to Barnston.

1 Stand Paten
A stand paten, diameter 8³/₁₀ inches, with a narrow gadrooned border and simple mouldings and shallow depression. On the surface of the plate is the inscription in script lettering: 'Birkenhead Chappel 1736'.

The paten has a stand with almost vertical sides, 2 inches high. The foot mouldings repeat the gadrooning, and end in a narrow flange. The diameter of the foot is 3³/₈ inches.

There are four marks on the surface of the paten: (i) Maker's mark RO within a heart-shaped frame Hugh Roberts (Grimwade 2382); (ii) Britannia; (iii) Lion's head erased; (iv) Date letter C (cycle XII), 1698/99, London.

2 & 3 Communion Cups (see nos 4 & 5)
Two identical communion cups. Each is 9 inches high, and has a bell-shaped bowl 4½ inches deep with almost straight sides tapered with a reeded rim, diameter 4³/₁₀ inches, which stands upon a slender moulded stem of baluster form, having an inset below the bowl followed by a concave moulding, and an S-shaped moulding, a step and shoulder, a large step. The diameter of the foot is 4¹/₁₀ inches. On the side of each bowl is an elaborate coat of arms and the presentation inscription (as found on other pieces of the suite), and sacred monogram: 'Presented by Francis Richard Price Esq 1828'.

One of these cups is on loan to Barnston Church.

There are five marks: (i) Maker's mark RE above EB within a quatrefoil, Rebecca Emes and Edward Barnard I (Grimwade 2309); (ii) Lion passant guardant; (iii) Leopard's head; (iv) Date letter M (cycle XVIII), 1827/28, London; (v) Duty mark.

4 Plate Paten (see nos 2, 3 & 5)
A paten, 8 inches diameter, having a deep depression and a bold border with ovolo decoration divided by a billet. In the centre is the sacred monogram with nails and cross. It carries the same inscription and has the marks as nos 2, 3 and 5, and was on loan to Barnston church in 1984.

5   FLAGON (see nos 2, 3 & 4)
A flagon 13 inches high, rim diameter 4½ inches and base diameter 6⅗ inches, with straight sides and an ornamental lip. It has a waist band inscribed with horizontal reeds, broken at intervals by diagonal straps. There is a band of circles beneath the rim. The lid, which is damaged, is domed with a double moulding. The scroll handle is ribbed and ornamented with acanthus leaves and topped by an acanthus leaf. The handle joins the body of the flagon with an oval collar. Marks and inscription are as on nos 2, 3 and 4.

BLACON
(HOLY TRINITY)
(see **CHESTER** HOLY AND UNDIVIDED TRINITY)
Deanery of Chester

BOWDON
ST MARY THE VIRGIN
Deanery of Bowdon

A fine array of plate existed at Bowdon until the Reformation when in 1559 Robert Booth of Dunham bequeathed: 'A silver challice with a patten and xx shillings of money .. to be contynewally prayed for their'. It is not known if his wishes were carried out, but over a century later William Meredith of Ashley Hall and his wife Mary who came from Lincolnshire, gave a flagon and stand paten on which their names were inscribed. In 1759, Mary, Countess of Stamford, gave them to Carrington (St George) when the family endowed the newly built church there in the estate and parish of Bowdon (see Carrington). These pieces are now at Partington.

The disposal of the Merediths' gift is explained by the Benefactors' Board in Bowdon Parish Church which states that Oliver Bellefontaine, gentleman gave to buy gilt plate for the Communion table £105. According to Bowdon Parish register Mr Oliver Bellefontaine came from Dunham Hall and was buried 5 June 1744. His bequest consisted of two large silver flagons, two silver cups and two silver salvers, one large and one small. None of this plate has survived, as it was all stolen in 1744 and never recovered in spite of a promised reward of 20 guineas (*Adam's Weekly Courant*, 10 May 1774), and it was replaced by a similar set the following year. No more plate was given to Bowdon until 1910 when a gold chalice and paten, a copy of a chalice from Iceland, now in the Victoria and Albert Museum, were given by the Gore family.

1   ALMS DISH
A large plain silver gilt alms dish, diameter 18 inches, with a 2½-inch moulded edge and a single depression and overall height of 2½ inches. In the centre of the plate are engraved large sacred symbols IHS with cross and nails surrounded by rays.

It is engraved on the back: 'Bowden Church in Cheshire 83 oz = 14 pw'.
There are four marks on the rim: (i) Maker's mark (now much worn) LO above a five point star within a shaped shield, Seth Lofthouse (Grimwade 1945); (ii) Britannia; (iii) Lion's head erased; (iv) Date letter K (cycle XII), 1705/06, London. (Plate 30.)

2 & 3 COMMUNION CUPS
Two matching silver-gilt communion cups, each 8⅘ inches high, with bell-shaped bowls 3⅗ inches diameter and 4⅕ inches deep. The rim has a single moulding. The stem is divided by a substantial knop with a moulded waist. The base is moulded with a step and shoulder. Beneath the foot, 4½ inches in diameter, is an inscription: 'Bowden Church Cheshire' and the record of their weights: no. 2: 'W.16.17', no. 3: '16.2'.
The side of the bowl is engraved with the sacred symbols as on the alms dish (no. 1).
There are four marks struck beneath the foot: (i) Maker's mark IC divided by a midway pellet within a rectangle, John Carter II (Grimwade 1214); (ii) Lion passant guardant; (iii) Leopard's head crowned; (iv) Date letter Gothic U (cycle XV), 1775/76, London. (Plate 32.)

4   SALVER PATEN (see nos 2, 3, 5, 6 & 7)
A circular silver gilt salver paten, resting on three scroll feet, with ornamental moulded rim 8½ inches diameter. The sacred symbols are inscribed on the surface, and underneath are the inscriptions 'Bowden Church Cheshire', and the weight 'W.23 16'. The marks are as on nos 3, 5, 6 and 7. (Plate 32.)

5   SALVER PATEN
A circular silver gilt salver paten following the design of no. 4, but smaller: diameter 6¾ inches, weight 'W11.18'. The marks are as on nos 3, 4, 6 and 7.

6 & 7   FLAGONS
A matching pair of silver gilt flagons, overall height 14½ inches. Each has vertical sides with slender moulded waistband to mark the end of the flagon at the junction of the body with the splayed base which terminates in a bold step and shoulder and a further moulding and very short flange. The rim diameter is 5⁷⁄₁₀ inches and base diameter 9 inches. The high domed lid is attached to the S-scroll handle with an elaborate hinge and an open corkscrew thumb. The handle ends in a shaped terminal with corkscrew mouldings on the top side and horizontal moulds with shaped edge, and joins the side of the flagon with an oval collar. The spout rises slightly above the rim and terminates against the side of the flagon in an ornamental shell. The lid is not marked in either flagon, but the four marks (as found on nos 2, 3, 4 and 5) are found on the side of the flagon. The inscription and sacred symbols are the same and the weights are inscribed: no. 6: 'Wt 84.16' and no. 7: '84.15'. (Plate 31.)

BRERETON
St Oswald
Deanery of Congleton

1   COMMUNION CUP
A commonwealth cup 9½ inches high. Its plain, slightly everted bucket-shaped bowl is 5¹/₁₀ inches deep. The rim is 5¹/₁₀ inches in diameter. The bowl turns sharply to the stem which has a skirt slightly below the bowl, before sweeping down towards the foot, scored with five concentric lines, diameter 5¹/₁₀ inches. The side of the bowl is engraved with the arms of Smithwick and is inscribed: 'The gift of William Smithwick of Smithwick Esqr to the Church of Brereton'.

There are four marks on the side of the bowl: (i) Maker's mark, indistinct, perhaps an animal, within a plain shield; (ii) Leopard's head crowned; (iii) Lion passant guardant; (iv) Date letter Q (cycle IX), 1653/54, London.

2   FLAGON (see no. 3)
A flagon 12 inches high having almost vertical sides, the junction of body and foot marked by a moulded band ⅖ inch wide. The diameter of the base 7¾ inches. The lid is domed, flat cap and the rim moulded. The S-scroll handle is surmounted by a heart-shaped thumbpiece. The side is engraved with a coat of arms with plumes.

There are four marks: (i) Maker's mark PP above a motif (?fleur-de-lis) within a trefoil frame; (ii) Lion passant guardant; (iii) Leopard's head crowned; (iv) Date letter Gothic C (cycle X), 1660/61, London.

3   STAND PATEN (see no. 2)
A stand paten which may have had a communion cup (replaced about 1722/23) has generous proportions and has been used as a paten cover. It has a diameter of 7¾ inches with a rim 1¹/₁₀ inches wide with a single scored line marked near the edge of the border. There is a shallow depression. It stands on a slender blocked stem, giving an overall height of ⁹/₁₀ inch. The coat of arms engraved on the plate and the marks are the same as the flagon (no. 2).

4   COMMUNION CUP (see nos 5 & 6)
A communion cup 9⁷/₁₀ inches high with a bell-shaped bowl, rim diameter 5³/₁₀ inches, which has apparently been renewed or extensively repaired. The bowl is 5 inches deep and curves to the spool-shaped stem which is divided by a simple knop ⅗ inch deep with very narrow collars. The base is moulded with a shoulder and stepped. On the side of the bowl is the Brereton coat of arms in a lozenge and the inscription: 'The Gift of the Honble Mrs Eliz^{bth} Brereton to the Church of Brereton'.

Below the rim are four marks: (i) Maker's mark Pa with a small animal crouching and facing right below, within a plain shield, Humphrey Payne (Grimwade 2118); (ii) Britannia; (iii) Lion's head erased (repeated beneath the base); (iv) Date letter (worn) perhaps G (cycle XIII), 1722/23, London.

5   STAND PATEN (see nos 4 & 6)
A stand paten to accompany nos 4 and 6. It consists of a plain plate, diameter 7¾ inches, with a narrow moulded rim and single depression. It stands on a spool-shaped stem and a blocked base on which are three concentric lines. The arms, inscription and marks are as on nos 4 and 6.

6   ALMS DISH
A heavy alms dish 8¾ inches in diameter with a moulded rim 1¼ inches wide and a single depression. The marks, arms and inscription are as on nos 4 and 5. The date letter is clearly G (cycle XIII), 1722/23, London.

BRUERA
ST MARY
Deanery of Malpas

1   COMMUNION CUP
A communion cup 7 inches high, weight 7 oz. Troy. The bell-shaped bowl is 4 inches deep and has an everted rim, diameter 4¼ inches. The stem is divided by a narrow knop ¼ inch deep, and has been repaired close to the bowl. The foot is stepped, the shoulder moulded and has a flange. The base diameter is 4 inches. An additional charm of this cup is the quality of the engraving. On one side of the bowl are the sacred symbols, and on the other an oval containing a representation of Christ the Good Shepherd holding a crook in his right hand and a lamb across his shoulders. He is bare-footed and wears a flowing robe. Between these two motifs is an inscription: 'The Gift of the Revd Mr Rob: Fogg to the Chappel of Church on Heath 1726'.

There are four marks on the side of the bowl: (i) Maker's mark (imperfectly struck) perhaps IO or IC within an oval frame; (ii) Leopard's head crowned; (iii) Lion passant guardant; (iv) Date letter S (cycle XI), 1695/96, London.

There is also a Sheffield plate flagon which bears the names of the vicar and wardens in 1823.

BUGLAWTON
ST LUKE THE EVANGELIST
Deanery of Congleton

The church was built in 1840 and the original silver, still in use, comprises two communion cups, a stand paten and an alms plate. All bear the date letter Gothic D (cycle XIX), 1839/40, London and the maker's mark for Joseph Savory II and Albert Savory (Grimwade 1853). As this is out of the range of this survey it is not described fully.

BUNBURY
ST BONIFACE
Deanery of Malpas

Only one amendment need be made to the survey of the plate at Bunbury by Sir Leonard Stone. It is now established that the small plate paten (no. 1) which was attributed to Griffith Edwardes II of Chester, is the work of his father, Griffith Edwardes I, also a Chester Goldsmith, who died between 1603 and 1607.

Regular annual inventories of the church plate at Bunbury were made from 1758. In 1791 the churchwardens' accounts contain a reference to 'the stealing of our Church plate', but no evidence of the theft has been found.

Reference:
Stone, pp.1-11.

1   PATEN

A small plate paten with a slight depression. Diameter $3^{1}/_{5}$ inches, weight 3.3.19, with a rim $^{3}/_{5}$ inch wide enriched by three scored concentric lines.

There is a single mark on the rim: GE above a motif in a trefoil now identified as Griffith Edwardes I of Chester (Compendium 2773). (Plate 34.)

This plate paten is similar to that by John Lingley of Chester at Baddiley.

2   COMMUNION CUP

A communion cup $8^{1}/_{2}$ inches high. The diameters of rim and base are the same, $4^{1}/_{5}$ inches. The bell-shaped bowl with slightly everted lip has a capacity of a little over one pint, and an inscription on the side believed to have been added about 1834. The bowl joins the stem with mouldings and has a heavily moulded knop. The considerable moulded foot has a pronounced shoulder.

On the side of the bowl are the four marks: (i) Maker's mark RC above a pheon surmounted by small pellets within a heart-shaped frame; (ii) Leopard's head crowned; (iii) Lion passant guardant; (iv) Date letter P (cycle VIII), 1632/33, London. (Plate 33.)

3   STAND PATEN

A stand paten $8^{7}/_{10}$ inches in diameter with a moulded rim and shallow depression. It stands upon a wide stem curving slightly towards a moulded base $3^{1}/_{2}$ inches in diameter. The overall height is $2^{1}/_{2}$ inches, and the weight is 14.11.16.

There are four marks: (i) Maker's mark script HP in quatrefoil with motifs, Humphrey Payne (Grimwade 1061); (ii) Britannia; (iii) Lion's head erased; (iv) Date letter A (cycle XIII), 1716/17, London. (Plate 33.)

4 & 5 FLAGONS

Two matching flagons. The height of each is 12 inches, the rim diameter 4½ inches, the capacity 3¾ pints and the weight 50.9.21. There is a high domed lid and a thumb rising slightly above the dome. The rim is moulded and a reed moulding marks the division between body and base. The foot is moulded and the diameter is 7¼ inches. The handle is an S-scroll and on the side of the body the sacred symbols. Underneath the base is an inscription:

> The Gift of Phoebe
> Wife of Richd Davenport
> of Calvely Esq
> To the Parishioners of Bunbury
> in the County of Chester
> in the year of our
> Redemption MDCCXXXVI.

See also flagon at Heswall, no. 3.

There are four marks: (i) Maker's mark TP within an oval frame, Thomas Parr II (Grimwade 2870); (ii) Lion passant guardant; (iii) Leopard's head crowned; (iv) Date letter V (cycle XIII), 1735/36, London. (Plate 33.)

6 & 7 ALMS PLATES

A pair of matching alms plates, each of diameter 10 inches with a wide plain rim and a deep depression. Overall height 1 inch. The plates are inscribed: 'For the Offertory at the Parish Church of Bunbury'.

There are four marks: (i) Maker's mark RB, Richard Bayley (Grimwade 2262); (ii) Leopard's head crowned; (iii) Lion passant guardant; (iv) Date letter b (cycle XIV), 1747/48, London. (Plate 33.)

8 COMMUNION CUP

A communion cup based on the design of no. 2 but just failing to achieve its proportions. It has a bell-shaped bowl with rim diameter 3⁹⁄10 inches. Height 7⁹⁄10 inches, diameter of the base 4¼ inches, capacity ½ pint. Weight 17.18.8. The bowl is inscribed 'For the Offertory of Bunbury Church'.

There are five marks on the side of the bowl: (i) Maker's mark WB, William Bateman II (Grimwade 3038); (ii) Lion passant guardant; (iii) Leopard's head crowned; (iv) Date letter t (cycle XVIII), 1834/35, London; (v) Duty mark.

BURLEYDAM
ST MARY AND ST MICHAEL
Deanery of Nantwich

When Dr Samuel Johnson visited Combermere at the beginning of what was to be his tour in North Wales in July 1774, he noted that the communion plate 'is handsome'.

He was accompanied by Mr and Mrs Thrale and in a fuller account of the visit Mrs Thrale recorded:

> On this day we heard Divine Service performed in a chapel my uncle built about a mile from the house at Burleydam where stood an old tattered place unfit for the purpose. It is a neat plain edifice and the Communion Plate of suitable value. Sir Linch says the whole cost him six hundred pounds but I know not how far he is to be believed …

The replacement church at Burleydam was opened in 1769 and although altered and added to in later years still has the church plate admired by Dr Johnson and Mrs Thrale. This consists of a suite of communion cup, paten, stand paten and flagon, and is of the highest order, made by Augustin Le Sage in 1769/70, the date the chapel was built. Each piece has a rococo arms of Cotton engraved upon it, and on some the crest of Cotton.

Reference:
Bristow, p.98.

1   COMMUNION CUP (see nos 2, 3 & 4)
A communion cup 8 inches high, parcel gilt with a bell-shaped bowl 3¾ inches deep having an inverted rim, diameter 3⅞ inches. The bowl stands upon a moulded stem with a gadrooned knop and below this a further narrower band of gadrooning. The base spreads out toward a further band of gadrooning, a quarter cavetto moulding and a step. The base diameter is 4½ inches. The coat of arms is engraved on the side of the bowl and the crest of the Cotton family on the foot spread.

There are four marks on the side of the bowl: (i) Date letter O (cycle XV), 1769/70, London; (ii) Leopard's head crowned; (iii) Lion passant guardant (repeated under the base); (iv) Maker's mark AL under a figure of a communion cup and above a five-pointed rowel – all within a quatrefoil frame, Augustin Le Sage (Grimwade 57) (repeated under the base).

2   PATEN (see nos 1, 3 & 4)
A very plain paten, 5½ inches diameter with a plain rim forming a single depression on which are engraved the coat of arms of the Cotton family. On the underside of the rim are three marks, very badly struck: one was that of the maker, the others are illegible.

3   STAND PATEN (see nos 1, 2 & 4)
A stand paten 6⅞ inches diameter, having a gadrooned rim and a single depression. It rests upon a spool-shaped stem, 1¾ inches high. This spreads to a band of gadrooning and a step. Base diameter 2¾ inches. The arms are engraved on the surface of the plate, and on the underside there are four marks as on the communion cup (no. 1).

4   FLAGON (see nos 1, 2 & 3)
A flagon, 12¾ inches high overall, having a double pear-shaped body, at its widest diameter, 5¼ inches. The curved oval top incorporates the lip and is covered by a lid, domed and ribbed towards a flowered finial. The edge of the rim is gadrooned, which embraces the lip. There is a loop handle to which the lid is hinged. This is of broken form, the edges enriched by a string of graded beads moulded on either side. The bottom of the handle is attached to the underside of the widest part of the body, where it divides into two leaves. The body rests upon a splayed foot which has a repeat of the gadrooning and a step. Diameter of base 4¼ inches. There is a coat of arms on the front of the body and an engraved crest on the side.
   There are four marks, as on the communion cup (no. 1), placed in a circle under the base of the bowl.

BURTON
St Nicholas
Deanery of Wirral, South

In 1995 the church silver was stolen and has not been recovered. The lost plate was recorded as follows:

Reference:
Commission; 1549/50 'One chales and ringe of ii Belles'.

1   COMMUNION CUP (see nos 2 & 3)
A parcel gilt communion cup with a bell-shaped bowl, 8½ inches high, the depth of the bowl 4½ inches. The spool-shaped stem is divided by a very narrow band with small vertically lobed edges. The stem has simple plain moulding beneath the bowl. The foot is moulded and the base has a narrow band of gadrooning – diameter 4⅖ inches. On the side of the bowl the sacred symbols. Inscribed on the penultimate moulding of the foot:

BURTON CHURCH

AD 1809
Ex dono Ricardi Congreve Armigeri.

There are five marks under the foot: (i) Maker's mark SH within a rectangle, Solomon Hougham (Grimwade 2536); (ii) Lion passant guardant; (iii) Leopard's head crowned; (iv) Date letter O (cycle XVII), 1809/10, London; (v) Duty mark.

2   ALMS PLATE (used as a paten) (see nos 1 & 3)
An alms plate 12½ inches diameter with a gadrooned edge and 1¼-inch rim with a single depression, in the centre of which is a raised cross 2½ inches diameter, on which are engraved the sacred symbols. The marks are as those on nos 1 and 3.

3   EWER (see nos 1 & 2)
The ewer is reported as being about 15 inches high, with a long handle and a spout. The body was bulbous, with a reeded [?gadrooned] edge, with the same inscription as found on the other pieces. The marks were as on nos 1 and 2.

CALVELEY
Deanery of Malpas

Calveley Hall chapel, a small one-time private chapel, was connected with the Hall, now demolished. It was purchased by local residents and linked with the work of the Parish of Bunbury in the middle of the 20th century. All but one item of the plate is Sheffield plate.

1   COMMUNION CUP
A communion cup 6½ inches high, of goblet form, with a rim 3³⁄₁₀ inches diameter. The depth of the bowl is 3⁷⁄₁₀ inches. The stem is of trumpet form, sweeping down to a plain reeded step. Diameter 3 inches.

On the side of the bowl are five marks: (i) Maker's mark PB above AB within a square, Peter and Ann Bateman (Grimwade 2140); (ii) Lion passant guardant; (iii) Leopard's head crowned; (iv) Date letter A (cycle XVII), 1796/97, London; (v) Duty mark.

CARRINGTON
ST GEORGE
(now at PARTINGTON)
Deanery of Bowdon

The church has been closed and the plate transferred to Partington nearby (see **BOWDON**).

1 FLAGON

A flagon, originally at Bowdon until 1759, when Mary, Countess of Stamford bought and gave it and the stand paten (no. 2) to Carrington, 9½ inches high with a flat cap lid hinged to an angular thumb and an S-scroll handle which ends in an angular terminal. The base is splayed and a single reeded band marks the junction between body and base. Below this the base splays out to the foot, diameter 6½ inches. On the splay is an inscription: 'Bought by Mary, Countess of Stamford and given for the use of St George's Chapel, Carrington 1759'.

On the side of the flagon beneath an engraving of the sacred symbols with rays, an inscription:

> Donum
> Willelmi Meredith
> de Ashley
> In usum Eucharistiae
> Ecclesiae S.M. de Bowdon
> Com: Cestr
> 1688

On the top of the flat cap lid and on the side of the flagon are four marks: (i) Maker's mark – a cypher PR of script form with pellet below in a shaped shield (Jackson, 1921, p.140) (repeated on the handle); (ii) Leopard's head crowned; (iii) Lion passant guardant (repeated under the foot); (iv) Date letter l (cycle XI), 1688/89, London. (Plate 35.)

2 STAND PATEN

A stand paten, also originally from Bowdon, 8¼ inches diameter with a 1-inch-wide rim edged with reed moulding. The overall height is 2 inches. It stands upon a plain trumpet stand which was added at a later date and the base is hollow, diameter 3¾ inches. The sacred symbols are engraved on the centre of the plate. The rim bears an inscription: 'Maria Meredith Willelmi Uxoris Filii Henrici Robinson de Whaploade in Com Lincoln pro Eucharistiae Donum Ecclesiae B.M. de Bowdon AD 1688', and a repeat of the English inscription found on the flagon (no. 1).

There are four marks, as on the flagon (no. 1), and the lion passant guardant is repeated on the base.

3 COMMUNION CUP

A communion cup 7³⁄₁₀ inches high purchased by Mary, Countess of Stamford, to complete the silver at Carrington. It has a bell-shaped bowl and a rim diameter 3⅗ inches, sweeping down to a stem divided by a moulded knop ¾ inch deep and a moulded foot 3⅗ inches diameter.

On the side and repeated under the foot the inscription: 'The Gift of Mary Countess of Stamford to St George's Chapel at Carrington 1759'.

There are four marks under the base: (i) Maker's mark MF within a lozenge, Magdalen Feline (Grimwade 2028); (ii) Lion passant guardant; (iii) Leopard's head crowned; (iv) Date letter D (cycle XV), 1759/60, London.

Magdalen Feline was one of the Huguenot silversmiths living in London. The Stamfords were great patrons of the Huguenots. Magdalen Feline also made a toilet set for the Countess which, with other Huguenot silver, is at Dunham Massey Hall. The property was acquired by the National Trust under the will of Roger, 10th Earl of Stamford. (Plate 36.)

CHEADLE
ST MARY
Deanery of Cheadle

1   COMMUNION CUP

An early 17th-century communion cup with almost vertical sides and bucket-shaped bowl, 8 inches high and rim diameter 4 inches. The sides of the bowl turn abruptly at the bottom to meet the stem divided by a knop ½ inch deep and 1⁴⁄₅ inches wide. The base is stepped with a shoulder and damaged by crushing. The foot diameter is 4⅕ inches.

The cup is inscribed: 'This Boule and Challis Belonges To The Parrish Church of Cheadle'. (The 'Boule' has not survived.)

The maker's mark, RW above either a pellet or a motif within a heart-shaped shield (Compendium 7502), has been repeated four times, though poorly struck, on the side of the bowl. The mark has not been identified with certainty, but if from nearby Manchester, could well be that of Robert Welshman.

Reference:
Brocklehurst, nos 15 and plate IV, 26.

2   PATEN or ALMS DISH

A large paten (perhaps used as an alms dish), 9½ inches in diameter with a rim 3½ inches wide and set at a slight angle to a single angular depression. There are no mouldings. A coat of arms is engraved on the surface of the plate, and on the back is an inscription:

Deo Opt Max:
DD
R.Royston Rect de Cheade
tu ne despici Christe
AD 1722

There are four marks: (i) Maker's mark WM above a five-point star in a simple shield (imperfectly struck); (ii) Leopard's head crowned; (iii) Lion passant guardant; (iv) Date letter capital Gothic I or J (cycle X), (1666/67), London.

3   STAND PATEN

A stand paten diameter 10 inches with a moulded rim ⅖ inches wide, forming a slight depression. The plate stands upon a curved waist, 1³⁄₁₀ inches wide and has a simple moulded foot 3 inches in diameter. In the centre of the plate the sacred symbols IHS, cross and nails within a wreathlike surround having stiff foliage.

There are four marks: (i) Maker's mark LA beneath a seated animal, possibly a dog, within a frame with semi-circular head, Thomas Langford I (Grimwade 1894); (ii) Britannia; (iii) Lion's head erased (repeated under the foot); (iv) Date letter C (cycle XIII), 1718/19, London.

4   FLAGON

A flagon, overall to top of the thumb 12 inches, with almost vertical sides 11½ inches high. It has a domed lid. The bottom of the flagon is marked by a reeded girdle and is stepped and moulded. Diameter of base 6½ inches. The S-scroll handle ends in a heart shaped terminal.

On the side of the flagon an inscription:

> The Gift of
> Mrs Eliz Jackson Widow
> to Cheadle Church
> in Cheshire
> ye 26 Apr 1734

There are four marks inside the lid and on the side of the flagon: (i) Maker's mark TF below a small fleur-de-lis and above a five point star within a lobed frame, Thomas Farren (Grimwade 2749); (ii) Leopard's head crowned; (iii) Lion passant guardant; (iv) Date letter Q (cycle XIII), 1731/32, London.

5 & 6   COMMUNION CUPS

Two identical communion cups (one in parcel gilt) of goblet form. Each is 6 inches high with rim diameter 3⅕ inches. The curve of the bowl sweeps down the stem of trumpet form and to the foot, diameter 3 inches. The cups are severely plain except for a narrow band of pellets.

Although an inscription states they were given by the Rector in 1875, the five marks on the base are: (i) Maker's mark Gothic JL within a rectangular frame Joseph Lock (Grimwade 1492); (ii) Leopard's head crowned; (iii) Lion passant guardant; (iv) Duty mark; (v) Date letter I (cycle XVII), 1804/05, London.

CHELFORD
St John the Evangelist
Deanery of Knutsford

1 COMMUNION CUP

A communion cup of possibly domestic origin supplied some years after the Commonwealth for the use of the church. It is 6¾ inches high and has a deep cylindrical bowl and a baluster stem and circular foot. The rim diameter is 4 inches. The bowl is pricked with the initials L above I E in a surround of scrolls centring in a heart, and the inscription is: 'The Gift of Mrs Elizabeth Baskerville relict of Thomas Baskerville of Old Withington Esq 1677'.

There are four marks on the bowl: (i) Maker's mark RF above a five-point star within a heart-shaped frame; (ii) Lion passant guardant; (iii) Leopard's head crowned; (iv) Date letter P (cycle IX), 1652/53, London.

2 STAND PATEN

A stand paten with broad gadrooned rim, diameter 9 inches on a trumpet-shaped stand. The paten stands 2¼ inches high and is engraved on the reverse side of the plate: 'The Gift of the Revd. John Parker A.M. to Chelford Chapel 1759'.

There are four marks: (i) Maker's mark DB with star above and inverted crescent within a squarish frame; (ii) Leopard's head crowned; (iii) Lion passant guardant; (iv) Date letter q (cycle XI), 1693/94, London.

3 ALMS PLATE

An alms plate with gadrooned rim, diameter 9½ inches, and inscribed on the reverse side: 'The Gift of John Parker Esq to Chelford Chapel 1765'.

There are four marks: (i) Maker's mark Gi beneath a five-point star within a lobed frame John Gibbons (Grimwade 823); (ii) Britannia; (iii) Lion's head erased; (iv) Date letter O (cycle XII), 1709/10, London.

4 ALMS PLATE

An unidentified alms plate with gadrooned rim, but having a different maker's mark.

5 FLAGON

A plain flagon 13¼ inches high with a domed lid and spreading cylindrical base. Diameter 7¾ inches. It has an S-scroll handle and a corkscrew thumb. It is dated 1760 on the handle.

There are four marks: (i) Maker's mark TW with C above and W below within a double circle, Thomas Whipham II and Charles Wright (Grimwade 2976); (ii) Lion passant guardant; (iii) Leopard's head crowned; (iv) Date letter D (cycle XV), 1759/60, London.

6   TAZZA

A continental bowl of tazza form, 7½ inches in diameter, the centre repoussé and chased with a representation of the Adoration of the Magi. The border is chased and engraved with birds and formal foliage. It is mounted on a circular foot bearing the Sterling mark. Its past history is not known, but it was given to the church by the Dixons of Astle Hall in 1945/46. (See Chelford parish magazine, June 1946, 'Some Chelford Notes', by Audrey C. Walsh.)

THE CHESTER CITY CHURCHES

When the Commissioners of 1553, under Bishop Bird and others who were to act for the King, examined the City churches, they recorded the plate and goods found in eleven places of worship. In addition to the Cathedral these were St Bridget, St Giles 'Spittell in Boughton', Holy Trinity, St John the Baptist, St John's Hospital (Northgate), St Martin, St Mary super Montem, St Michael, St Olave, St Oswald, St Peter. By the time Ball drew up his inventory in 1907, many changes had taken place.

St Oswald's (housed in the south transept of the Cathedral) had been moved to a new site on the Parkgate road in 1871, and dedicated to St Thomas, thus continuing the dedication of a small chapel which had once stood nearby and had been overlooked by the Commissioners. St Bridget's in Bridge Street had been demolished to make way for the access road to the new Grosvenor Bridge, a new St Bridget's being built nearer the bridge only to be demolished later in the same century. St Martin's, though rebuilt, closed in the mid-19th century, reopening for a short period as the church for Welsh-speaking Cestrians, and was later demolished. St Giles at Boughton had been demolished during the siege of Chester in the Civil War, a new church dedicated to St Paul being erected in 1830 close to the place of numerous public executions. Christ Church in St Oswald's Parish had been built in 1838 and later formed into a separate parish. St John without the Northgate, in the years before its closure was commonly referred to as 'Little St John's', to distinguish it from the parish church of St John the Baptist, occupied a wing of the Blue Coat School outside the Northgate, though formerly linked with the Northgate prison.

By 1979 drastic reorganisation of the churches and parishes of Chester had taken place; a number of churches were either turned over to other uses or demolished, fittings, furniture and plate were, in many cases, dispersed, and some lost sight of, making any attempt to record the plate, its significance to former parishes and its present whereabouts difficult. It was therefore decided to examine the list of plate in Churches drawn up by Ball, to link the early plate with the churches where it has historical significance, and indicate its present location.

Holy Trinity in Watergate Street has found a new worship centre at Blacon and the building has become the City Guildhall. Unlike St Bridget's,

St Michael's in Bridge Street was saved from demolition, and became the City Heritage Centre. St Olave's, after being linked to St Michael's for a while, and having survived a serious fire, is now redundant and no longer a place of worship. St John's without the Northgate has ceased to be a church. St Mary's near the castle is now an offshoot of the County Record Office and its furniture dispersed, and St Martin's has been demolished to make way for the ring road.

Only a few remain, fulfilling the purpose for which they were built, lovingly cared for over the years and, in many cases, supplied with splendid church plate. The following inventory will attempt to put on record the present whereabouts and, in some cases, the fate of the silver made before 1837.

CHESTER
(THE BISHOP OF CHESTER'S PRIVATE CHAPEL)
Deanery of Chester
(see also **CHESTER** ST MARTIN)

1   COMMUNION CUP (for use when visiting the sick)
On the formation of the Chester Team of churches the Archdeacon passed this cup, originally at Chester St Martin's, for use in the Bishop's Private Chapel. A silver, parcel gilt, communion cup (unmarked) but without paten or paten cover, standing 5 inches high, with a bell-shaped bowl and pronounced everted rim, diameter 2½ inches. The stem has a wide moulded knop and the foot is convex, meeting the stem in a curiously abrupt manner, its only relief being a scribed line. The base diameter is 2½ inches. The weight of the cup is 4 oz.

On the side of the bowl is the inscription:

> The
> Gift of Mrs
> DIGHTON SALMON
> For the use of the Poor
> Sick Communicants of
> St Martin's Parish
> In Chester
> 1731

Mrs Salmon gave a number of similar communion cups to the City churches. As these were the work of Richard Richardson I, one can safely assume that this cup was his work and that his marks and those of the Chester Assay would have appeared on the now missing paten cover. (Plate 37.)

CHESTER
CHRIST CHURCH
Deanery of Chester

The church which dates from 1876, and contains some interesting plate of an earlier period, replaced a building which had been consecrated in 1838 as a daughter church in St Oswald's Parish. The early plate here probably survived the rebuilding, although the earliest piece, the stand paten of 1725, was given to the church in 1897. It is rich in plate later than 1874, but this lies outside the scope of this present record.

References:
Ball 1907, p.123ff.
Pevsner and Hubbard, p.150.

1 STAND PATEN

A stand paten, diameter 5½ inches, with a moulded rim and a slight depression on which are the four marks. It stands 1½ inches in height, the stand having a moulded base, diameter 2½ inches. There is an inscription on the underside recording the fact that it was given to the church in 1897.

There are four marks: (i) Maker's mark (much worn), two initials, the second an A beneath a crown within a shaped frame with lobed top. Ball interpreted this mark as 'WA with two-handled vase above in a shaped shield', William Allen I, who entered this mark in 1725 (Grimwade 2997); (ii) Lion passant guardant; (iii) Leopard's head crowned; (iv) Date letter K (cycle XIII), 1725/26, London.

2 COMMUNION CUP (see no. 3)

This is the first of two dissimilar cups of the same date and by the same maker, William Bateman I, which were given to the church at the time of the building of the original church.

It stands 6¾ inches high and has a rim diameter of 3½ inches. It has a campana-shaped bowl, the top three-quarters being concave, the rest sweeping down to meet a concave stem which ends in a moulded foot, diameter 3½ inches. Ball was under the impression that this cup had been altered in shape, but there seems to be no reason to believe this as the marks below the rim are clear and intact. On one side of the bowl are engraved the sacred monogram with rays, cross, IHS and nails, and the words 'Christ Church 1838'.

There are five marks: (i) Maker's mark W.B within a shaped frame, William Bateman I (Grimwade 3037); (ii) Lion passant guardant; (iii) Leopard's head crowned; (iv) Date letter f (cycle XVIII), 1821/22, London; (v) Duty mark.

Reference:
Ball 1907, p.126.

3   COMMUNION CUP (see no. 2)
A communion cup reflecting a much earlier shape, which one might expect to find in the 17th century, but bearing the William Bateman I mark as found on the communion cup no. 2.

It stands 6¾ inches in height and has a plain beaker-type bowl with everted rim below which are the marks. The rim is 3½ inches in diameter and the bowl 4¼ inches deep. The bottom of the bowl is angular and supported by a spool stem and moulded base, diameter 3¼ inches. The bowl is inscribed 'Christ Chirch 1838' and also has the sacred monogram (as on cup no. 2). There is a disc repair behind this. The five marks are as on the previous cup.

Reference:
Ball 1907, p.126.

4   ALMS PLATE
Ball records a pair of these plates in 1907. One remains, diameter 9 inches and ⅞ inches in height with a deep depression and moulded rim. The border is curved and there are two gothic capital Cs (for Christ Church) in the centre of the depression.

There are four marks: (i) Duty mark (of William IV); (ii) Date letter S with the Sheffield crown within a rectangular frame, 1838/39; (iii) Lion passant; (iv) Maker's mark D & S within a rectangular frame, Dixon & Son.

Reference:
Ball 1907, p.127.

CHESTER
HOLY AND UNDIVIDED TRINITY
Deanery of Chester
(transferred to Blacon)

The ancient site in Watergate Street was abandoned as a parish church in recent years and the building became the City Guildhall, though retaining a number of interesting monuments. The original plate belonging to the church was transferred to the new parish church of Holy Trinity at Blacon.

1   COMMUNION CUP (see no. 2)
This is the earliest and most splendid of the Chester Elizabethan communion cups. It bears the mark of William Mutton (a sheep's head within an ornamental shield) (Compendium 1) – the earliest known Chester maker's mark – and is dated from the churchwardens' accounts for 1570 when it cost, along with the communion paten (no. 2), £6 18s.10d. Made as a companion to the communion paten, it is 7⅜ inches high and has a deep bowl splaying at the rim to a diameter of 4¾ inches. The stem has a knop with small collars above and below, decorated with six ovals and small pellets, an unusual feature, almost

echoing a medieval treatment. There are two bands of enrichment between mouldings, one immediately below the bowl and another at the base of the stem, each of the same applied decoration, consisting of a series of circles, triangles and ovals forming a regular repeating pattern not found on any other cup in the Chester area, but very like the enrichment on the communion cup at Llandyfrydog, Anglesey, which is also the work of William Mutton.

The bowl carries two bands of inscriptions in capitals, some of which are joined. The top band situated immediately below the rim reads: '+ DRINKE YE AL OF THIS FOR THIS IS MI BLOVD OF THE NEWE TESTAMENT +' (a leaf separating each word). Below this, running round the middle of the bowl, the text is continued on the second band with a leaf separating each word as before: '+ WHICHE IS SHED FOR YOV AND FOR MANE +'.

If the spelling is any guide, the text is closer to the Edwardian Prayer of Consecration (1549) than to that in the revised book of 1559. The suggestion that the inscription was added to the cup some years after it was made seems based upon the observation that the engraving of the letters appears to cut into the solitary William Mutton mark. This is not conclusive evidence, and the case against this is strengthened by the spelling and the fact that one would not expect to find a perfectly plain cup in 1570. The bands of the inscription and the decoration on the stem are gilt (see the cup at Gawsworth, no. 1).

References:
Ball 1907, p.51ff.
Ridgway 1968, p.55 and plate 13.

2   PATEN (see no. 1)
A perfectly plain communion paten made in 1570 to accompany the communion cup (no.1) bearing the single William Mutton mark. It is 7½ inches in diameter, formed with a single depression and a rim ¾ inch wide scribed with four concentric lines as the only relief. The mark is punched on the rim.

References:
Ball 1907, p.51ff.
Ridgway 1968, p.55 and plate 13.

3   STAND PATEN
Although this stand paten bears the London assay mark for 1694/95 it came to the church through the will of Elizabeth Booth of Dunham Massey who died 11 December 1734. She was buried in the south transept of Chester Cathedral which then served as the parish church of St Oswald, where a memorial records that she was 96 at the time of her death. It bears the coat of arms of Booth of Dunham (argent three boars heads erect and erased), in a lozenge-shaped shield. There is no inscription, but 'E Booth' has been scratched on the underside. Beneath the coat of arms is a cypher K.L.A. of adorsed letters. When the churchwardens received the bequest, they recorded on 23 December 1734:

Received a silver salver left by will of Madam Elizabeth Booth late dr of Sir John Booth engraven a cypher of the letters K and H, with the arms of the family of Booth of Dunham Massey to hold Communion bread.

The stand paten, diameter 11½ inches, is 3½ inches high and has a gadrooned edge to both the rim and the splayed trumpet foot.

There are four marks: (i) Maker's mark BV with an inverted crescent above and a star below in a quatrefoil, Abraham Buteux (Grimwade 249); (ii) Leopard's head crowned; (iii) Lion passant guardant; (iv) Date letter r (cycle XI), 1694/95, London.

Reference:
Ball 1907, p.58.

4 & 5   A Pair of Identical Flagons

These flagons were a gift to the church, and the churchwardens' accounts record: 'Two noble flagons given by an unknown person to the Church of Trinity, and were first used June 9 1728'.

Each flagon stands 14½ inches high including a tall domed lid, diameter 4¾ inches, hinged to a scroll thumbpiece and S-scroll handle which terminates in a plain shield and attached to the body of the flagon by an oval collar. The rim is reeded and the straight sides slightly batter, rising from a narrow reeded girdle below the handle terminal and splaying towards a moulded spreading foot 7⅞ inches in diameter and 2½ inches high. Below the lid is an inscription: 'To the honour of God and the use of ye Parish Church of ye Holy Trinity in ye City of Chester June ye 8 1728'. Each flagon weighs 57 oz.

Both are fully marked on the base and also on the underside of the lid: (i) Maker's mark WD beneath a leaf in a shaped shield, William Darker (Grimwade 3078). Two flagons were made for Chester St John the Baptist (nos 8 and 9) by the same maker and are assayed for 1729/30; (ii) Lion passant guardant; (iii) Leopard's head crowned; (iv) Date letter M (cycle XIII), 1727/28, London. (The date is printed as 1757 in Ball.)

Reference:
Ball 1907, p.60ff.

6   Communion Cup

A plain communion cup, 7 inches in height with a bell-shaped bowl, rim diameter 3⅞ inches having a wide stem and slender moulded knop on a wide moulded foot, diameter 3¾ inches. According to the churchwardens' accounts it was purchased for £4 1s. 6d.

There are five marks: (i) Maker's mark RR within a rectangle, Richard Richardson II Type 5a (Compendium 7385); (ii) Lion passant guardant; (iii)

Leopard's head crowned; (iv) Chester City coat; (v) Date letter b (series 4), 1752/53, Chester.

Reference:
Ball 1907, p.61.

CHESTER
ST JOHN THE BAPTIST
Deanery of Chester

Towards the end of Edward VI's reign, the inventory of goods at St John's showed they had been allowed to keep '1 Chalyce of sylver with a patent gilts ... vii ownces'. Other goods were also listed, reflecting the Protestant trend and fashion, for they included a white damask cope which had been turned into a table cover, and a 'payre of organs'. The list reflects, as it did in the case of the other City churches, the retention of a bare minimum for church use. The nature and ultimate fate of the other plate at St John's is not known. Some may have been restored during the short reign of Queen Mary, but the earliest surviving silver at St John's is a London-made cup of 1633. Whether this remained at St John's during the Civil War cannot be established, but seems unlikely. More likely, as in other City churches, it was provided by the wardens as part of the replacement plate at the time of the Restoration, and the inscription and date upon it seem to suggest this. It is of domestic character and would be available at the time even though second-hand when purchased. A large paten was provided in 1664. Ball lists a paten, 1650, but this is confusing as he describes a Ralph Walley alms dish of 1683 and omits reference to it in his list. Another Chester goldsmith, Richard Richardson I, provided a paten in 1717 and also made a communion set for use when visiting the sick (cup and paten) which Mrs Dighton Salmon gave to the church in 1725/26. The two flagons (London 1729/30) and two alms plates (London 1735) complete the list of early plate.

References:
Ball 1907, p.33ff.
Morris, p.153.
Scott, pp.20-21, illustrated.

1   COMMUNION CUP

A cup of 1633 with bell-shaped bowl, possibly of domestic origin, which may have been added to the church plate some time after the Restoration. A similar, though not identical, cup was provided by the same wardens in 1674 (see no. 3).

The cup is $6^{1}/_{8}$ inches high and the bowl rim diameter is $3^{3}/_{5}$ inches. It has a moulded baluster stem and a disc, concave foot scribed on the edge. An inscription on the bowl reads 'This is the Communion cup of St John's', and on the foot is a second inscription: 'R.B. and T.B. Churchwardens, 1674'. The initials stand for Randle Batho and Thomas Bird. Under the foot is scratched a weight 8 : 10 and the single mark of the lion passant guardant.

There are four marks on the bowl below the rim: (i) Maker's mark (?)I. T with a mullet or (?)pellet below in a double-edged heart-shaped frame. The mark is rubbed. Ball recorded the mark as I.T. above a mullet as on a similar cup by the same maker at St John without the Northgate (no. 1) (see Jackson, p.114); (ii) Leopard's head crowned; (iii) Lion passant guardant; (iv) Date letter q (cycle VIII), 1633/34, London.

Reference:
Ball 1907, p.40.

2   PATEN

A large heavy paten, diameter 11⅗ inches with the border, 2⅗ inches wide forming a single depression. On the border is a long inscription: 'The Gift of Mrs Margaret Jones to the Church of St John Baptist in Chester to Cary the Consecrated Bread upon at the Holy Sacrament of Bread and Wine to be kept Solie for that use and Woe be to those that Commit Sacriledge 1667'. This is accompanied by an elaborate coat of arms (Mersey of Sale impaling Dutton of Hatton) not apparently connected with the donor, although the Dutton family had been associated with the licensing of Cheshire Minstrels which took place at St John's Church.

The weight 20.9.00 is scratched underneath and there are four marks: (i) Maker's mark, now worn, was recorded by Ball as 'R.H. with two pellets and rose below in heraldic shield'. Ball's rose would appear to be a star or mullet below the initials, and the presence of pellets is disputed; (ii) Leopard's head crowned; (iii) Lion passant guardant; (iv) Date letter G (cycle X), 1664/65, London.

Reference:
Ball 1907, p.43.

3   COMMUNION CUP

A communion cup of goblet form resembling, and probably a deliberate copy of the communion cup of 1633 (see no. 1) though made 1672/73 and presented to the church in 1674. Each carries the same inscription, in the same positions. On the bowl: 'This is the Communion Cup of St Johns'; on the foot: 'R. B. and T. B. Churchwardens, 1674'.

The cup stands 6⅛ inches high, the bowl 3¼ inches deep, the rim slightly everted, diameter 3⅗ inches. The baluster stem splays out to a foot, diameter 3½ inches.

There are four marks on the side of the bowl, and the lion passant guardant mark is repeated beneath the foot, along with a scratched weight record 8 : 8: (i) Maker's mark (rubbed) G G with a star or mullet between. Ball recorded it as 'with fleur-de-lys below', in a shaped shield; (ii) Leopard's head crowned;

(iii) Lion passant guardant; (iv) Date letter P (cycle X), 1672/73, London (not 'R in black letter capital of the year 1684-5, as Ball recorded).

References:
Ball 1907, p.44.
Scott, p.21, illustrated.

4 ALMS DISH

A large circular alms dish with a diameter of 8⅞ inches, formed of a single depression. There is a flat rim 1½ inches wide on which is engraved leaves resembling butterflies and berry-like beads through which the stem passes. The centre of the depression has an inscription in script which records:

John Thomason
Joseph Maddock
Church Wardens
1683

Surrounding this is engraved a border of conventional leaves in six pairs. The marks are punched above the inscription and help to balance it. These consist of the mark of Ralph Walley, RW within a shaped shield (Compendium 7503), punched twice, between which is a sterling mark in two lines within an ornamental shield. This piece is believed to be the earliest recorded piece by this Chester goldsmith.

References:
Ball 1907, p.42, illustrated.
Brocklehurst, no. 46 and plate X.
Jackson 1911, p.140ff, illustrated.
Ridgway 1968, p.182 and plate 40.

5 PATEN

A paten 8½ inches in diameter, with a moulded rim of incised lines and a shallow depression. The weight scratched beneath is 10 oz. 8 dwt. There is an inscription in script characters: 'Thomas Hiccock and Thomas Bridge Church Wardens 1719'.

There are five marks: (i) Maker's mark Ri, in shaped shield, Richard Richardson I Type 3 (Compendium 6815); (ii) Britannia; (iii) Lion's head erased; (iv) Chester City coat; (v) Date letter R (series 2), 1717/18, Chester.

Reference:
Ball 1907, p.44.

6 COMMUNION CUP (for use when visiting the sick) (see no. 7)

A communion cup for use when visiting the sick (with paten cover, see no. 7). The height of the cup is 5⅝ inches and the rim diameter 2⅞ inches. The bowl is bell-shaped and the stem, divided by a plain knop, spreads to a moulded foot. There is an inscription on the side of the bowl which reads: 'The Gift of

Mrs Dighton Salmon for the use of the poor sick Communicants in the Parish of St John the Baptist, Chester 1725'.

There are five marks on the side of the bowl: (i) Maker's mark Ri within an ornamental shield, Richard Richardson I Type 3 (Compendium 6815); (ii) Lion passant guardant; (iii) Leopard's head crowned; (iv) Chester City coat; (v) Date letter Z (series 2), 1725/26, Chester.

References:
Ball 1907, p.46, illustrated.
Ridgway 1968, p.167.

7   PATEN COVER (see no. 6)

A paten cover for the cup (no. 6), diameter 3¼ inches, formed of a single depression to fit over the cup mouth and having a narrow flange. The stand is of spool form and the flat base is inscribed 'D. S. 1725', the initials of the donor. There are five marks as on the cup (no. 6).

8 & 9   FLAGONS

Two almost identical flagons given to the church by Mrs Dighton Salmon, whose servants were recorded in the churchwardens' accounts as having been given 1s. when they delivered the gifts.

They are of baluster jug form, with a well formed lip, but without a lid. Each stands 10¾ inches in height with a rim diameter of 4½ inches and moulded foot diameter 4½ inches. On the front of the flagon, opposite to the scroll handle is an inscription:

The
Gift of Mrs
Dighton Salmon
To the Church of St
John Baptist in
Chester 1731

(a small winged angel's head below).

The weights are scratched underneath: 40.15 and 42.10.

There are four marks on the base: (i) Maker's mark W D with rose above within a trefoil frame, William Darker (Grimwade 3079) (see Holy and Undivided Trinity (nos 4 and 5) for flagons by the same maker); (ii) Lion passant guardant; (iii) Date letter O (cycle XIII), 1729/30, London; (iv) Leopard's head crowned.

References:
Ball 1907, p.47.
Scott, p.21, illustrated.

10 & 11   Alms Plates

Two matching plates diameter 10 inches with 1¼-inch rim forming a single depression. Weight marks are scratched beneath: 10 oz. (Ball inaccurately recorded 19 oz.) and 15 oz. 11dwt., and each has an inscription. On one rim: 'In usum offertorii ad eodem B: Johanni Baptistee Sacrum Apud Cestrienses A D 1735', and on the other: 'Hilarem datorem diligit Deus'.

Each has the same set of marks: (i) Maker's mark RB, Richard Bayley (Grimwade 2262). Compare the Alms Plate (no. 5) at St Peter's Church, dated 1736/37, by the same maker; (ii) Lion passant guardant; (iii) Date letter V (cycle XIII), 1735/36, London; (iv) Leopard's head crowned.

Reference: Ball 1907, p.48.

Chester
St John without the Northgate
(redundant)
Deanery of Chester

In the years immediately before its closure, it was commonly referred to as Little St John's, to distinguish it from the parish church of St John the Baptist.

Originally the site of the hospital of St John the Baptist church on the north side of the Northgate, it was later incorporated in the Blue Coat Hospital School (now closed). The City Northgate gaol was situated alongside Little St John's and a narrow bridge, known as the Bridge of Sighs, passing over the town ditch and later canal, linked the two buildings. The old gaol was closed and demolished in 1808, along with the Northgate.

In 1553, the Commissioners left with the chaplain a silver parcel gilt chalice and paten weighing 10 oz., and some other church goods. In the 19th century a Britannia metal communion set consisting of a flagon, two cups, a paten and a plate made by James Dixon & Sons of Sheffield, *c.*1840 had been used at the replacement gaol.

The Corporation Assembly Minutes, 26 March 1801 (AB/5.f.80) record the decision to loan to Little St John's a silver ewer left to the Corporation by Colonel Roger Whitley in 1680, for use in the Communion Service, from 1801 to 1840. In 1840 a new flagon was given to the church by George Brydges Granville, and the Whitley ewer was returned to the City Plate collection. The plate from Little St John's has been deposited with the plate from St Oswald's at St Thomas of Canterbury's Parish Church on Parkgate Road.

The plate listed by Ball in 1907 still exists, except for the 'Chalice 1781' whose present whereabouts is not known (see no. 4).

1   Communion Cup (see no. 2)

A heavy communion cup which closely resembles a cup of 1633 given to St John the Baptist's Parish Church (no.1) in 1674. The cup stands 7³/₁₀ inches high. The bowl, of goblet form, rim diameter 4 inches, has sloping sides and is 3½ inches deep, supported by a baluster stem leading to a splayed base 3⅘ inches in diameter. There is a later inscription:

> 'The Gift of John Thomason Alderman and Justice of the Peace to the new Chappell Belonging to the Hospitall of St John Baptist without the Northgate in the City of Chester 1717'.

Scratched beneath the base is the weight, 12.10.12.

There are four marks below the rim: (i) Maker's mark I.T above a mullet within a double-edged heart-shaped frame (see Chester St John the Baptist (no. 1), and Jackson, p.114); (ii) Leopard's head crowned; (iii) Lion passant guardant; (iv) Date letter D (cycle IX), 1641/42, London.

References:
Ball 1907, p.112.
Grosvenor Museum Exhibition, 1973.

2   STAND PATEN

A stand paten, 5⅗ inches in diameter with a narrow slightly moulded rim and pronounced dip towards a ¼-inch depression. The stand is compressed by damage, but has a single step to a 3-inch-diameter base. The original height was about 2½ inches. A weight record has been inscribed below the plate – 5.16.0. and there is an inscription on the surface: 'The Gift of Mrs Alice Thomason Wid; to ye new Chappell belonging to ye Hospll of St John Bapt without ye Northgate in ye City of Chester 1717'.

There are five marks: (i) Maker's mark Ri within an oval, Richard Richardson I Type 4; (ii) Britannia; (iii) Leopard's head erased; (iv) Chester City coat; (v) Date letter rubbed but probably Q (series 2), 1716/17, Chester.

References:
Ball 1907, p.113.
Ridgway 1968, p.170.

3   STAND PATEN

The origin of this stand paten is not known beyond the record given in script on the surface that it was the gift of John Graham the incumbent in 1864, which was about a century after it was made. In the absence of a date letter and maker's mark, the form of the Hibernia figure appears to confirm this.

Stand paten diameter 6¹⁄₁₀ inches, overall height 1¾ inches. The plate has a narrow, slightly moulded rim and a shallow depression. The stand foot is of trumpet form, splaying towards a narrow flat base, diameter 2¾ inches.

On the underside of the plate are two marks: (i) Hibernia; (ii) Irish Harp and Crown (Dublin).

Reference:
Ball 1907, p.113.

4 CHALICE 1781

Ball lists a cup of 1781 as being amongst the plate at St John's, but an extensive search at St Thomas's church has not disclosed its present whereabouts. Ball's record is given here in the hope that the description might lead to its recovery:

> This vessel has apparently never been used in the chapel, probably on account of its non-ecclesiastical character. It is a loving cup or goblet, without handles, and 6½ in. high. The bowl is decorated with a well-executed design of true lovers' knots and floral garland ornament in repousse, and is an elegant and chaste cup. At the base of the bowl and at the edge of the foot is a neat bead ornamentation. The cup bears no inscription. The hallmarks are: (1) the London date letter "f" in small roman of the year 1781; (2) leopard's head crowned; (3) lion passant, and (4) the maker's mark, I.R., in plain oblong shield (John Robins, London). [Perhaps Grimwade 1623.]

Reference:
Ball 1907, p.114.

CHESTER
ST MARY ON THE HILL
(also ST MARY SUPER MONTEM)
Deanery of Chester

When the individual parishes of St Bridget and St Martin ceased to exist, their plate was transferred to St Mary on the Hill, once referred to as St Mary Super Montem, and this became known officially as the Parish of St Bridget and St Martin. The plate at St Mary's was then removed to the new church of St Mary without the Walls at Handbridge on the other side of the Dee, where it remains, and the account of its history is given under Chester St Mary without the Walls.

CHESTER
ST BRIDGET
(demolished)
Deanery of Chester

Originally the Parish Church of St Bridget stood opposite to St Michael where Bridge Street and Lower Bridge Street meet and where once stood the south gate of the Roman entrance to Deva.

St Bridget's received numerous bequests. In 1528 Elizabeth Hurlstone of Chester bequeathed 'on Chales off sylv wt on vestmet', but in 1553 the

Commissioners left to the church only one chalice of silver and a gilt paten weighing xii ounces.

St Bridget's was the parish church of the Edwardes family of Chester Goldsmiths, and their memorials remained in the church until, with the building of the new Grosvenor Bridge at the beginning of the 19th century, a new road, Grosvenor Street, necessitated the demolition of the church and a new St Bridget's was built on the site of St Mary's nunnery near the castle. The plate was transferred to it. In 1891 the new St Bridget's was demolished, and the original dedication and plate were again transferred to St Mary's on the Hill which became officially the Parish of St Bridget and St Martin.

It is surprising that any plate survived. The plate was retained at this church until that too closed in 1973 and the buildings were acquired by the Cheshire County Council to extend the County Record Office.

In 1907 Ball reported the plate from St Bridget's as a silver gilt flagon and two patens 1696, a communion cup of 1718, a communion cup of 1783 and two later patens of 1890/1.

At the same time, the older silver of the original St Mary's was transferred to the new church at Handbridge (St Mary without the Walls), and the plate from St Bridget's was purchased by the Grosvenor Museum, Chester, in 1988, where it is now on display.

References:
Ball 1907, p.79ff.
Earwaker, 1898.

CHESTER
St Mary on the Hill
(St Bridget's)
Deanery of Chester

The circumstances which brought about the transfer of the early plate from this ancient church, in 1887, to St Mary Handbridge and the depositing to take its place of the plate formerly in the parish church of St Bridget, Chester, on the demolition of St Bridget's, is described under St Mary without the Walls (Handbridge). The plate from St Bridget's was retained at St Mary on the Hill until that church too became redundant in 1973, when the building was acquired by Cheshire County Council.

The list of plate surveyed by Ball in 1907 comprised: two patens and a flagon – all 1696; a communion cup by Richard Richardson I – 1718; a communion cup (London) – 1783; and two patens given to St Mary's in 1891. All except the last on Ball's list, came from St Bridget's, which originally stood opposite to St Michael's where Bridge Street and Lower Bridge Street meet. Together they flanked what had been the south gate of the Roman fortress.

Among numerous bequests made to the church was, for example, in 1528 when Elizabeth Hurleston of Chester bequeathed: on Chales off sylv wt on vestmet – (Lancs. and Chesh. Wills, Chetham Society xxxiii).

By 1553 the Commissioners left at the church only one chalice of silver and a gilt paten weighing xii ounces. St Bridget's became the parish church of the Chester Goldsmith family of Edwardes, and their memorials remained in the church until, with the coming of the new Grosvenor Bridge, a new road was cut (Grosvenor Street) which necessitated the demolition of St Bridget's. A new St Bridget's was then built nearer the Castle, to which the plate was transferred. This new church had a short life and was demolished in 1891, less than a century afterwards, and again the plate was transferred, this time to St Mary on the Hill, which then became the Parish of St Bridget and St Martin. It is surprising that any plate survived.

References:
Ball 1907, p.79ff.
Earwaker 1898.

1 FLAGON

A fine silver gilt flagon, overall height 14 inches, with a rim diameter of 5¾ inches and a base diameter of 9 inches was fully recorded (inaccurately) by Ball in 1907. Earwaker described the flagon a few years earlier as a silver-gilt flagon with an inscription on the bottom 'St Bridget's Chester, Chas Price, Saml Nickson Churchwardens 1810'. It was, however, of much earlier date.

It was given originally to St Bridget's by one Mrs Hannah Swan who also gave two patens (see nos 2 and 3). Ball described the flagon as follows:

> This is a handsome piece of plate, of finer workmanship and decorative treatment than is generally to be found of its period of manufacture. It stands 13¾ in. high, has a diameter of 5 6-8 in., and at the foot 8⅛ in. It has a lid and thumbpiece without a lip. Around the centre of the lid, and at the edge of the base is a handsome tongue moulding. It is an example of the Britannia period and bears the following hallmarks: Maker's mark, Ro, in heart-shaped shield (Hugh Roberts, Newgate Street, London), (2) the figure of Britannia (3) leopard's head and (4) the London date letter, A, in Court hand of the year 1696 [in fact 27 March-28 May 1697 (cycle XII)]. This is the earliest example in Chester of the Britannia period, being made during the first year that the new standard was adopted.

Beneath the foot is inscribed:

St Bridget's Chester.
Chas. Price, Saml. Nickson,
Churchwardens,
1810

The inscription was added at a much later date, presumably when it was repaired, as it was presented with the two patens next described, by Mrs Hannah Swan, as the inscription appearing on the patens makes clear. The Ro mark referred to by Ball is Grimwade no. 2382 Hugh Roberts. The flagon is evidence that Hugh Roberts was using his mark at least a year before he entered it at Goldsmiths' Hall, April 1697 (when the surviving register there begins).

Purchased by the Grosvenor Museum, Chester, in 1988, and on display in the Ridgway Gallery. (Plate 38.)

References:
Ball 1907, p.80.
Earwaker 1898, p.230.

2 & 3   TWO PLATE PATENS

A matching pair of plate patens, diameter 9⅝ inches, formed of a single depression, with a broad moulded edge 1¼ inches wide, on one of which is an inscription recording their history: 'This and such an other with a guilt Flaggon Cup and Couer are the gift of Mrs Hannah Swan to St Bridget's Parish'.

They bear the same hallmarks as are found on the flagon (no. 1) and were made by Hugh Roberts. It would seem from the inscription that the gift may have included not only the silver flagon and the two patens but also a cup and paten cover, but if so, nothing is known of these two items and they were not known to Earwaker at the end of the 19th century. Weight 15 ounces each. The surfaces are heavily scored with knife cuts.

Purchased by the Grosvenor Museum, Chester, in 1988, and on display in the Ridgway Gallery. (Plate 39.)

Reference:
Ball 1907, p.81.

4   COMMUNION CUP

A plain communion cup, 6¾ inches in height with a wide deep bowl, bell-shaped, the rim diameter 3⅝ inches. The bowl has a slightly everted rim and is inscribed: 'Thomas Bolland, James Johnson, Church Wardens 1720'. The bowl curves round towards the stem which is divided by a narrow girdle and curves outwards to a step and a well proportioned shoulder which is separated from the foot by two mouldings. Base diameter 3⅝ inches. A weight record has been inscribed beneath the foot, 10-1-0.

Below the rim are five marks: (i) Ri within a shaped shield, Richard Richardson I Type 3 (Compendium 6815); (ii) Britannia; (iii) Lion's head erased; (iv) Chester City coat; (v) Date letter S (series 2), 1718/19, Chester.

Purchased by the Grosvenor Museum, Chester, in 1988, and on display in the Ridgway Gallery.

References:
Ball 1907, p.82 (illustrated).
Ridgway 1968, p.167.

5   COMMUNION CUP

This cup would appear to be a deliberate copy of the communion cup (no. 4), though the base mouldings are damaged and the inscription reads: 'Benjn Scott, J. Williams, Church Wardens 1784'.

There are four marks on the side of the bowl below the rim: (i) Maker's mark (rubbed): (ii) Lion passant guardant: (iii) Leopard's head crowned: (iv) Date letter h (cycle XVI), 1783/84, London.

On loan to Huntington New Parish in October 1985.

Reference:
Ball 1907, p.82 and illustrated opp. p.83.

CHESTER
St Martin
(demolished)
Deanery of Chester

An early foundation rebuilt at various times, St Martin's once formed a small separate parish, but was later linked with St Bridget's and located at the church of St Mary on the Hill. When this church in turn closed it became an annexe to the Chester County Record Office.

Ball states that in 1553 the Commissioners delivered to Thomas Trubshaw and Roger Cottrell a chalice of silver and a paten parcel gilt weighing thirteen ounces, noting at the same time that they considered other goods delivered to the churchwardens were of so small value that they were given to the poor of the parish.

When Ball recorded the silver at St Martin's in 1907 the church possessed 'a small chalice 1731, chalice of 1804, ditto 1804, credence paten 1805'. Most of this silver has now been traced as follows:

The 1731 cup is kept at the private chapel of the Bishop of Chester (see under Chester, Bishop's Private Chapel). One of the 1804 chalices was handed over to Huntington new parish, but present whereabouts not known. The other 1804 communion cup was purchased by the Grosvenor Museum Chester in 1988, and is now on display in the Ridgway Gallery. The stand paten was lent to Huntington new parish (see Huntington).

Reference:
Ball 1907, p.117.

CHESTER
St Mary without the Walls
(Handbridge)
Deanery of Chester

When the parish of St Bridget with St Martin was established in 1887, the ancient parish church of St Mary on the Hill became the church of the new parish and the silver belonging to St Bridget's and St Martin's was transferred to it. At the same time the new Church of St Mary, built across the River Dee at Handbridge in 1885-87, became the new parish of St Mary and the plate which had been in use at the older St Mary's was transferred to Handbridge. It is for this reason that it is now described, as Ball described it, under St Mary's Handbridge, otherwise known as St Mary without the Walls.

The wardens' accounts at St Mary's are unique amongst Chester church records in that they begin in 1536 and reveal the fate of the collection of silver which had accumulated, although there are no records of any plate being purchased at this early period. As the Reformation proceeded, with the threats of so much silver being alienated, one Elyn Clarke laid claim to a chalice as her property. The incident is recorded in the churchwardens' accounts in 1547:

> Md that the viiit day of January in the yeir of or lorde god MCCCCXLVIJ Elyn Clarke wydowe comyth before the hole pishe demandynge ther & them one certain chalysse And so Thomas wiswall & Ric' Strete the beyng Churche wardense wth advise & cosent of the hole pisheners did delyvr the same chalisse unto the said Elyn as her awne.

Her fears were justified, for around 1550/51 altars were being demolished and many church goods were being sold.

> It' one sylv' crosse Dooble gylt sold by W Ball & Tho Browne vz lviii unces the sylv senser xxviii unces ... xxi li/s
>
> x
>
> s   li   s
> One gyld chales sold by mr ball of xv unc ... iii xv
>
> One other chales sold by Thoms Rogerson of ... sold to
> li
> Mr vawdrie for iii
>
> The third gild was mistres clerks

In 1553 the Commissioners did their work, and left only a chalice and paten weighing 10 oz. A hurried restoration of the church took place in Queen Mary's short reign and a spirited attempt was made to replace and restore articles which had suffered desecration and loss in the previous reign. This included the church plate, hence the entry in the churchwardens' accounts 1553/54: 'Itm payd to Lawrans the gold smythe for mendynge of the pyx xvi'; the following year Roger Ledsham provided a pewter Holy Water Bucket for 3s 3d and, in 1556/57, Laurence Done was paid 4s for a censer.

Queen Mary died in 1558 and gradually most of the reminders of the old days were done away with. About this time the older communion plate was exchanged for a new cup and cover paten made by the Chester goldsmith William Mutton. These pieces are referred to by Randle Holme in an inventory of goods drawn up by Thomas Johnson and Thomas Welshman in 1631: 'a communion Cupp of silver & cover of the same'. Mutton also provided similar cups for St Michael's, Holy and Undivided Trinity and several churches in Cheshire and North Wales.

The church was near to the castle and suffered considerably during the Civil War siege and later in 1659 at the time of the Cheshire Rising when the church was used as a prison. The Elizabethan cup and paten survived, as did an oval dish given in 1639, but the Communion Table had disappeared and fourpence was spent in looking for it.

In 1683 the Chester goldsmith Nathaniel Bullen made a paten in accordance with the bequest of Thomas Barlow who had been a churchwarden at St Mary's in 1675/76.

A London-made flagon was purchased by the wardens in 1712 for £25 16s 0d, and Thomas Robinson, the Chester goldsmith, supplied a flagon ring or stand for it. Some years later, in 1758, a new communion cup and paten were ordered from another Chester goldsmith, Richard Richardson II, at a cost of £7 2s 3d, who used as his model the earlier Elizabethan cup. It is possible that he also added the stand to the Bullen paten at the same time, thus turning it into a stand paten.

After the new St Mary's church had been built in 1887, more gifts were made to enrich the church plate. These included some early silver: an alms dish of 1822, an 18th-century mote spoon and some old silver mounts to the service books which were valued at ten guineas. These pieces had no connection with the earlier church.

Eventually the ancient church of St Mary was abandoned and became a part of the County Record Office – many of its old possessions were distributed.

References:
Ball 1907, p.87.
Earwaker 1898.
Holmes.

1 COMMUNION CUP (see no. 2)

Communion cup made about 1570, 7¾ inches in height, having the William Mutton sheep's head mark. The sides of the bowl curve slightly inwards and lack the pronounced splay at the rim found on the other two Mutton cups in the city at St Michael's and at Holy and Undivided Trinity. The rim, diameter 4¼ inches, took a paten cover (see no. 2) as distinct from having a plate paten. An inch below the rim is an engraved band of conventional foliage between interlacing borders. The conventional foliage at the intersections is formed from an extension of the stem of the main enrichment. The interlacing borders are engraved with a rocking ornament, also found at Stoak Church, Cheshire. The stem is spool-shaped and has a plain rounded knop with collars above and below. There is a narrow band of enrichment consisting of a ladder and billet immediately below the bowl, which is repeated at the base of the stem.

The foot is splayed, the shoulder being compressed, and around the edge of the foot is a further band of enrichment of tongue and dart form.

References:
Ball 1907, p.89, and illustrated opp.p.89.
Brocklehurst, no. 3.
Earwaker 1898, p.23.
Oman, plate 63b.
Ridgway 1968, p.58 and plate 18.

2   PATEN COVER (see no. 1)
A paten cover, diameter 4⅖ inches, height 1⅕ inches, to accompany the communion cup no. 1), also made by William Mutton and carrying his mark. It is made with a single depression with a slight reeded flange to fit over the rim of the cup. The foot is plain and splayed, having a solid base on which is a simple interlacing decoration similar to that on the cup, forming four compartments filled with conventional foliage.

3   PATEN
In the churchwardens' book there appears the following observation:

> Memorandum thatt sume takeinge notice of the wantt of a silver plate to serve the bread att Comunions: the 29th September 1638 Mrs Elinor Anderton, wife of Mr Matthew Anderton Esqr did bringe to Mr Seddon, our then Curate, a little broade silver Dish with two eares, to be bestowed on the p'ish and remaine in the church for the same use for ever.

It is not known how long this plate remained in the church, for in 1639, despite the request that it should 'remain in the church for the same use for ever', there is a further note and memorandum made by the wardens:

> Memorand: that Mrs Ales Whitbe widdow, after the death of her late husband, Edward Whitbe, Esq, late Recorder of this Citty, did give and bestowe upon the Church a longe silver plate, with a foot under itt to serve the Comunion bread, and a square quishion with fringe and tassels of cloath att issue branched for the deske for the Comunion table, to remain for the Church use for ever, and were given in Anno Dni 1639.

Mrs Whitbe had been a generous supporter of the church as early as 1618, and had also had an interest in the welfare of St Olave's. Her husband had been Recorder of the City and had died in 1639. She died the following year.

The plate, possibly of domestic origin, is oval in shape, formed of a single depression, with a perpendicular side and stands on a foot. Made in

London in 1638/39, the marks are rubbed, and the maker's mark is illegible. An inscription reads: 'The Gift of Mrs Ales Whitbe to the Parish Church of St Maries 1639'.

4   PATEN (converted into a STAND PATEN)
A large paten, diameter 9⅜ inches with a stand probably added by Richard Richardson II in the 18th century, giving a total height of 2⅜ inches. Scribed in the centre of the plate are two concentric circles, and between these guide lines is an inscription: 'The gift of Thomas Barlow of Upton to St Mary's Church in Chester 1683'.

Thomas Barlow was one of the churchwardens in 1675/76 and died in September 1683. The wording of the churchwardens' accounts when Randle Holme was paid for 'Puttinge Thomas Barlow's Leagisie down upon the Table of guifts' indicates that he had left the plate, or money for its purchase, in his will. The paten was made by Nathaniel Bullen, the Chester goldsmith, and it bears no marks except the conjoined NB struck twice, Nathaniel Bullen Type 1 (Compendium 6147).

References:
Ball 1907, pp.95-96, illustrated.
Jackson 1921, p.387.
Ridgway 1968, p.127.

5   FLAGON (see no. 6)
The churchwardens' accounts for 1712 record: '£25.16s. paid Mr. Robinson, Goldsmith, for the silver flagon for the Sacremtt as appeers by his note'. In fact Thomas Robinson, the Chester goldsmith, did not make the flagon, but he did provide the flagon ring or stand for it (see no. 6).

A large flagon, 18 inches in height overall, has a domed hinged lid with screw thumb above an S-scroll handle. Opposite the handle is a lip, the reeded moulding of the rim continuing around the lip. Slightly below the junction of the bottom of the handle with the body of the flagon is a band marking the bottom of the body, and from here it splays out to a moulded base. Beneath the lip is an inscription: 'Stephen Stone and William Witter Churchwardens 1712'.

There are four marks: (i) Britannia; (ii) Lion's head erased; (iii) Date letter R (cycle XII), 1712/13, London; (iv) Maker's mark Lo in shaped frame with key above and fleur-de-lis below, Nathaniel Lock (Grimwade 1948).

Reference:
Earwaker 1898, p.23, illustrated.

6   FLAGON RING or STAND (see no. 5)
The flagon ring bought to accompany the flagon (no. 5) is formed of a rim 9¾ inches in diameter and has three bracket feet in the form of scrolls joined to a base ring, giving a total height of 2¼ inches.

It bears the Chester marks: (i) Britannia; (ii) Lion's head erased; (iii) Chester City coat; (iv) Date letter L (series 2), 1711/12, Chester; (v) Maker's mark Ro in a shaped shield, Thomas Robinson Type 2 (Compendium 6956).

References:
Ball 1907, p.96.
Ridgway 1968, p.180.

7   COMMUNION CUP (see no. 8)

In 1758 the wardens ordered a new communion cup and paten from Richard Richardson II, the Chester goldsmith, for which they paid £7 2s 3d. For some reason they ordered an exact copy of the Elizabethan cup and paten cover made by William Mutton (see nos 1 and 2), and it is therefore an interesting piece of 18th-century antiquarianism.

It stands 8½ inches in height, rim diameter 4¼ inches and depth of the bowl 4½ inches. The sides of the bowl are straight and taper towards the stem, which is divided by a plain knop. The base, diameter 4½ inches, is moulded and carries a repeat of the decoration found on the 16th-century communion cup referred to. The bowl also carries a repeat of the Mutton engraving of conventional foliage between double margins divided into four sections.

On the side of the bowl, between the rim and this decoration, are five marks: (i) Maker's mark RR (inverted), Richard Richardson II Type 5a (Compendium 7385); (ii) Lion passant guardant; (iii) Leopard's head crowned; (iv) Chester City coat; (v) Date letter very indistinct but evidently i (series 4), 1759/60 (not 1734 as stated by Ball), Chester.

8   PATEN COVER (see no. 7)

A paten cover made by Richard Richardson II and dated 1759/60 to accompany the reproduction of the Elizabethan communion cup made by William Mutton, and copying the paten cover made by him (see no 2).

The following plate was supplied at the time of the building of St Mary's Handbridge, 1887, and given by benefactors to supplement the silver transferred from St Mary on the Hill.

9   ALMS DISH

An alms plate or dish, 9 inches in diameter, having a single depression and a gadrooned rim, otherwise quite plain apart from a later text and inscription recording the gift in 1887 by Mr A.W. Butt and then valued at £7 10s.

There are five marks: (i) Maker's mark (inverted) I.W. for John Whittingham (Grimwade 1746); (ii) Lion passant; (iii) Leopard's head; (iv) Date letter g (cycle XVIII), 1822/23, London; (v) Duty mark.

Reference:
Earwaker 1898, p.17.

10   MOTE SPOON

A list of gifts preserved amongst church records states that a 'sacramental spoon' was the gift of Mrs Tarver and that at the time it was valued at 10s. The small mote spoon given to the church to be used for the removal of foreign bodies in the wine, whatever its original use and purpose, follows the usual 18th-century pattern and is of domestic type having a small perforated bowl and a sharp pointed handle. The hallmarks are almost illegible but appear to have included the maker's mark I M on the stem.

References:
Ball 1907, p.98 (incorrect).
Earwaker 1898, p.17.

11   SERVICE BOOK MOUNTS

At the time of building, Mr John F. Lowe, a Chester goldsmith, presented the church with 'old silver mounts for service books', then valued at ten guineas. These have recently been traced and are now preserved in the church, attached to four service books:

> i   On a *Book of Common Prayer*: Four ornate corners and a clasp mount in two parts, the clasp missing. The maker's mark D.H. within an oval;
> ii   Placed in 1933 on a 1928 copy of the Prayer Book: consists of four ornate corners. On the two clasps and hasp the maker's mark I.W. within an oval and, on the hasp, script capital initials and the date 1794. On the corners an unidentified (foreign?) town mark, the letters D.H within an oval, and the date letter v within a square, and another unidentified mark;
> iii   The *Book of Common Prayer* with four corners and clasp and hasp complete, but no marks;
> iv   Communion Book, mounted with four corners and clasp and a small silver crucifix. No marks.

CHESTER
ST MICHAEL
(redundant)
Deanery of Chester

At the Reformation, St Michael's was left with a chalice and paten, overgilt, weighing 18 ounces, and these presumably remained in use until William Mutton, the Chester Goldsmith and churchwarden at St Michael's, provided a new communion cup and paten, probably taking the older silver in part exchange. Whether he actually refashioned the newer set from the older cannot be proved, though it has been suggested. Of other goods allowed to remain were green and red satin vestments altered to form 'a carpet for the Communion table and a red cope to make a carpet for the pulpit'. After a lull in reforming zeal during the reign of Mary, William Mutton, a bigoted Protestant reformer, continued the work of destruction at St Michael's and elsewhere as his powers increased with civic advancement. The accounts show that he sold the timber from the rood loft for 3s 4d in 1568 and in 1578 sold 220 pounds of lead, which he found when demolishing the church cross, for 18s. He provided a number of City and neighbouring churches with communion plate, and it was reasonable to suppose that he would provide his own church with a new set. There is no reference to the Wardens having purchased it so we may give William Mutton the benefit of the doubt and believe he may have presented the communion cup and cover to his parish church.

A list of vestments and other goods made in 1560 includes: 'Item a challes. of sylver & gyllte by extemacyone To the vallowe of xviii ounsse in weghte', and a similar list four years later gives: 'A Challis silvere and gilte that wayes in wegt extemasione xviii ounses'.

The plate was acquired by the Grosvenor Museum in 1988, and is on display in the Ridgway Gallery.

Reference:
Ball 1907, p.63ff.

CHESTER
ST OLAVE
(redundant)
Deanery of Chester

The dedication alone establishes this as an early foundation, possibly linked with the Scandinavian or Danish colony of early times. A small medieval church, it was once a parish church linked with St Mary on the Hill, but after a long period was placed under the neighbouring St Michael's church.

Following many spells of disuse it was reopened after the Second World War as a young people's centre before being damaged by fire. Later St Olave's was declared redundant, and St Michael's became a Heritage Centre. The plate from both churches was purchased by the Grosvenor Museum, Chester.

St Olave's had received a 'chales' and other goods by the will of Margaret Hawarden of Chester (proved 1520/21) who had directed it to be delivered 'to the reves of the said parish for to serve God Saynt Olave and all Sayntes ther wt as longe as they may last'. In 1553 the Commissioners left the church with a small chalice and paten weighing only 6 ounces, which may have been the same set.

According to a note in the *Cheshire Sheaf* a contributor had found, amongst archives, a scrap of paper and a record dated 15 November 1666 which read:

> That in the time of the late warrs the silver boule and cover given by Dannat ... were or was by long hydinge in obscure and moyst places to preserve it and them, from the hands of sacrilegious persons soe canckred that they were ... wholly made, to the use intended, unserviceable ...

and it went on to say that a public meeting agreed the 'plate and cover should be sold', and 50s was received. Dannat's identity is not known. The only surviving plate associated with St Olave's which can be now identified is a flagon, the gift of Mrs Elizabeth Booth in 1728. When St Olave's ceased to be a place of worship it was given to St Michael's Church, but when that church closed it passed into the keeping of the Chester Team Ministry. In 1988 the silver from both churches was purchased by the Grosvenor Museum, Chester, where it is on display in the Ridgway Gallery.

Reference:
Cheshire Sheaf, 3rd series, vol.VI, 1906, p.6, no.942.

CHESTER
ST PAUL
(Boughton)
Deanery of Chester

The church was erected in 1830 as a perpetual curacy vested in the vicar of St John the Baptist. It has since become a separate parish and the church has been rebuilt. It retains some of its original plate, including a communion cup earlier than the foundation and some later and Sheffield plate items.

The information is taken from Ball, as the author has not seen the plate and was unable to obtain information from the incumbent.

Reference:
Ball 1907, p.139ff.

1   COMMUNION CUP
A communion cup almost 7 inches in height, having a slight repoussé decoration on the bowl below the rim and a tongue decoration at the base. The stem is plain, ending in a moulded base on the edge of which is an inscription: 'St. Paul's Chapel, Boughton, Chester. The Gift of G. B. Granville, Esq., a Trustee, 26th Octr., 1830'. The hallmarks are those of the London Assay office, including that of the maker Samuel Hennell and the date letter for 1804/05.

2   COMMUNION CUP
Ball states that this communion cup is 'an exact counterpart of the chalice of 1804 and was evidently manufactured from it as a model'. He also states that the inscription reads: 'St Paul's Chapel Boughton Chester 1832', and that the sacred monogram and rays are engraved on the side of the bowl. The cup was made by William Bateman and assayed at London 1830/31.

There are also two silver patens with the London hallmarks of 1894/95, and a Sheffield plate flagon and two small Sheffield plate patens with an inscription on each indicating that they were given in 1832.

CHESTER
St Peter
Deanery of Chester

As in so many churches in Chester the Commissioners stripped St Peter's of all but a gilt chalice and paten which could be those referred to in an inventory of goods made in 1650 in which there is more pewter than silver:

> One Gold cup with a covr (and lether Case) Wt. 13½z
> One Gold plate the gift of Mr Will Edwards wt 6z
> Two pewter potts or flaggons & 4 dishes for the collections,
> the gift of Mr John Mountford
> One other pewter flaggon 4 lb½
> One old dish for the poores bread 4 lb. 6z
> One dish for Baptizings 3 lb
>
> > This we changed for a bason wt 2 1 4z.
> > marked PC on the bottom
>
> Two pewter plates 1 lb 4½z.

The use of the word 'gold' probably indicates silver gilt; the 'dish for baptizings' had been purchased in 1647 or 1648 for 4s 6d, and Will Edwards, the donor of the other 'gold plate' had been churchwarden in 1631/32. An inventory drawn up in 1672 includes: 'One silver Bowle with silver cover with case of leather for same' and 'One small silver plate', which were probably the same pieces referred to in the 1650 inventory. It is not known when these disappeared, but the earliest surviving plate at St Peter's is a London-made paten of 1708/09, followed by a cup and flagon of 1713. The Chester goldsmith Richard Richardson I was responsible for making the cup and flagon, and the nearness in date would suggest that he had also been asked to provide the paten. Later in the 18th century, another paten, a communion cup and a larger flagon were added and these complete the list of early plate at St Peter's, which is now a chapel of ease to St John the Baptist Church and the plate is stored in a bank.

References:
Ball 1907, p.103ff.
Simpson.

CHESTER: ST PETER

1   STAND PATEN

A stand paten, diameter 10 inches, with a single shallow depression formed by a slightly raised moulded rim, standing on a trumpet foot which has a moulded base. Total height 2⅞ inches. There is no inscription.

There are four marks on the surface of the paten: (i) Maker's mark MA with a bird above the A within an oval, Willoughby Masham (Grimwade 1981); (ii) Leopard's head erased; (iii) Britannia; (i) Date letter N (cycle XII), 1708/09, London. (Plate 42.)

Three salvers by the same London goldsmith were added to the City plate when Hugh Starkey was mayor in 1701.

2   COMMUNION CUP

A communion cup made by Richard Richardson I of Chester who also provided the flagon (see no. 3). An inscription on both the cup and flagon records: 'This cupp with a silver flagon is the gift of Mrs Sibill Philleps to the Parish of St Peters in Chester Anno Dom 1716'. The cup is 9 inches in height and has a bell-shaped bowl, diameter 4½ inches. The stem is broad and in the place of a pronounced knop is a moulded band. The base, diameter 4⅝ inches, has a series of bold mouldings.

There are five marks on the side of the bowl: (i) Maker's mark Ri within a shaped shield, Richard Richardson I Type 3 (Compendium 6815); (ii) Britannia; (iii) Leopard's head erased; (iv) Chester City coat; (v) Date letter N (series 2), 1713/14, Chester.

References:
Ball 1907, p.105, illustrated.
Ridgway 1968, p.166 and plate 85.

3   FLAGON

In 1716 Mrs Sibill Philleps also gave the flagon to accompany the communion cup (no. 2), the inscription being slightly changed. It stands 14 inches in height with a high moulded domed lid to which is attached a scroll thumb-piece hinged to the top of an S-scroll handle, ending in a shield-shaped terminal. The rim diameter is 5½ inches. The side of the flagon is scribed with two lines where the handle is attached to the side at the top, and there is a narrow girdle slightly above the handle attachment at the bottom, which is repeated immediately above a moulded base, diameter 7⅞ inches. The inscription reads: 'This flagon with a silver cupp is the Gift of Mrs Sibill Philleps to the Parish of St Peters in Chester Anno Dom 1716'.

There are five marks on the side of the flagon below the rim, which are repeated on the top of the domed lid: (i) Maker's mark Ri within a shaped shield, Richard Richardson I Type 3 (Compendium 6815); (ii) Britannia; (iii)

Leopard's head erased; (iv) Chester City coat; (v) Date letter N (series 2), 1713/14, Chester. (Plate 42.)

References:
Ball 1907, p.105, illustrated.
Ridgway 1968, p.166 and plate 84.

4   FLAGON

A second flagon was given to St Peter's in 1720. An inscription engraved on the front reads: 'The gift of Mr Henry Crosby to the Parish Church of St Peter in Chester 1720'.

Made in London, the flagon is 9½ inches in height and the rim diameter is 4⅛ inches. The lid is domed and moulded and has a scroll thumb-piece hinged to a scroll-shaped handle. There is a narrow moulded band below the rim, otherwise the sides of the flagon are plain, resting on a moulded base, diameter 4⅞ inches. Beneath is a scratched weight 32.7.0.

There are four marks: (i) Maker's mark E L with mullet below in a heart-shaped shield ?George Ellis (Grimwade 604); (ii) Leopard's head erased; (iii) Britannia; (iv) Date letter D (cycle XIII), 1719/20, London.

Reference:
Ball 1907, p.106.

5   ALMS PLATE

Ball described this piece as a paten. Its diameter is 10 inches, formed of a single depression with a moulded rim and 1⅝-inch edge, around which is an inscription: 'The Legacy of Mrs Marg^t Crosby to the Parish Church of St Peter in Chester. 1736'.

There are four marks: (i) Maker's mark RB, Richard Bayley (Grimwade 2262) who also supplied St John's church with two alms plates made in 1735/36 (see under Chester St John the Baptist, nos 10 and 11); (ii) Leopard's head crowned; (iii) Lion passant guardant; (iv) Date letter a (cycle XIV), 1736/37, London.

Reference:
Ball 1907, p.107.

6   COMMUNION CUP

Ball inaccurately attributes this cup to 1785, but also suggests an earlier date of 1762, which is in fact correct. It closely resembles the earlier cup (no. 2) made by Richard Richardson I, though it is slightly smaller, a little under 9 inches in height, and the stem is more slender, with a half-way girdle and a moulded base.

The bowl is bell-shaped, having on it an engraved sacred symbol of IHS, nails, cross and rays, and beneath this an inscription: 'The Parish of St Peter's Chester'.

There are five marks: (i) Maker's mark RR within a rectangle, Richard Richardson II Type 5a (Compendium 7385); (ii) Lion passant guardant; (iii)

Leopard's head crowned; (iv) Chester City coat; (v) Date letter m (series 4), 1762/63, Chester. (Plate 42.)

This cup was copied in the 20th century by Lowe & Sons and now forms part of the plate at Bunbury Cathedral, near Perth, Western Australia, a gift from the parishioners of Bunbury, Cheshire.

References:
Ball 1907, p.107.
Ridgway 1985, p.157 and plate 58.

CHESTER
St Thomas of Canterbury (also St Oswald)
Deanery of Chester
(see also St John without the Northgate)

From medieval times the south transept of Chester Cathedral served as the parish church of St Oswald. In 1871 a new church was erected in Parkgate Road to serve as a parish church and was dedicated to St Thomas of Canterbury – the dedication of a small chapel nearby which had been destroyed during the siege of Chester in the Civil War. In 1881 this new church became the parish church of St Oswald. The parish was also linked with the church of St John without the Northgate, known as Little St John's. In the reorganisation of the Chester parishes, which brought these two churches into the Chester Team Ministry, the chapel of St John without the Northgate was closed and its plate transferred to St Thomas's church which also incorporates the work (and plate) of the earlier St Oswald's.

The plate which came to St Thomas's from St John's Church, Northgate, is listed under Chester St John without the Northgate and the plate which was transferred from the south transept of the Cathedral is dealt with below.

1 & 2 Two Communion Cups

These two cups form a matching pair. Each is 9 inches in height having a bell-shaped bowl with reinforced rim, diameter 4¾ inches. The stem, which is divided by a flattened knop (on one cup repaired) having two plain mouldings above and below, sweeps down to a moulded foot, base diameter 4⅗ inches. The words 'St. Oswalds' are engraved in script on the side of the bowl.

There are four marks: (i) Maker's mark, Humphrey Payne (Grimwade 1061); (ii) Lion passant guardant; (iii) Leopard's head crowned; (iv) Date letter K (cycle XIII), 1725/26, London.

Reference:
Ball 1907, p.135.

3 & 4 Two Stand Patens

Two stand patens forming an identical pair to accompany the two communion cups (nos 1 and 2), each formed by a single depression 8⅖ inches in diameter, having a narrow moulded rim. The stand foot is plain, 2$^{9}/_{10}$ inches high, having a single step and moulded foot, base diameter 3½ inches. On the surface of the paten are the words 'St. Oswalds', as well as the marks which are the same as those on the communion cups.

Reference:
Ball 1907, p.136.

5   ALMS DISH

An alms dish belonging to the same set as nos 1 to 4, 12½ inches in diameter, having a 1¼-inch moulded rim and a single deep depression. Total height 1¼ inches. The dish is inscribed 'St. Oswalds' and the four marks on the rim are the same as on nos 1-4 and 6.

Reference:
Ball 1907, p.136.

6   FLAGON

The baluster-shaped flagon is in the form of a large heavy jug with a lip, the rim continuing over the lip to form a moulded bridge. There is no lid. It stands 11½ inches overall and has an overall width of 8¼ inches. The rim diameter is 4$^{1}/_{10}$ inches. The foot moulded, and the diameter of the base is 5½ inches. The handle is an S-scroll, broken at the top and having a plain leaf. The bottom of the handle ends in a plain scroll and is joined to the extreme part of the body with an oval collar. The lip is plain apart from a simple mould ending in a compressed pear shaped drop. There is a long inscription (incorrectly recorded by Ball) which reads:

This Sett of Communion Plate was the
Voluntary Gift of the Vicar and Parishioners
of St Oswalds by Contributions Anno
Dom. 1725/6
Wm Normanton Jam^s Wright Church Wardens

There are four marks below the rim as on the other pieces (nos 1-5).

Reference:
Ball 1907, p.136.

7   COMMUNION CUP (for use when visiting the sick (see no. 8)

The cup is 5¾ inches in height. The bowl is bell-shaped, 3 inches deep, with a slightly everted rim, diameter 2$^{9}/_{10}$ inches. The sides of the bowl slope into the stem without mouldings. This is divided by a plain knop and has a stepped and moulded base, diameter 2¾ inches. There is an inscription engraved on the side of the bowl: 'The Gift of Mrs Dighton Salmon for ye use of ye Poore Sick Communicants of ye Parish of St Oswalds in ye City of Chester 1725'.

There are five marks on the side of the bowl below the rim: (i) Maker's mark Ri within a shaped shield, Richard Richardson I Type 3 (Compendium 6815); (ii) Lion passant guardant; (iii) Leopard's head crowned; (iv) Chester City coat; (v) Date letter badly struck but would appear to be Y (series 2), 1724/25, Chester (not Z as recorded by Ball).

Reference:
Ball 1907, p.148.

8   PATEN COVER (see no. 7)
Paten cover to accompany no. 7 for use when visiting sick communicants. Diameter 3½ inches, having a slight depression to fit over the mouth of the cup. The stand is blocked, diameter 1¼ inches, having two incised lines following the rim, and the date 1725.

There are only two marks on the surface of the paten: (i) Maker's mark Ri within a shaped shield, Richard Richardson I Type 3 (Compendium 6815) (as on the cup no. 7); (ii) Lion passant guardant.

Reference:
Ball 1907, p. 148.

CHRISTLETON
ST JAMES
Deanery of Chester

1   ALMS BASIN
This basin is the earliest piece of plate at Christleton and its present use as an alms basin is determined by its current function. It was located by the Revd A.A. Guest Williams, Rector of Christleton (a known authority on silver) and was given by Mrs Richmond in memory of Walter Richmond (son of George Richmond the painter).

The basin is 13 inches diameter, has a plain rim ³⁄₁₆ inch wide with two reeded lines on the edge, and a considerable depression, giving a height of 3¼ inches. There are two weight marks on the base, one of which is 29, and the pricked initials W above TE.

There are four marks on the rim: (i) Date letter S within a plain shield (imperfect) (cycle VI), 1595/96, London; (ii) Lion passant guardant; (iii) Leopard's head crowned; (iv) Maker's mark RC above a fleur-de-lis within a shaped frame (unidentified).

2   FLAGON
A flagon 13 inches high having a domed lid, rim diameter 4⅛ inches and a screw thumb above a scroll handle. The lid has only the maker's mark and the lion passant guardant on the rim, and the scroll handle, which ends in a heart-shaped terminal, has the maker's mark. The sides of the flagon are

almost vertical down to a reeded girdle and continue below this to a step and moulded shoulder and a narrow flange. Base diameter 7 inches.

On the side of the flagon is an inscription in script letters within an oval leafy cartouche: 'The Gift of the Revd Doctr Philip Egerton to the Parish of Christleton'.

There are four marks on the side of the flagon: (i) Maker's mark CL above a pellet with a heart-shaped frame, Joseph Clare I (Grimwade 353); (ii) Leopard's head crowned; (iii) Lion passant guardant; (iv) Date letter G (cycle XIII), 1722/23, London.

(At the funeral of Dr Egerton (published in 1728) the preacher refers to him as having given 'New altar fittings at his own expense including a valuable and noble flagon of plate'.)

3   COMMUNION CUP (see no. 4)
A communion cup 8½ inches high with a bell-shaped bowl 4½ inches deep, rim diameter 4¼ inches, with an everted lip. The bowl turns to a spool-shaped stem which is divided by a narrow moulded knop. The foot has a double shoulder, the lower one larger, and ends in a narrow flange, base diameter 4½ inches.

There is an inscription on the side of the bowl in script: 'The Challic of Christleton Church John Wither Peter Cappur Ch: Wardens 1723 +'.

There are five marks on the side of the bowl: (i) Maker's mark Ri within a heart-shaped shield, Richard Richardson I Type 3 (Compendium 6815); (ii) Lion passant guardant; (iii) Leopard's head crowned; (iv) Chester City coat; (v) Date letter W (series 2), 1722/23, Chester.

4   STAND PATEN (see no. 3)
A stand paten, diameter 6½ inches, with a narrow moulded rim set at an angle, leading to a depression angled to the paten surface, standing upon a stem which is now damaged and compressed, ending in a double shoulder moulding. Base diameter 3¼ inches and the height would have been about 2½ inches. There is an inscription on the foot of the paten in script letters, in a circle: 'This salver Belongs to the Parish of Christleton 1723'.

There are five marks as found on the communion cup (no. 3).

5   ALMS DISH
An alms dish, diameter 9¾ inches, with no edge, the sides curving round to form a curve total height one inch. In the centre of the dish are inscribed the sacred symbols in rays. On the base is an inscription: 'A Gift to the ALTAR of the Parish Church of CHRISTLETON in Cheshire 1764'.

There are five marks on the outside surface of the dish: (i) Maker's mark RR within a rectangle, Richard Richardson II Type 5b (Compendium 7386); (ii) Lion passant guardant; (iii) Leopard's head crowned; (iv) Chester City coat; (v) Date letter N (series 4), 1763/64, Chester.

6   COMMUNION CUP (for use when visiting the sick) (see nos 7 & 8)
A parcel gilt bell-shaped communion cup standing on a baluster stem, 3½ inches high – the lip of the bowl moulded and everted. Base diameter 1¾ inches, on the side IHS and rays.

There are five marks on the side of the bowl: (i) Maker's mark WK in a rectangle, William Kingdon (Grimwade 3213); (ii) Duty mark; (iii) Lion passant; (iv) Date letter s (cycle XVIII), 1833/34, London; (v) Leopard's head.

7   PATEN COVER (for use when visiting the sick) (see nos 6 & 8)
A companion paten cover to no. 6, made to fit over the mouth of the cup, strongly made with a short stand, diameter 11¹³⁄₁₆ inches. The cover is 3⅛ inches diameter and is solid. The rim is moulded and raised, the edge is marked underneath with the five marks found on the communion cup (no. 6). On the surface are the IHS and rays.

8   CRUET (see nos 6 & 7)
A round cruet, diameter 1¾ inches and 3½ inches high, with a screw top. On the side are the symbols IHS with rays. The base is concave, on which are the marks as on nos 6 and 7.

CHURCH HULME
(HOLMES CHAPEL)
ST LUKE
Deanery of Congleton

1   STAND PATEN
A stand paten 9¾ inches diameter with a slightly everted rim 1⅛ inches wide, having a moulded edge and forming a single depression. Total height 1½ inches. The paten stands upon a concave stem, moulded and blocked, having small mouldings around the edge, diameter 3 inches.

There is an inscription in script letters on the edge of the paten alongside the four marks: 'The gift of Thomas Hall of Cranage, Iron Master, to the use of the Communicants of the Chappelry of Church Hulme for ever in memory of his dear Children (Anna and Cotton Hall) who were both interred in the Chancell of the said Chappell in the Month of Aug[t] Ano Dom 1700'.

The four marks are: (i) Maker's mark LO above a star within a shaped shield, Seth Lofthouse (Grimwade 1945); (ii) Britannia (inverted); (iii) Lion's head erased; (iv) Date letter E (cycle XII), 1700/01 London.

See the gift of a stand paten by Thomas Hall to Bodfari St Stephen and the note on Church Lawton below.

Reference:
Ridgway 1997, p.41.

2 Flagon

A flagon 12¼ inches high, the corkscrew thumb rising a further ¼ inch above the top of a domed lid hinged to the top of a scroll handle attached to the side of the barrel with a collar. The rim is moulded, diameter 4½ inches. The inside depth of the flagon is 9⅛ inches and is marked on the outside by a moulding below which the base curves outwards to a shoulder and a step. Diameter 7¼ inches. On the side an inscription: 'This belongs to the Chappel of Church Hulme'.

The four marks are found inside the lid and on the side of the flagon: (i) Maker's mark BA within a quatrefoil, Richard Bayley (Grimwade 116); (ii) Britannia; (iii) Lion's head erased; (iv) Date letter D within a plain shield (cycle XIII), 1719/20, London.

3 Stand Paten

A stand paten 9⅜ inches diameter having a ¼-inch moulded rim and a single depression. The paten stands on an inward sloping stand ending in a shoulder and flange, diameter 3¾ inches. On the surface of the paten an inscription: 'This Belongs to the Chappel of Church Hulme'.

There are four marks: (i) Maker's mark IS below a star within a rectangle surmounted by a three-quarter circle frame, James Smith I (Grimwade 1643); (ii) Lion passant guardant; (iii) Leopard's head crowned; (iv) Date letter G (cycle XIII), 1722/23, London.

4 Communion Cup

A large cup, 10 inches high, with a bell-shaped bowl, rim diameter 4½ inches everted. The bowl 4¾ inches deep, curves around with a single moulding to the stem which is divided by a substantial circular knop, having a plain girdle. The knop is 1¹/₁₀ inches deep and 2¼ inches diameter. The stem ends in a step and shoulder, diameter of base 4¹/₁₀ inches.

There is an inscription in script lettering on the side of the bowl: 'This belongs to the Chappel of Church Hulme'.

There are four marks on the bowl: (i) Maker's mark (rubbed) TT below a crown and small rose within a shaped frame, Thomas Tearle (Grimwade 2938); (ii) Leopard's head crowned; (iii) Date letter H (cycle XIII), 1723/24, London; (iv) Lion passant guardant.

5 Communion Cup (see no. 6)

This communion cup is smaller than no. 4 and may have been used for administration to sick communicants. It is 5¼ inches high with a bell-shaped bowl, 3 inches deep, and an everted rim diameter 2⁵/₁₆ inches. The stem is divided by a bowl-like knop and the base (slightly damaged) is moulded, diameter 2⅝ inches.

There is an inscription which begins on the accompanying paten '[Given] to Holmes Chapel 1779'.

There are five marks on the side of the bowl: (i) Maker's mark RR within a deckled frame, Richard Richardson III Type 1 (Compendium 7405); (ii) Lion passant guardant; (iii) Leopard's head crowned; (iv) Chester City coat; (v) Date letter a (series 5), 1776/77, Chester. (This was the year Richard Richardson IV took over the family business.)

6   PATEN COVER (see no. 5)

A paten cover to accompany no. 5, made to fit over the mouth of the cup. Overall height 1 inch. The paten has a narrow flange 3/16 inch deep. The grip forms the foot when used as a paten, and is blocked. On the plate is engraved: 'Given'. The inscription is continued on the communion cup (no. 5) ['to Holmes Chapel 1779'].

There are no marks, but its date and maker are established by those on the cup.

CHURCH LAWTON
ALL SAINTS
Deanery of Congleton

In his survey for the Commission of 1548, Sir Thomas Venables reported that a 'Chalise' at Church Lawton was being held as a security for a loan.

In 1699 Thomas Hall, son of Edward Hall, gave a paten to Bodfari and to Lawton Church, by 'William Hall Ironmaster'.

An advertisement was placed in the *Staffordshire Advertiser*, 15 July 1816, by Samuel Pointon and John Hall the churchwardens, offering a reward of ten guineas for information concerning a thief who broke into the church through a bricked-up doorway and stole a flagon, a communion cup and a salver, all of silver. (Eighty years later, a brass alms dish showing the figures of Adam and Eve was recovered from a neighbouring canal by someone who thought it was gold.) The churchwardens' accounts refer to the theft:

June 14 1816   Paid to Hannah Oakes for ale that four men had when in search of the plate 2/-;

July 5 1816   Paid to Mr Chambers of Congleton for 100 advertisements 16/-;

Sept 2 1816   Paid to Mr Chambers for advertisements and being put in Stafford paper £1-4-0.

There then follows a curious entry: 'Sept 4 1816 Paid Mr Farrell for reward £10-0-0'. Does this mean that the silver was recovered? The following year the squire of Lawton, William Lawton, provided a replacement suite of silver consisting of a communion cup, a paten and a flagon. He also supplied a second communion cup matching the cup of 1817, but made in 1835/36 by a different goldsmith.

References:
Cox 1975.
Lancashire and Cheshire Historic Society Journal, vol.109, 1959, p.102.

1 COMMUNION CUP (see nos 2 & 3)

A communion cup 7 inches high, having a bell-shaped bowl with an enforced and everted rim, diameter 3⁷⁄₁₀ inches. The bowl a little over 4 inches deep. The bowl stands on a trumpet-shaped stem ending in a shoulder moulding and a large step. The diameter of the base is 3⁷⁄₁₀ inches. On the side of the bowl is a representation of IHS and cross surrounded by eight broad radiating rays of engraved lines. Above and below this an inscription: 'Presented from Wm Lawton Esqr to the Parish of Lawton 1817'. Weight 11¾ oz.

Below the rim five marks: (i) Maker's mark W B with a pellet between in an irregular frame, William Bateman I (Grimwade 3037); (ii) Lion passant guardant; (iii) Leopard's head crowned; (iv) Date letter b (cycle XVIII), 1817/18, London; (v) Duty mark.

2 PATEN (see nos 1 & 3)

A paten, diameter 8¼ inches, having a wide curved border edged with a narrow gadrooned rim, creating a single curved depression. On the surface of the plate a repeat of the sacred initials and cross and, following the curve of the plate, the same inscription as found on the communion cup (no. 1) and the flagon (no. 3).

3 FLAGON

A flagon 1¹⁵⁄₁₆ inches high, having a high domed lid and a pronounced shoulder and a moulding which overrides the moulded rim. Diameter 3⁹⁄₁₀ inches. The thumb is open and moulded hinged to a scrolled handle and joins the barrel slightly above a reeded girdle and attached to the barrel side with an oval collar. The barrel continues below the girdle until it turns in to a step and shoulder with a wide reeded step forming a base. Diameter 6⁷⁄₁₆ inches. The front of the barrel has the inscription and a repeat of the sacred initials and cross and the eight broad radiating rays.

The marks are the same as found on nos 1 and 2. Inside the lid the leopard's head crowned has been omitted.

4 COMMUNION CUP

The communion cup, supplied in 1835/36 by a different maker, is an almost exact copy of no. 1, slightly heavier (12¼ oz) and ¹⁄₁₆ inch shorter in height. The inscription is the same as the earlier pieces.

There are five marks below the rim: (i) Maker's mark CF within an oval, Charles Fox II (Grimwade 303); (ii) Lion passant; (iii) Leopard's head; (iv) Date letter u (cycle XVIII), 1835/36, London; (v) Duty mark.

CHURCH MINSHULL
St Bartholomew
Deanery of Nantwich

Communion Cup

A communion cup 7¾ inches high with a rim 3⅘ inch in diameter. The bowl is bell-shaped and 4⅖ inches deep. It rests upon a stem which is divided by a large flat band-like knop, with two wide slightly moulded collars, in all a little over an inch wide. Below the knop the stem curves down and outwards to a completely plain shoulder moulding and a narrow flange. The diameter of the base is 3⅘ inches.

There are five marks on the side of the bowl: (i) Maker's mark Bi beneath a pheon in an oval, John Bingley, Chester (Compendium 789); (ii) Britannia; (iii) Lion's head erased (repeated on the foot); (iv) Date letter D (series 2), 1704/05, Chester; (v) Chester City coat. (Plate 43.)

(The author acknowledges with grateful thanks the help of Mr Paul Cruxton, churchwarden of Church Lawton at the time.)

Reference:
Ridgway 1968, p.122.

CODDINGTON
St Mary
Deanery of Malpas

1   Stand Paten

A stand paten, diameter 8⅞ inches, having a narrow moulded rim ¼ inch wide forming a single depression on which is an inscription in a circle: 'Deo et Ecclesiae St^{ae} Mariae de Coddington D.D Caldecot Aldersey Anno Dom: 1725'.

The plate stands upon a concave stem separated from it by a plain moulding. The foot has suffered considerable damage, but originally ended in a step and shoulder and a flange. The diameter of the foot 3⅜ inches, and the original overall height was probably 2¾ inches.

There are four marks on the surface of the plate: (i) Maker's mark script HP with four-point star above and below, within a quatrefoil with ornamental spandrels, Humphrey Payne (Grimwade 1061); (ii) Lion passant guardant; (iii) Leopard's head crowned; (iv) Date letter K (cycle XIII), 1725/26, London.

2   EWER

An exceptionally fine ewer made to accompany the communion cup and paten (nos 3 and 4). It stands 11 inches high and has a baluster pear-shaped body and moulded domed lid, rising to a moulded finial. The V-shaped spout ends in a compressed bead and the pedestal foot is moulded. A broken S-scroll handle terminates in a shaped shield. The flat hinge placed on top of the handle extends to the rim and V-shaped thumb. Mouth diameter 4 inches, base diameter 5½ inches. On the front of the ewer is an elaborate coat of arms with mantling, and an inscription reading: 'Sacro Usui Eccles Stae Mariae de Coddington D D Gul Mafsie 1727'.

Underneath the foot, on the body of the ewer, are five marks: (i) Maker's mark RR adorsed within a shaped shield, Richard Richardson I Type 6 (Compendium 7376) (repeated on the lid). (After 1730 this mark used by Richard Richardson II, as Type 1); (ii) Leopard's head crowned (repeated on the lid); (iii) Date letter script B (series 3), 1727/28 Chester; (iv) Lion passant guardant; (v) Chester City coat.

This piece is on display in the Ridgway Gallery at the Grosvenor Museum, Chester, where it is on long-term loan.

Reference:
Ridgway 1985, p.136 and frontispiece.

3   COMMUNION CUP (see no. 4)

A communion cup 7¼ inches high with a moulded rim to a slightly everted bell-shaped bowl, diameter 3¾ inches, curving down towards a spindle-shaped stem divided from the bowl by a simple moulding. The stem is divided by a rounded knop with collars. Towards the base are two inscribed concentric lines before a step and shoulder and a flange on which is an incised line. The foot is slightly damaged. Base diameter 4 inches. On the side of the bowl an inscription: 'Coddington Parish W.P. G.S. ChW 1727'.

There are five marks on the bowl: (i) Maker's mark RR adorsed within an oval with indented sides, Richard Richardson I Type 7 (Compendium 7377); (ii) Lion passant guardant; (iii) Leopard's head crowned; (iv) Chester City coat; (v) Date letter script B (series 3), 1727/28, Chester.

4   PATEN (see no. 3)

A large dish-like paten, diameter 7¾ inches, with a plain border with the rim turned under, standing a little under an inch deep. There is an inscription engraved in a circle on the surface of the plate: 'Deo et Eccles Stae Mariae de Coddington Sacrum J S R d 1727'.

There are five marks on the rim: (i) Maker's mark RR adorsed within an oval with indented sides, Richard Richardson I Type 7 (Compendium 7377); (ii) Lion passant guardant; (iii) Leopard's head crowned; (iv) Chester City coat; (v) Date letter script B (series 3), 1727/28, Chester.

CONGLETON
ST PETER
Deanery of Congleton

There were two medieval chapels in Congleton: the Lower Chapel long since destroyed had, according to the Sheriff's report in 1548, 'a chales'; and the Higher Chapel, St Peter ad Vincula which now survives as the parish church of St Peter was mostly rebuilt in the 18th century. This was also recorded as having a chalice in the Sheriff's report in 1548. For long the church came under Astbury.

1 COMMUNION CUP
A communion cup 8¼ inches high, having a moulded rim, diameter 4⅛ inches, a bell-shaped bowl 4⅝ inches deep curving round to a stem divided by a round knop with very slight collars towards the foot, having a step and shoulder ending in a step – diameter 3⅞ inches.

There is an inscription on the side of the bowl: 'Deo et Sacris in Capella de Congerton W•S'.

There are four marks on the side of the bowl: (i) Maker's mark – script letters in an oval, perhaps beginning with an E; (ii) Leopard's head crowned; (iii) Lion passant guardant (repeated inside the foot); (iv) Date letter t (cycle XI), 1696/97, London.

2 STAND PATEN (see no. 1)
A stand paten to accompany communion cup (no. 1), originally gilt, diameter 7¾ inches, with an upward rim with a moulded edge one inch wide and a narrow reeded border. The depression is deep, making the depth of the plate ¾ inch. In the centre of the plate within a circle of leaves is the inscription in script letters: 'The Gift of Tho: Higginbotham Gen: to the Chappel of Congleton Anno Domino 1706'.

The plate stands upon a spool-shaped stem, divided from the plate by a moulding. The cavetto stem ends in a shoulder with a flange. The base is blocked and has three concentric lines engraved near the edge. The base diameter is 2⅞ inches. The overall height is 1¹⁵⁄₁₆ inches.

The marks on the rim are as on the communion cup no. 1.

3 STAND PATEN (see no. 4)
A paten, 8 inches in diameter, having a wide rim, ⅞ inch, with a reeded edge. There is a single depression. The plate stands upon a short stem, 1⅛ inches deep, separated from the plate and ending in a step. The base, on which there is a strike of the maker's mark, is blocked, having a slightly concave solid blocking on which are the sacred symbols surrounded by rays, and a reeded edge. Diameter 2¾ inches.

There is an inscription in two consecutive lines: 'Deo et Sacris in Capella de Congerton W:S'.

There are four marks on the flat of the plate: (i) Maker's mark F A with pellet between within an oval, John Fawdery I (entered mark 1697), (could be Grimwade 662 except for pellet); (ii) Britannia; (iii) Lion's head erased; (iv) Date letter D (cycle XII), 1699/1700, London.

4   Communion Cup

A communion cup 7^9/10 inches high, with a bell-shaped bowl and everted lip. Rim diameter 4^1/16 inches. The stem is divided by a plain round knop with very slight collars. The spindle-shaped stem ends with a shoulder and a step. The base is 3^9/16 inches in diameter. Under the base and inside the bowl are traces of gilding, suggesting the whole cup had once been gilt.

On the side of the bowl is inscribed in script letters in a straight line: 'The Gift of Tho: Higginbotham Gen: to the Chappele of Congleton anno Domini 1706'.

There are four marks on the side of the bowl: (i) Maker's mark PA within a lobed rectangle, Thomas Parr I (Grimwade 2120); (ii) Britannia (repeated under the foot); (iii) Lion's head erased; (iv) Date letter O (cycle XII), 1709/10, London.

5   Flagon

A flagon 11^7/8 inches high, rim diameter 5 inches, having a domed lid but no spout. There is an S-scroll handle joining below the reeded band, which has a heart-shaped terminal and an oval collar to moulded thumb. The base of the flagon has a reeded band and a reduced foot set in base. Diameter 6 inches. On the side of the barrel an inscription:

> This Flaggon was given for the
> use of the Comunion Service in this
> Chappell by Peter Shakerley of Somerford
> in this Parish of Astbury Esqr Eldest
> Son of Sir Geffrey Shakerley Knight
> by Katherine his First Wife Daughter
> of William Penington of Muncaster –
> in the County of Cumberland Esqr
> 1718

There are four marks on the top of the domed lid and on the side of the barrel and the maker's mark is repeated on the handle: (i) Maker's mark C L within a heart-shaped frame, Joseph Clare I (Grimwade 353); (ii) Lion's head erased; (iii) Britannia; (iv) Date letter C (cycle XIII), 1718/19, London.

(See the inscription on the flagons nos 7 and 8 at Astbury.)

6   ALMS DISH
An alms dish 9¾ inches diameter, with a ¾-inch rim, slightly moulded on the edge but forming a deep depression – in all ¹¹/₁₆ inches overall depth. There is an inscription in the centre of the bowl, 'Given by Contribution •• Ralph Malbon Minister 1721'. There are no marks.

COTEBROOK
ST JOHN AND HOLY CROSS
Deanery of Malpas

A note in the box in which these three pieces of silver are stored reads 'Given by C L Egerton 1875. Robert Hayson was Rector of Anderson or Winterborne Anderson Co. Dorset in 1673'. Robert Hayson is known to have been at Anderson in 1650 and when he died his successor was instituted on 20 March 1684/85.

Whether this applies to all the pieces is uncertain. No Elizabethan cup was recorded at either place in 1889, and the church is now redundant. The donor C.L. Egerton was Cecely Louise, the younger daughter of the 10th Baronet. She married the Earl of Selkirk in 1878, two years before the church was built, who laid the foundation stone.

Reference:
Nightingale.

1   COMMUNION CUP (see no. 2)
A gilt Elizabethan cup 7⅞ inches high, with straight sides and rim diameter 3⅛ inches, the depth of the bowl 3⅝ inches. The side of the bowl has a band of interlaced borders bare of decoration, but with a sprig of conventional foliage rising above and below at the crossing. The bowl turns sharply towards a stem of hour-glass form, divided by a round knop with collars. The knop is hatched with hyphens. The base consists of two steps, dividing shoulders, the last decorated with ovolos and triangles. The foot diameter 3¼ inches. There are no marks.

2   PATEN (see no. 1)
A paten cover, accompanying the communion cup (no. 1), fits very loosely, the rim of the cup being 3⅛ inches diameter. The height is ⅛ inch but is incomplete. On the slightly domed top there should be a spool-shaped base with a round top on which may have been inscribed the date (as at Pott Shrigley and on several Elizabethan paten covers of the period). There are no marks.

3   STAND PATEN
The plate is 4¹¹/₁₆ inches in diameter and slighty concave. It rests upon a stand with an overall height of 2 inches, the stand being 1½ inches having a single flange and open bottom. There are no marks, but it seems to be coeval with

the gift. On the surface, following the line of the rim, is the inscription: 'Dedit Robertus Hayson huius ecclesia Rector 1673'.

DARESBURY
ALL SAINTS
Deanery of Great Budworth

1   (STAND) PATEN (with later additions)
A stand paten, diameter 5½ inches, overall height 1⅞ inches and with a plain moulded rim. The stand has shoulder moulding and flange, the base diameter 2½ inches. Total weight 4¾ oz. Under the base of the stand is the Britannia mark, which establishes the fact that it was added after 1697. The surface of the plate has a plain hatched cross within an early cartouche, and has been drastically engraved with scrolls and flower heads at a much later date. Underneath the plate is the crest of a stork. The engraver of the later decoration has taken trouble not to interfere with the four marks on the plate:
    (i) Maker's mark SL with motif above and below within a shaped frame (not in Jackson); (ii/iii) (rubbed) presumably Lion passant guardant and Leopard's head crowned; (iv) Date letter R (cycle IX), 1654/55, London. (Plate 44.)

2   FLAGON
A flagon, overall height 12¾ inches, including a ramshead thumb which runs well above the domed and moulded lid to which it is attached. There is a reeded band beneath the 4½ inch diameter rim. The curved spout ends in a well made base support and terminates in a bead. An S-scroll handle attached to the side of the barrel with a round collar terminates with a shaped shield. There is a reeded band at the base which then allows the barrel to continue to a step and shoulder moulding and a moulded base, diameter 6⅞ ins. Weight 54 oz.
  An inscription below the spout:

The Gift of
Mr JOHN EATON
Deceas^d for the
use of Darsbury
(Chappelry)
1730

There are four marks on the top of the lid and on the side of the flagon: (i) Maker's mark (poorly struck) WD within a ?trefoil with rounded corners, William Darker (Grimwade 3079); (ii) Lion passant guardant; (iii) Leopard's head crowned; (iv) Date letter Q (cycle XII), 1731/32, London. (Plate 45.)

3   STAND PATEN
A stand paten with a shallow plate, diameter 10⅝ inches and moulded rim. It stands on a spindle stand, height 3¼ inches with a step and shoulder moulding. Base diameter 4¼ inches. Weight 22 oz.

On the underside of the plate is an inscription: 'The Gift of Rich[d] Brooke Esq[r] to Daresbury Church A.D.1746'.

There are five marks underneath the plate: (i) Maker's mark large capital RR separated by a midway pellet, the bottom sides of the shield frame curved inwards to the base. Richard Richardson II Type 3c and William Richardson II Type 1c (Compendium 7399); (ii) Lion passant guardant (repeated inside the stand); (iii) Leopard's head crowned; (iv) Chester City coat; (v) Date letter script V (series 3), 1746/47, Chester. (Plate 46.)

Reference:
Ridgway 1985, p.189 and plate 59.

4 COMMUNION CUP

A communion cup 8½ inches high, with a bell-shaped bowl and moulded rim, diameter 4¼ inches. The bowl turns gradually to the stem which is almost vertical, divided by a ribbed moulded band. The stem continues to a shoulder of gadrooning ending in a step, diameter 3¾ inches. Weight 13½ oz. There is a long inscription on the side of the bowl:

> Purchased with Money
> in the Dawn of Youth left behind
> by two lovely Sisters
> FELICIA and FRANCES ELISA HERON
> in Life and Death undivided
> who from a very early Age
> had by their own earnest Desire
> assiduously received the BREAD OF LIFE
> and
> THE CUP OF BLESSING

There are four marks on the side of the bowl: (i) Maker's mark RM over BS within a square frame, Richard Morson and Benjamin Stephenson (Grimwade 2374) (see also Disley communion cup no. 1); (ii) Lion passant guardant; (iii) Leopard's head crowned; (iv) Date letter capital Gothic S (cycle XV), 1773/74, London. (Plates, 47, 48.)

DAVENHAM
ST WINIFRED
Deanery of Middlewich

1 COMMUNION CUP

An Elizabethan parcel gilt cup, 7½ inches high with a bell-shaped bowl, rim diameter 4/10 inches and 5½ inches deep. The bowl has a band of decoration with double line borders which cross over and has sprigs of conventional foliage at the crossings – the decoration between the bands consists of conventional foliage. Beneath the bowl, divided by mouldings, is a spool-shaped stem divided by a round knop with collars. Beneath the stem a moulded inset followed by a shoulder, a reed band and a flange. The base is 4 inches diameter.

There are four marks on the side of the bowl: (i) Maker's mark a beaked bassinet (see Jackson p.97) (or bird's head erased); (ii) Leopard's head crowned; (iii) Lion passant guardant; (iv) Date letter Gothic n (cycle V), 1570/71, London.

2   Communion Cup

A communion cup 7¾ inches high with a goblet-shaped bowl, diameter 4 inches – the sides engraved, standing on a baluster stem with trumpet-shaped base and reeded foot, diameter 3¾ inches.

There are four marks on the side of the bowl: (i) Maker's mark WS within a rectangle; (ii) Leopard's head crowned; (iii) Lion passant guardant; (iv) Date letter q (cycle VIII), 1633/34, London.

3   Stand Paten

A stand paten, diameter 7⅕ inches with an oblique moulded rim and a single depression. It stands on a hollow trumpet-shaped stem, diameter 2½ inches. Total height 2 inches. Beneath the plate is inscribed:

W & T
1707
G & B

There are four marks: (i) Maker's mark a five-point star above letters which have been rubbed; (ii) Britannia; (iii) Lion's head erased; (iv) Date letter M (cycle XII), 1707/08, London.

Delamere
St Peter
Deanery of Middlewich

Salver

It may be assumed that the salver formed part of the plate supplied when the church, designed by the architect John Gunnery, was consecrated in 1817. Its date (1768/69) suggests that it may have been given by one of the masonic gentry who were instrumental in building the church.

The salver, which is now in need of repair, has a gadrooned edge. It is 8¼ inches in diameter and stands on three gadrooned feet.

There are four marks on the back: (i) Date letter Gothic N (cycle XV), 1768/69, London; (ii) Lion passant guardant; (iii) Leopard's head crowned; (iv) Maker's mark ?EC within a rectangle (inverted) Ebenezer Coker (Grimwade 550).

DISLEY
St Mary the Virgin
Deanery of Chadkirk

Construction of the church was started in 1527, but it was not consecrated until 1558. Records state that in 1769 the old plate was exchanged for '... two ewers, a chalice and cover and two oval plates, all nobly gilt'. These are still in use.

1   COMMUNION CUP (see no. 2)
A gilt communion cup having a cover (no. 2). The cup stands 9 inches high and has a bell-shaped bowl with an everted lip, rim diameter 4 inches and depth of bowl 3¾ inches. The base of the bowl has nine acanthus leaves set at intervals which cover three quarters of the bowl. The bowl is separated from a baluster-shaped stem by a band of small pellets and begins with a cavetto moulding and a moulded pear-shaped stem resting on a band of pellets leading to a shoulder and a further band of pellets forming the base. Diameter 4 inches. Beneath the foot is an inscription in script letters: 'Morson & Stephenson No. 98 Fleet Street Fcc^{rs}', and nearby the only mark: EV within a rectangle.

The mark and additional information gleaned from the inscription is of considerable interest. Grimwade does not record it positively, as the London records for 1758-73 are missing, and it may have been listed there. However, Grimwade records an EV mark (3561) among the unregistered marks as found on a candlestick of 1765, dishes of 1768 and a jug of 1770 and attributed it to Edmund Vincent. No other London Goldsmith about this time had these initials. The association of the mark and the name of the firm which claims to have made it adds an interesting piece of information. Grimwade reports that Edmund Vincent was the son of Arthur Vincent, a grocer of St Brides' Parish, and was apprenticed to Edward Feline on 6 July 1750. He was made free in 1763. He appears in the Parliament Report List 1773 as a plateworker, King's Arms Court, Ludgate Hill and in 1768 was at St Anne's, Soho. Richard Morson and Benjamin Stephenson moved from Fleet Street to Ludgate Hill in 1771, but had been prosecuted for selling gold watches 'worse than standard'. The avoidance of the Hall by using only the mark of Edmund Vincent and a claim to have made the Disley plate is of interest.

Reference:
Grimwade, p.689.

2   COVER (see no. 1)
A cover to the communion cup (no. 1). A dome with shoulder and a circle of pellets on the edge overlapping the rim of the cup and with a bezel inside the mouth of the cup. The cover rises 3½ inches to the top of the scroll finial (which at the time of this survey had been broken off). The sides of the cover rise in an ogee to a band of pellets from which three acanthus leaves spread out over

the cover. Above the pellets is a finial, thumb-like, curved and resembling a shell. There are no marks.

3 & 4   Two Dishes (Patens)
Two identical shallow oval silver dishes, provided as patens. The edge is waved and the border a narrow band of gadrooned decoration. Overall each dish measures 10⅛ inches wide. The rim is a little over one inch and forms an oval depression – in all ½ inch deep. There are no hallmarks on either dish, but the EV mark appears on only one of them.

5 & 6   Two Identical Ewers
Two identical gilt lidless circular ewers – each with an overall height of 13¼ inches. The broken scroll handle rises well above the rim of the jug to which it is attached. The rim rises to incorporate the spout partly covered by a moulded acanthus leaf. The handle is highly decorated and has a thumb knop on the top of a head. There is a cast leaf on the top side of the handle and another against the bowl. Below it are five graded pellets. The second part of the broken handle ends in a scroll attached to the side of the bowl in line with a band of pellets which divides the bowl at its widest part (5 inches wide). The pellets surround the rim of the ewer and are repeated round the neck. The main part of the body is of goblet form, decorated with seven swags of leaves tied with a bow. At the bottom of the bowl are nine acanthus leaves rising from a short stem divided by a circlet of pellets and below this the base spreads out to a bold shoulder ending in a base mould of pellets – diameter 4⅜ inches.

Inscribed below the base is the same inscription found on the chalice and the same mark, EV within a rectangle. There are no hallmarks.

DODLESTON
St Mary
Deanery of Chester

It is reported that in 1859 a 'pewter chalice and paten' were found in a priest's grave in the church at Dodleston and that they might have been taken to Chester Cathedral where one or two deans had been rectors of Dodleston later.

Terrier. 20 August 1778: 'Silver chalice about 7 ounces, and pewter patten and flagon'.

1   Communion Cup
A communion cup 6 inches high having a bell-shaped bowl, diameter 3¾ inches and 3¾ inches deep. The bowl rests upon a short stem 2¹⁄₁₀ inches in depth. The stem has a pointed knop and below this the stem passes into a step

and a shoulder followed by a flange, diameter 3⅝ inches. On the side of the bowl an inscription:

$$\left.\begin{array}{l}\text{James Doan}\\ \\ \text{Thos Potter}\end{array}\right\} \text{CW 1732}$$

There are five marks on the bowl: (i) Maker's mark WR conjoined within a rectangle, William Richardson I Type 2b (Compendium 9572); (ii) Lion passant guardant (repeated under the foot); (iii) Leopard's head crowned; (iv) Chester City coat; (v) Date letter script G (series 3), 1732/33 Chester. (There are traces of an earlier mark on the shoulder.)

2   STAND PATEN (see no. 3)
A stand paten 6⅖ inches diameter with a raised reeded rim ⅕ inch wide forming a shallow depression. The plate stands upon a spool-shaped stem with a moulded open foot and very slight flange, diameter 2⁹⁄₁₀ inches.

There are five marks on the underside of the plate: (i) Maker's mark PB over WB in a square frame (inverted), Peter and William Bateman I (Grimwade 2143); (ii) Lion passant guardant; (iii) Leopard's head crowned; (iv) Date letter K (cycle XVII), 1805/06, London; (v) Duty mark.

3   EWER
A classical ewer, overall height 11½ inches, having a domed lid and ball finial. The lip is combined with the Adam-style baluster body, the rim and lip have a reeded edge. The handle is ear-shaped and runs well above the finial. It is insulated at top and bottom, showing that its original use was for a hot liquid and that its later use was for wine. The handle joins the body with an elongated leaf fading into the side of the body with a sharp point. At the top the handle is attached by a leaf design which curls outwards.

Below the body is a trumpet-shaped stand which is divided from the base by reeded moulding, a shoulder, and a circular reeded step, diameter 4 inches.

There are five marks on the side of the body and on the inside lid: (i) Maker's mark PB over AB within a square frame, Peter and Ann Bateman (Grimwade 2140); (ii) Lion passant guardant; (iii) Leopard's head crowned; (iv) Date letter A (cycle XVIII), 1796/97, London.

EATON
CHRIST CHURCH
Deanery of Congleton

Although Eaton church was built in the middle of the 19th century, it inherited three pieces of 18th-century silver from a source not now known by the church officials.

1   FLAGON
A cylindrical flagon of Britannia silver, 12½ inches high, and rim diameter 3⅞ inches, having a domed lid with a button terminal and scroll thumb. There is an S-scroll handle. The body of the flagon is marked by a narrow band of reeding below which the foot splays outward to a shoulder moulding. The base has a narrow flange, diameter 6 inches. There is an engraving of the sacred symbols IHS surrounded by rays beneath the large curved spout which has been added at a later date. Weight 2 lb. 13 oz.

There are four marks, both on the side and inside the cover: (i) Maker's mark GA with crown above, with pellet on either side, inside a double circle, William Gamble (Grimwade 738); (ii) Britannia; (iii) Lion's head erased; (iv) Date letter Q (cycle XII), 1711/12, London.

2   STAND PATEN
A stand paten, diameter 7¾ inches, height 2½ inches, foot diameter 3 inches. The rim has a narrow moulded edge forming a single depression, in the centre of which are engraved the sacred symbols of IHS within rays. The initials I above I F are scratched, indicating a secular origin. The marks have been erased but would appear to be a date letter B, and a thistle (Edinburgh). Weight 9½ oz.

3 & 4   COMMUNION CUPS
Parcel gilt communion cups, height 8 inches, weight 10½ oz., each with the sacred symbols IHS surrounded by rays on the side of the bowl which is bell-shaped with everted rim. The sides curve round to a baluster stem, leading to a steep moulded foot and ending with a step and shoulder and a narrow flange.

There are four marks: (i) Maker's mark P•T with pellet between, in oval frame and having indents on top and bottom, Peter Tabart (?Grimwade 2237), or perhaps Peter Taylor (Grimwade 2239); (ii) Date letter n (cycle XIV), 1748/49, London; (iii) Lion passant guardant; (iv) Leopard's head crowned.

(Grateful thanks to Mr Paul Hibbert of Congleton for his invaluable help.)

ECCLESTON
St Mary the Virgin
Deanery of Chester

1   COMMUNION CUP
A communion cup, 7 inches high, rim diameter 4 inches. It has a plain bucket-shaped bowl with slightly everted rim and is 4⅜ inches deep. The bottom of the bowl turns sharply to a trumpet-shaped stem, ending in a step and shoulder moulding and a narrow flange, base diameter 4⅛ inches. Under the foot is engraved (contemporary with the age of the cup):

1683
R B   I P.

The parish Benefactions Board refers to this cup 'the silver cup was bought by the Parish'. There are no marks, but this might be the work of a Chester goldsmith. There is no accompanying paten. (Plate 49.)

2 PATEN
A paten, 8⅞ inches diameter, standing 1 inch high, with a narrow gadrooned border, leading to a curved rim 1 inch wide marking a deep depression. There is an inscription on the rim in script lettering: 'Ex dono T. Aumbry Rr de Eccleston 1746', which is confirmed by the record on the Benefactions Board: 'The Revd Mr Thomas Aumbry gave the silver plate'.

Knife marks on the face of the paten show it was used either as a credence paten or as a paten for consecration.

On the rim are four marks: (i) Lion passant guardant; (ii) Maker's mark (imperfectly struck), T above two initials, the first being an R. The T is in a squarish lobe and the other marks may also be in lobes. The bottom of the mark is missing and it has not been identified; (iii) Leopard's head crowned; (iv) Date letter a (cycle XIV), 1736/37, London.

3 FLAGON (JUG)
A very heavy jug, often referred to as a beer jug, but introduced to the church to serve as a flagon. It stands 9½ inches high, but the broken scroll handle and the spout rise above the rim, making an overall height of 10½ inches. The handle is capped and ends with a rounded terminal. The moulded rim, diameter 4⅞ inches, carries over the top of the spout which terminates against the body of the jug with a moulded cast shell. The body is pear-shaped, standing on a tucked-in pedestal foot which spreads out towards a shoulder and plain step; base diameter 5⅜ inches.

The donor is referred to in the inscription on the side of the flagon: 'Roger Ormes/Donarium Ecclesiae de/Eccleston/in Com Cestr Ano Dom/1746', and confirmed on the Benefactions Board as 'a silver decanter to be used at the Communion'.

There are four marks struck beneath the foot on the base of the body: (i) Lion passant guardant; (ii) Leopard's head crowned; (iii) Date letter l (cycle XIV), 1746/47, London; (iv) maker's mark script JB in a rectangle, John Berthellot (Grimwade 1179). (Plate 50.)

4 SALVER
A salver given to the church presumably to replace the paten (no. 2). It is 6 inches diameter, having a narrow rim edged with tiny pellets forming a shallow depression. It stands upon three ball and claw feet, making the overall height ¾ inch. An inscription on the underside of the plate records the gift in about 1904.

There are five marks: (i) Maker's mark H I above two letters, the latter a D, in a square frame. The mark has not been identified; (ii) Lion passant guardant; (iii) Leopard's head crowned; (iv) Date letter l (cycle XVI), 1786/87, London; (v) Duty mark.

FARNDON
St Chad
Deanery of Malpas

1 Paten Cover

The paten cover of stand form, 6 inches diameter, has a flange with two incised lines. The stand, diameter 2⅝ inches, is blocked with a series of circumscribed lines, and rests on a concave stem. It has a depression to house the original cup rim.

This paten cover may be connected to the earlier communion cup referred to in an inscription on a Victorian cup (made in London 1860/61) now in use at St Chad's: 'Received in exchange for a cup the gift of John Speed'. There seems to be no evidence to show who this John Speed was, but among members of the Speed family in the 16th and 17th centuries in Farndon, the most notable was John Speed, the cartographer, dating probably from 1552-1629. There was also a David Speed, Mayor of Holt in 1606, whose name appears on the Holt Mace made by John Lingley of Chester that year.

The form of the paten cover, the type of assay marks and the form of the maker's mark provide the only clues to support the belief that it belonged to the communion cup replaced with the Victorian cup: (i) Date letter imperfectly struck, but seems to be e (cycle VIII), 1622/23, London; (ii) Lion passant guardant. The form of this mark confirms cycle VIII rather than the later cycle XI suggested by Hubbard in Pevsner's *Cheshire*; (iii) Leopard's head crowned; (iv) Maker's mark RM above a motif (heart?) in shaped frame (Jackson p.114).

Reference:
Ridgway 1968, p.48.

2 Flagon

A flagon, overall height 13 inches, having a domed lid, with shoulder moulding and flange overriding the rim of the barrel, diameter 4⅛ inches. The open thumb is hinged to the top of the S-shaped handle, which curls around in an eccentric manner at the top, terminates just above a reeded girdle with a heart-shaped terminal, and joins the barrel with an oval collar. Beneath the girdle the sides continue downwards then turn to a shoulder moulding ending in a step. Diameter 7¹/₁₀ inches. The bottom of the flagon is some way below the girdle and in line above the shoulder mouldings.

There is a representation of the sacred symbols surrounded by rays on the front of the barrel and an inscription below the girdle: 'The Gift of Francis Fletcher of Farndon to Farndon Church 1781'.

There are four marks on the side of the flagon: (i) Maker's mark WV within a rectangle, William Vincent (Grimwade 3357); (ii) Lion passant guardant; (iii) Leopard's head crowned; (iv) Date letter f (cycle XVI), 1781/82, London.

3   COMMUNION CUP
A communion cup 7½ inches high, with a goblet-shaped bowl, diameter 4 inches, standing on a trumpet-shaped stand and a reeded step. It is inscribed: 'The Gift of Mrs Anne Fletcher to the Church of Farndon 1791'.

There are five marks: (i) Maker's mark (rubbed); (ii) Lion passant guardant; (iii) Leopard's head crowned; (iv) Date letter r (cycle XVI), 1792/93, London; (v) Duty mark.

FOREST CHAPEL
(MACCLESFIELD)
Deanery of Macclesfield

1   COMMUNION CUP (see no. 2)
A communion cup 7½ inches high with a bell-shaped bowl, 3³⁄₁₀ inches deep and a moulded rim 3⁷⁄₁₀ inches diameter. It rests upon a stem from which it is divided by a simple moulding, and is divided by a round knop forming a waist band, in all ⅖ inches deep. The foot has three mouldings and ends with a moulded flange, diameter 3⅖ inches. On the side of the bowl is inscribed: 'FOREST CHAPPELL 1732'.

The cup has the imperfectly struck mark of EF with a bird with displayed wings above and a six-point star below, within a shaped frame, Edward Feline (Grimwade 576). The mark is imperfectly struck four times on the side of the bowl, and four times underneath the bowl of the cup. There are no other marks. (Edward Feline was a Huguenot who entered his mark at Goldsmiths' Hall in London on 25 September 1720.)

2   PATEN COVER (see no. 1)
A paten cover, made to fit over the communion cup (no. 1), 4⅗ inches diameter and total height 1 inch. The knop or base has a diameter of 2⅕ inches with a concave stem. On the centre of the plate is inscribed IHS. There are slight signs of a mark (?Edward Feline) but no other marks.

FRODSHAM
ST LAWRENCE
Deanery of Frodsham

An inventory made in 1622 records 'one silver Cuppe with cover, a pewter standing Cuppe, a pewter bottle'. In 1637 an inventory records the 'Silver Cuppe and Cover' and 'One pewter Cuppe' remained, but no mention is made of the 'pewter bottle'. Two pewter flagons had been added.

By May 1671 the pewter cup had disappeared and a pewter dish had been added. The silver cup probably disappeared when the Revd Francis Gastrell (Vicar 1740-42) supplied new communion plate in 1763.

Reference:
Cheshire Sheaf, 3rd series, vol.I, 1896, p.92, no. 100.

1 & 2   COMMUNION CUPS

Two communion cups, one 9 inches high, the other slightly smaller, with bell-shaped bowls, rim diameter 3⅞ inches. Each stem is divided by a small band knop ½ inch deep and sweeps down to a moulded base, diameter 4½ inches.

There are four marks on the side of the bowl: (i) Maker's mark WC within a rectangle, Walter Crisp (Grimwade 3051); (ii) Lion passant guardant; (iii) Leopard's head crowned; (iv) Date letter capital Gothic H (cycle XV), 1763/64, London.

3   ALMS DISH

An alms dish 13 inches in diameter with a single rim 1⅝ inches wide and a simple edge moulding, depression, and a central boss 3 inches in diameter. The rim is inscribed: 'FRODSHAM CHESHIRE The Gift of F. Gastrell'. On the underside the maker's mark only is repeated four times, WC within a rectangle frame as on the communion cups 1 and 2 and flagons 4 and 5.

4 & 5   FLAGONS

Two matching flagons, one weighing 65.9 and the other 65.1 as engraved on the base of each.

Each has an overall height of 14⅝ inches and has a high, domed lid hinged upon an S-scroll handle with the hinge attached to an openwork knot-like thumb, and to the top of the handle where it terminates in a moulded drop ending in a single band. The bottom of the handle is attached to the bottom of the barrel by an oval collar and ends in a plain curved heart-shaped shield. A reeded band marks the division between body and base, the latter curving down to a bold moulding. On the sides of the flagons is the same inscription as on no. 3: 'FRODSHAM CHESHIRE The gift of F. Gastrell'. On the lid and side of each flagon are four marks and the maker's mark repeated on the handle, as on nos 1, 2 and 3.

6 & 7   STAND PATENS

Two matching stand patens intended to accompany communion cups nos 1 and 2, but by a different maker and slightly later in date.

Each has a plate of 7 inches in diameter, a narrow rim and single depression. The stem is trumpet form and has a pronounced bulbous moulding towards the base. Inscribed: 'FRODSHAM PARISH 1766'.

On the under-side of the plates are four marks: (i) Date letter capital Gothic L (cycle XV), 1766/67, London; (ii) Leopard's head crowned; (iii) Lion passant guardant; (iv) Maker's mark G•C in rectangular frame with pellet between, ?George Cowles (Grimwade 3582).

8   EWER
A large ewer probably from designs by Robert Adam. It stands to an overall height of 18¼ inches – the strap handle rising above the lid. The body is urn-shaped, held in a 2-inch deep gadrooned cup, and tapers to a narrow neck which is encircled by a band of corded wire, and at the junction of body and neck a further and wider band of ovolos. The top of the urn body is 6 inches in diameter. The strap handle is edged with cording and has a spine of beads. The handle, which rises well above the hinged lid, fits inside a similarly edged rim of the ewer, giving place for the spout. An acanthus or natural foliage motif is found at the junction of the handle and body.

At the base of the urn-shaped body is a further band of guilloche decoration and small four-petal flowers within each compartment. The base is trumpet-shaped and circular, with a further narrow reeded band and a generous embellishment of large ovolos and a plain step. On the side of the body are engraved the sacred symbols within rays and an inscription: 'The Gift of Elizabeth Hyde Spinster to the Parish Church of Overton in the County of Cheshire'.

On the side of the base, diameter 4⅗ inches, are the marks, which are repeated on the underside of the lid: (i) Makers' mark MB IF both within rectangles, Matthew Boulton and James Fothergill; (ii) Lion passant guardant; (iii) Birmingham mark of an anchor; (iv) Date letter B (1774/75), Birmingham.

A pair of ewers, very similar to the Frodsham ewer, was presented for use in St Mary's Chapel, Birmingham in 1774.

Reference:
Delieb and Roberts, illustrated op. p.40.

9   WINE STRAINER
It is not known when this wine strainer, or funnel, came to the Church. In an inventory by Butts of Chester compiled in 1933 in the time of the Revd Canon Myers, it is referred to as 1795, but the source of this information is not known.

The circular funnel head, diameter 4¾ inches, is moulded and leads to a spout joined to the head, 4¾ inches in length, narrowing slightly and curving towards the outlet. There is a simple reed moulding inside the mouth and a pierced strainer within. Overall length 6 inches. It bears no assay marks, but is inscribed 'PARISH OF FRODSHAM'.

Gawsworth
St James the Great
Deanery of Macclesfield

1   COMMUNION CUP (see no. 2)
This cup interested Charles Oman who observes:

> The unmarked and undated communion cup and paten at Gawsworth, Cheshire, I am inclined to assign to the beginning of the reign of Elizabeth I ... the fact that they are inscribed with a text from the Vulgate Version of John VI.63 indicate that they were made before Beza's translation came into general use. I am not prepared to exclude the possibility that they may have been produced towards the close of the reign of Edward VI ...

A communion cup 6½ inches high with a rim diameter of 4⅕ inches. The bowl is 3½ inches deep and has straight sides curving at the bottom to a spindle-shaped stem divided from the bowl by a small moulding. The stem is dominated by a considerable rounded knop of a major feature tricked with five rows of hyphens and on either side two rounded collars. Below the knop the stem passes into a band of ladder ornament followed by a shoulder and a further band of ladder ornament and a flange, diameter 4¹/₁₀ inches.

On the side of the bowl are two bands of inscription, one beginning an inch below the rim and the second 2⁷/₁₀ inches below the rim:

BAND 1: + CARO(leaf)non(leaf)PRODEST(leaf)QVI CQVAM
BAND 2: + SPITVS(leaf)EST(leaf)QVI(leaf)VIVIFICAT

The inscription is gilt. There are no marks.

Reference:
Oman, pp.231 and 311

2   PATEN (see no. 1)
A plate paten to accompany communion cup no. 1, 5⅕ inches diameter. It has a flat edge ⅗ inches wide with a single curved depression. It is inscribed on the edge in the alphabet used in the first half of the 16th century (and as on the communion cup) between lines and in gilt. Reading from outside the rim: +ERBA(leaf)QVE(leaf)EGO(leaf)LOQVOR(leaf)SPIRITVS(leaf)SUNIT(leaf)ET(leaf)VITA. Unmarked. (See Chester Holy and Undivided Trinity no. 1.)

3   COMMUNION CUP
An enormous communion cup, 15⁷/₁₀ inches high with a moulded rim and a rim diameter of 6½ inches. The bowl is of bell shape, everted, and is 7½ inches deep. It stands on a stem divided by a flattened and moulded band knop and ends with a large shoulder and a moulded step to a foot, diameter 6 inches.

On the bowl is an inscription: 'The Gift of Wm Hall A M Rect^r of Gawsworth 1763' with the sacred symbols and rays.

There are four marks on the side of the bowl: (i) Maker's mark (inverted) S W (1 midway pellet) within a rectangle, Samuel Whitford I (Grimwade 2661); (ii) Lion passant guardant; (iii) Leopard's head crowned; (iv) Date letter Gothic capital H (cycle XV), 1763/64, London.

GOOSTREY
ST LUKE
Deanery of Congleton

The churchwardens' accounts in 1639 refer to the old communion cup being sold for £1 9s. 6d., but there is no reference to one being bought.

1 STAND PATEN

A stand paten, diameter 9⅛ inch, having a moulded rim and a deep depression. It stands upon a wide stem with a moulded base of a step and shoulder, base diameter 3¾ inches, overall height 3 inches. The initials D I, for Dorothy Jodrell who gave the paten in 1719 are inscribed on the paten. Weight 16 oz.

There are four marks: (i) Maker's mark W A beneath a motif (?a bird) in shaped frame, Samuel Wastell (Grimwade 2990 or 2991); (ii) Lion's head erased; (iii) Britannia; (iv) Date letter K (cycle XII), 1705/06, London.

2 COMMUNION CUP (see no. 3)

A communion cup 9 inches high with a bell-shaped bowl and a rim diameter of 4½ inches, standing on a tall stem divided by a narrow moulded band. Below the stem the base is well moulded with three shoulders, to a foot diameter 4⅛ inches. The side has a representation of the sacred symbols surrounded by rays. Given, along with the flagon (no. 3), by Randle Armstrong, 1759.

There are four marks on the side of the bowl: (i) Maker's mark script F W within a rectangle, Fuller White (Grimwade 733); (ii) Leopard's head crowned; (iii) Lion passant guardant; (iv) Date letter Gothic capital D (cycle XV), 1759/60, London.

3 FLAGON (see no. 2)

Randle Armstrong gave £20 towards the purchase of this flagon and a chalice for the use of Goostrey Chapel in 1759.

A flagon without spout, 13 inches high, having domed lid and open thumb, hinged to an S-scroll handle. The rim, diameter 3¾ inches, is moulded. A band of reeding marks the junction of the body with a deeply splayed base which curves outwards to a simple moulding and a very pronounced shoulder, ending in a narrow flange – diameter of base 7¾ inches. The sacred symbols surrounded by rays on the side. Weight 50 oz.

There are four marks on the side of the flagon, corresponding to those on the communion cup (no. 2).

GRAPPENHALL
ST WILFRED
Deanery of Great Budworth

1   FLAGON
A flagon 13¼ inches high with a domed lid and no lip, having a plain cylindrical body, rim diameter 4⅝ inches, with straight sides on which is an inscription beneath sacred symbols:

> The Gift of M^{rs}
> Johanna Blackburne
> of Bridge End to
> Gropnal Church
> 1765

There is an S-scroll handle terminating in a shield with ogee head. The body of the flagon is marked by a reeded band and below this the foot spreads outwards to mouldings and a step. Diameter of base 8⅜ inches.
   There are four marks on the side of the flagon and inside the lid: (i) Maker's mark F midway pellet C within a rectangle, Francis Crump (Grimwade 672); (ii) Lion passant guardant; (iii) Leopard's head crowned; (iv) Date letter Gothic capital L (cycle XV), 1766/67, London.

2   COMMUNION CUP (see no. 3)
A parcel gilt communion cup 8½ inches high with a goblet-shaped bowl, rim diameter (slightly everted) of 4⅘ inches. Depth of bowl 5 inches. It stands upon an almost straight stem separated from the bowl by narrow mouldings. The stem is also divided by a narrow band of mouldings and ends with a shoulder and a step to a foot, diameter 4 inches. There is an inscription on the side of the bowl beneath the sacred symbols and surrounded by rays:

> The Gift of M^{rs}
> Sarah Blackburne
> August 1797

There are five marks on the underside of the foot: (i) Maker's mark WH within a rectangle, William Hall (Grimwade 3163); (ii) Lion passant guardant; (iii) Leopard's head crowned; (iv) Date letter capital B (cycle XVII), 1797/98, London; (v) Duty Mark.

3   PATEN COVER (see nos 2, 4 & 5)
A paten cover, diameter 5 inches, to accompany the communion cup (no. 2). It fits over the cup but if treated as a paten, the base is blocked and inscribed with the sacred symbols IHS surrounded with rays. The edge of the plate is curved to a depth of ⅖ inch and the total height is 1³⁄₁₀ inches. On the plate is inscribed: 'The Gift of Mrs Sarah Blackburne. August 1797'. Marks as on cup no. 2.

4 & 5   Alms Dishes (see nos 2 & 3)

Two identical alms dishes, 9 inches diameter, with a 1⅕-inch border moulded at the edge, forming a depression but giving way to a central boss decoration 2¾ inches wide, on which is a repeat of the sacred symbols surrounded by rays. Under the boss are the same marks as on nos 2 and 3.

6   Communion Cup (for use when visiting the sick) (see no. 7)

A communion cup for use with the sick, parcel gilt, 3³⁄₁₀ inches high, with bell-shaped bowl but with a moulded rim and angled base, standing on top of a stem divided by a moulded band and ending in a step: diameter 1⅖ inches. Sacred symbols surrounded by rays on the side of the bowl.

There are five marks on the bowl: (i) Maker's mark H H in rectangle, Hyam Hyams (Grimwade 1005); (ii) Lion passant; (iii) Leopard's head; (iv) Date letter k (cycle XVIII), 1825/26, London; (v) Duty mark.

7   Paten Cover (for use when visiting the sick) (see no. 6)

Paten cover, diameter 3⁷⁄₁₀ inches, to fit over the cup no. 6. An angular top with a step edge, a cavetto stand to a plate on which are the sacred symbols IHS surrounded with rays. The edge has the five marks as found on the cup.

Great Barrow
St Bartholomew
Deanery of Chester

1   Communion Cup (see no. 2)

A communion cup, parcel gilt, 8½ inches high with a rim diameter of 5½ inches, having a bucket-shaped bowl with almost straight sides, 4⅞ inches deep and slightly everted rim. On the sides of the bowl are engraved the two coats of arms of Bridgman and the City of Chester, each in a wreath of foliage. The bowl rests upon a trumpet-shaped stem leading to a shoulder and wide flange – diameter 5¼ inches.

There is only one mark on the side of the bowl, T D with five-point mullet above and below, with tiny rings on either side of each mullet, within a square frame with clipped corners.

This mark is found on the patens supplied to the Cathedral by Henry Bridgman in 1662, and also the cup given to the Cathedral to replace the two cups also donated to the Cathedral at the time of the Restoration. (Plate 51.)

References:
Brocklehurst, no. 20.
Glynne, p.120.
Ridgway 1980.
W.I. Scrapbook.

2   PATEN COVER (see no. 1)

A paten cover, diameter 6½ inches, to accompany the communion cup no. 1. The rim has a single depression which fails to match the diameter of the cup. The foot, 2⅞ diameter inches, is blocked and bears a large engraving of the Arms of Bridgman. There is only one mark, as on the communion cup. (Plate 51.)

3   FLAGON (JUG)

Among silver given to the church by Mr Hugh Lyle Smyth of Barrowmore at Christmas 1888, was a flagon, an alms dish and a strainer spoon. The alms dish is outside the present survey, and the strainer spoon has been missing for some time.

The flagon supplied with a plain spout is of tankard form, with a domed lid, 7¼ inches high but with a solid curved cast thumb of corkscrew type, embracing a leaf, making an overall height of 7¾ inches. The domed lid is moulded, and the moulded rim, diameter 4⅓ inches, rises over the spout top. The scroll handle has a thumb which is hinged to the top of the handle with graded mouldings. The bottom joins the barrel with a round collar a little below a reeded band and ends with a plain shield terminal. The foot has a band of reeding followed by a shoulder and step, diameter 5½ inches.

The name of the church and the parish is inscribed on the barrel, and the initials ID with a pellet between is inscribed on the handle. An inscription beneath the base records the gift.

The flagon is fully marked on the underside of the lid and on the side of the barrel, and the maker's mark is repeated on the handle: (i) Britannia; (ii) Lion's head erased; (iii) Date letter capital C (cycle XIII), 1718/19, London; (iv) Maker's mark Gothic Ja with a motif above with ornamental shield, possibly John Jackson I (very like Grimwade 1092). (Plate 52.)

GREAT BUDWORTH
ST MARY AND ALL SAINTS
Deanery of Great Budworth

1   COMMUNION CUP (see no. 2)

A communion cup, once gilt, 8½ inches high. The bell-shaped bowl is well splayed to a rim 4⁷⁄₁₀ inches diameter. There is a band of conventional foliage 1½ inches below the rim with interlacing borders forming six panels with sprigs at the intersections placed alternately up and down. The stem is wide, having collars above and below the knop. Above and below the stem are bands of tongue and dart enrichment, and after a shoulder moulding on the foot there is a further band followed by moulding. The foot is 3⁹⁄₁₀ inches. On the side of the bowl is the mark of a sheep's head, William Mutton, Chester, *c.*1570. Weight 8 oz. 4 dwts.

References:
Brocklehurst, no. 2.
Ridgway 1968, pp.58-59 and plate 16.

2 PATEN (see no. 1)

A plate paten, once gilt, to accompany the communion cup no. 1. It is 5¾ inches in diameter, having a rim ⅘ inches wide and incised concentric lines on the surface, with a single deep depression. The sheep's head of William Mutton of Chester (Compendium 1) is struck on the rim. Weight 4 oz.

3 STAND PATEN

A stand paten, 9⅞ inches inches diameter, inscribed on the underside of the plate 'Great Budworth', along with a simple coat of arms. The plate rests upon a moulded stand. Overall height 2½ inches. Weight 17 oz. 8 dwts.

There are four marks: (i) Maker's mark (?)CK with pellet below in a heart-shaped frame, Charles Kandler I (Grimwade 341); (ii) Leopard's head crowned; (iii) Lion passant guardant; (iv) Date letter h (cycle XIV), 1743/44, London.

4 & 5 FLAGONS

The parish accounts under 1714/15 include the information: '10 Die January Two pewter fflagons and a Pewter dish'. These were apparently discarded when the silver flagons were provided. For this a general meeting was held on 1 January 1716/17 at which was passed a resolution to purchase plate. The same resolution was passed on four consecutive years before the purchase was actually made. The first resolution on 1 January 1716/17 reads:

> Plate shall be bought for ye use of the communicants of the said parish in such manner as by the present curate and such as he shall choose to his assistance therein think fit

and in 1720 the following items record the actual purchase of flagons:

Pd to Mr Richardson for the Communion Pleat as by receipt	£34.11s. 0d
for horse hire & expenses to Chester when we paid the leather sum	3s. 6d
Pd for ye carriage of the Pleate from Chester with the cases without	3s. 6d
Pd for soudering one of them at Northwish and the messenger to and from Budworth	2s. 0d

[Richard Richardson acted as an agent for Joseph Clare I.]

Two matching flagons, each 12½ inches high, of bellied form and pear-shaped body with a moulded rib around the shoulder and a spout terminating in a drop. A domed cover has a baluster finial and broken scroll handle and curled thumb. The body curves around towards a circular foot which is moulded, with a shoulder and flange, 4¾ inches diameter. Weight (1) 48 oz. (2) 47 oz. 14 drm. There is an inscription on the body of the flagon, beneath the spout:

'The Communion Plate Belonging to the Parish Church of Great Budworth in Cheshire 1719'.

There are four marks: (i) Maker's mark CL above a pellet within a heart-shaped frame, Joseph Clare I (Grimwade 353); (ii) Lion's head erased; (iii) Britannia; (iv) Date letter D (cycle XIII), 1719/20, London.

Reference:
Brocklehurst, no. 40 and plate VI.

6 COMMUNION CUP (for use when visiting the sick) (see no. 7)
A small communion cup 4¾ inches high with a bell-shaped bowl, diameter of rim 2¼ inches and 2¼ inches deep, on a stem divided by a small reeded knop. The base ends with a shoulder moulding and a flange, diameter 2⅜ inches. The bowl is inscribed: 'Great Budworth'.

There are five marks on the cup: (i) Maker's mark RR within a rectangle, Richard Richardson II Type 5b (Compendium 7386); (ii) Chester City coat; (iii) Leopard's head crowned; (iv) Lion passant guardant; (v) Date letter n (series 4), 1763/64, Chester.

References:
Brocklehurst, no. 50.
Ridgway 1985, p.157.

7 PATEN (see no. 6)
A plate paten, diameter 3⅘ inches to accompany communion cup no. 6. There is a plain edge ⅖ inch wide on which is inscribed 'Great Budworth', and a single depression. Total depth ⅖ inch. There are five marks on the edge corresponding with those on the communion cup (no. 6) although in a different order, and the date letter is inverted.

8 SALVER
The churchwardens' accounts record: '1766 bought from Mr. Richardson Communion Plate £12.16.2'.

A salver, diameter 13 inches, with a pie-crust border, standing on three feet. Engraved in the centre with IHS in rays. Inscribed on the back: 'GREAT BUDWORTH 1766'. Weight 28oz. 14drm.

There are four marks: (i) Date letter Gothic capital L (cycle XV), 1766/67, London; (ii) Lion passant guardant; (iii) Leopard's head crowned; (iv) Maker's mark (rubbed) R R with midway pellet in rectangle, Richard Rugg (Grimwade 2420) or Robert Rew (Grimwade 2422).

Richard Richardson acted as agent for London makers.

9 & 10 TWO COMMUNION CUPS
Two almost identical communion cups (no accompanying patens), the difference lying in the height, one being 9⅜ inches and the other 9¾ inches – the rims being 4⁹⁄₁₆ inches and 4⅝ inches respectively. The bowl of each is

goblet-shaped, 5½ inches deep, separated from the stem by a reeded band 1¼ inches diameter. Below this band the stem is splayed to a band of reeding 1⅜ inches and 1½ inches diameter – it then splays to the foot, 4½ inches diameter with a narrow band of reeding. On the side of each bowl is an inscription beneath a representation of the sacred symbols IHS in a circle with rays: 'The Communion Plate belonging to the Parish Church of Great Budworth in Cheshire'.

There are five marks on the underside of the base: (i) Maker's mark HC above IE within an oval frame, Henry Chawner and John Emes (Grimwade 977); (ii) Lion passant guardant; (iii) Leopard's head crowned; (iv) Date letter A (cycle XVII), 1796/97, London; (v) Duty mark.

GUILDEN SUTTON
ST JOHN THE BAPTIST
Deanery of Chester

COMMUNION CUP

A parcel-gilt communion cup 5¾ inches high, with a goblet-shaped bowl, rim diameter 3¼ inches, standing on a pedestal stem – base diameter 3⅛ inches. It is inscribed: 'The gift of Revᵈ P W Hamilton Minister Guilden Sutton 1831'.

The four marks, apparently omitting the duty mark: (i) Maker's mark (rubbed) script (?)J followed by a script H, Jonathan Hayne (Grimwade 1408); (ii) Lion passant guardant; (iii) Leopard's head crowned; (iv) Date letter f (cycle XVIII) 1821/22, London.

HALTON
ST MARY
Deanery of Frodsham

John Cheshire's portrait can still be seen in the library he built at Halton in 1730. Although the books he gave have been considerably depleted, the fine suite of silver with which he equipped the church is still intact and in use.

1 COMMUNION CUP (see nos 2 & 3)

A communion cup 8¾ inches high, having a bell-shaped bowl, with everted lip, rim diameter 4¼ inches and 4½ inches deep. The side of the bowl carries the coat of arms of John Cheshire. The stem is divided by a moulded band. The foot is moulded with a shoulder and a flange. Base diameter 4⅜ inches.

The four marks are on the bowl: (i) Maker's mark T T with five-petal rose and crown above them, within a shaped frame, Thomas Tearle (Grimwade 2938); (ii) Lion passant guardant; (iii) Leopard's head crowned; (iv) Date letter Q (cycle XIII), 1731/32, London.

2   STAND PATEN (see nos 1 & 3)
A paten, rim diameter 8⅛ inches, to accompany the communion cup (no. 1), with a rim producing a single depression. It stands upon a spindle-shaped stem and has a blocked foot, diameter 4⅜ inches. The overall height is 1⅝ inches. The paten carries the same coat of arms and the assay marks as no. 1.

3   FLAGON (see nos 1 & 2)
A flagon 13½ inches high, having a cylindrical body and a high moulded and domed lid ending in a lobed finial. The lid is attached to the top of an S-scroll handle with an open ram's head thumb. The bottom of the body is marked by a narrow reed moulding followed by a shoulder, a step and a flange. The diameter of the base is 7¼ inches. On the side of the flagon is a long inscription within an oval border, and beneath this the coat of arms of John Cheshire:

> This flagon
> Chalice & Paten are ye Gift
> of Sʳ John Che∫shyre Knight
> His Majisties Sergeant at Law
> To the use of the Chappell of Halton
> in the Dioces and County of Chester
> For the Administration of the
> Blessed Sacrament to the Honour
> of God and Edification of the
> Communicants there
> the 7 day of July in ye year
> of our Lord 1731

The marks are the same as on nos 1 and 2.

HANDLEY
ALL SAINTS
Deanery of Malpas

1   COMMUNION CUP
A communion cup 7⁹⁄₁₀ inches high with a rim diameter of 3⁷⁄₁₀ inches. The bowl is 3⁹⁄₁₀ inches deep. The bowl has a band, ⅗ inch wide, of conventional foliage between two incised lines which are continuous and do not cross over. The bowl stands upon a spindle stem divided by a round and collared knop. Above and below the stem are offsets containing a decoration made by a small wheel, which repeats every seven diagonal stokes. The foot has a shoulder and moulding followed by a band of ovolos and spandrels.
    There is no paten, but a Victorian stand paten suggests when the Elizabethan paten may have disappeared. There are no marks.

2   JUG
A jug, used as a flagon, 8¾ inches high, made of generous silver – the rim being ⅛ inch thick, and external measurement of rim 3⅛ inches. There is a single moulding which envelops the spout. The handle is broken scroll. A third of the way down the baluster bowl is a narrow band of reeding. The bowl ends in a foot consisting of a hollow step and repeated shoulder, ending in a step. Base diameter 4¼ inches. Engraved on the side of the bowl, beneath the spout are the sacred symbols IHS surrounded by rays, and an inscription:

> The gift of the Revd Thos Ince Rector
> to the Parish Church of Handley
> 1747

The four marks on the side of the bowl are repeated on the underside of the base, and the maker's mark is repeated on the handle: (i) Date letter T (cycle XIII), 1734/35, London; (ii) Maker's mark R midway pellet B within a rectangle frame, Richard Bayley (Grimwade 2262); (iii) Leopard's head crowned; (iv) Lion passant guardant.

HARGRAVE
ST PETER
Deanery of Malpas

1   BEAKER (see no. 2)
A beaker supplied as a communion cup in 1700. It stands 3⅞ inches high with a rim diameter of 3¹/₁₀ inches. There are signs of an incised hairline ¹/₁₀ inch below the rim. The sides of the beaker, which show marks of hammering, are straight and the base is arc offset with a four-reeded band, diameter 2⅛ inches. On the side is an inscription:

> Beati
> Qui esuriunt et Sitiunt Justitiam
> Hargreave C
> an 1700

('Blessed are they who hunger and thirst for righteousness'
– Matt. 5. 6 (Vulgate).)

There is a single maker's mark struck twice on the side of the beaker: AT within a square frame (possibly Dutch). (Plates 53, 54.)

2   PATEN (see no. 1)
A companion to the beaker, and carrying the same maker's mark but with a different inscription. It is 6 inches in diameter and has a ½-inch-wide rise

angled towards a pie crust edge ½ inch wide. The base is 4¼ inches. On the plate is an inscription in Latin:

> Chap de Hargreave
> ut sit Christi Amoris
> debita Comemoratio
>
> Desiderata Fercula
> Vovit
> Benevolus

('So that it may be an owed reminder of the love of Christ') or ('A well wisher dedicates (offers) these much needed vessels in order that they may be a fit commemoration of the Love of Christ'). (R.V.H. Burne, Archdeacon of Chester, 1959.)

The maker's mark, as on the beaker, is struck twice (not clearly) on the base. (Plate 55.)

3 JUG (FLAGON)

A jug, commonly called a beer jug, used as a flagon. Height from rim to base 9 inches. The moulded rim, diameter 3¼ inches, continues over the spout and rises above the rim of the jug and follows the curve of the baluster body to a depth of 3½ inches. The body curves around to a curved base followed by a concave moulding and a step. The S-shaped handle has a pronounced curving feature at the top scroll and terminates at the bottom with a heart shape. The top of the handle has been deliberately notched to help with pouring as there is no leaf feature there. On the point of the body beneath the spout is a representation of the IHS with rays. The scroll is attached to the body with an oval collar.

On the inside of the base, diameter 4¾ inches, is an inscription in script: 'The Gift of M G to Hargreave Chapel 1784'.

On the bottom of the body are four marks: (i) Maker's mark WC within a rectangle, either William Cowley (Grimwade 3055) or William Caldecott (Grimwade 3059); (ii) Lion passant guardant; (iii) Leopard's head crowned; (iv) Date letter i (cycle XVI), 1784/85, London.

HARTHILL
ALL SAINTS
Deanery of Malpas

1 STAND PATEN

Among the more recent plate at Harthill is a confection of a stand paten having a diameter of 5¼ inches with a reeded border and a central boss on which are inscribed the sacred symbols surrounded with rays. The plate is a recent addition – and has no marks. However, it has been placed upon a somewhat damaged open-ended stand inside which is a single mark of ID with a star between. This appears to be the mark of a Chester goldsmith, Joseph Duke I, whose work is known between 1769 and 1780.

Reference:
Ridgway 1985, p.77.

2   Communion Cup

A parcel gilt communion cup 8½ inches high, with a bell-shaped bowl 4¾ inches deep. The rim, diameter 4¼ inches, is strengthened with a plain moulding. The bowl curves to a stem divided by a reeded band curving to a reeded step followed by a shoulder and step. Base diameter 4 inches. On the side of the bowl are the sacred symbols surrounded by rays within a scroll on which is inscribed in Roman capitals in two lines 'All things come of thee O Lord/and of thine own do we give thee'.

There are four marks: (i) Maker's mark imperfect, but appears to be in script letters JG with a star between, John Gorham (Grimwade 1343); (ii) Lion passant guardant; (iii) Leopard's head crowned; (iv) Date letter S (cycle XV), 1773/74, London.

3   Flagon

A spoutless flagon 11 inches high with a reeded rim diameter 3⅜ inches. The domed lid is 1¾ inches high. The body of the flagon has straight, slightly tapering sides to a reeded girdle 6¾ inches below the rim. Below this the base follows the line of the body and then spreads out to a rounded step and shoulder followed by a narrow shoulder, the base being 6¾ inches. The flagon has a scroll handle and a ram's head thumb with openwork topped by a shell motif with scrolls on either side. The IHS with rays are on the side of the body.

There are four marks on the side: (i) Maker's mark (imperfectly struck) script capital F followed by a C, Francis Crump (Grimwade 674); (ii) Lion passant guardant; (iii) Leopard's head crowned; (iv) Date letter capital Gothic T (cycle XV), 1774/75, London.

4   Alms Dish

An alms dish, diameter 10 inches, with a plain 1¼-inch border.

The four marks are on the underside of the border: (i) Maker's mark I midway pellet C, John Carter II (Grimwade 1214); (ii) Date letter U (cycle XV), 1775/76, London; (iii) Lion passant guardant; (iv) Leopard's head crowned.

HASLINGTON
St Matthew
Deanery of Nantwich

1   COMMUNION CUP (see nos 2, 3 & 4)
A parcel-gilt communion cup 6¾ inches high, having a bowl diameter 4 inches with reeded edge. The bowl is of goblet type, having almost straight sides which curve round towards the bottom and join the stem with two narrow mouldings. The stem has a round knop ⅗ inches deep, without collars. Above the knop is a cavetto mould 7/10 inches deep and below the knop the stem sweeps down to a moulding and a step, diameter 3⅖ inches. On the side of the bowl the sacred symbols IHS surrounded by rays.

Under the foot is an inscription in script letters: 'Haslington Chapel Cheshire. Rebuilt by the Revd Sir Thos Broughton Bart 1811'.

There are five marks: (i) Maker's mark IC in a rectangle (upside down), John Clarke II (?Grimwade 1220); (ii) Lion passant guardant; (iii) Leopard's head crowned; (iv) Date letter Q (cycle XVII), 1811/12, London; (v) Duty mark.

2   PATEN COVER (see nos 1, 3 & 4)
A paten cover to accompany the communion cup (no. 1), of stand form with a plain blank top. The plate is 6⅕ inches. There is an edge ½ inch wide, with four concentric lines. It forms a slight depression and in the centre of the plate are the sacred symbols surrounded by rays. The stem is cavetto and leads to a wide moulded, yet narrow flange. On the underside of the plate is the inscription (as on the cup) and the same assay marks.

3   FLAGON (see nos 1, 2, & 4)
A flagon, 9½ inches high, with a domed lid, and reeded moulded rim diameter 4 inches. The lid is hinged to the top of the S-shaped handle with a pierced curved ornament with an open heart-shaped opening. The handle has a heart-shaped terminal.

The barrel is 6½ inches deep with straight sides, and a spout ending in a couple of beads. It curves around at the base to a moulded pedestal 1 7/10 inches deep, ending with a reeded step – diameter 3¾ inches. There is a representation of the sacred symbols on the side of the barrel. There are three marks inside the lid and five below the rim, the same as on nos 1, 2 and 4.

4   ALMS DISH (see nos 1, 2 & 3)
An alms dish, diameter 9 inches, having a 1 1/10-inch moulded edge with a single depression. The marks, inscriptions and sacred symbols are the same as on nos 1 to 3.

II
The Plates

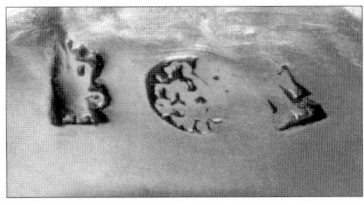

1. CHESTER CATHEDRAL: Chalice, London 1496/97. See page 1.

2. CHESTER CATHEDRAL: Marks on chalice, London 1496/97. See page 1.

3. CHESTER CATHEDRAL: Communion cup. See page 1.

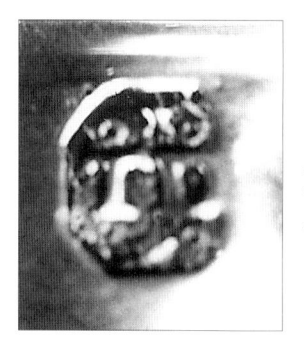

4. CHESTER CATHEDRAL: Maker's mark TD on communion cup and on paten covers (opposite). See pages 1-2.

5. CHESTER CATHEDRAL: Two paten covers. See page 2.

6. CHESTER CATHEDRAL: The arms of Bridgman on front of paten cover. See page 2.

7. CHESTER CATHEDRAL: Two stand patens, London 1662/63. See page 2.

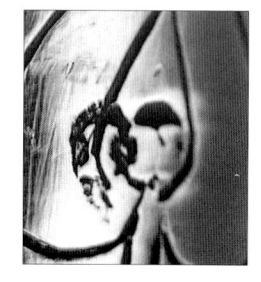

8. CHESTER CATHEDRAL: Pair of flagons, London 1662/63. See page 2.

9. CHESTER CATHEDRAL: Maker's mark on one of flagons. See page 3.

10. CHESTER CATHEDRAL: Alms dish, London 1673/74. See page 3.

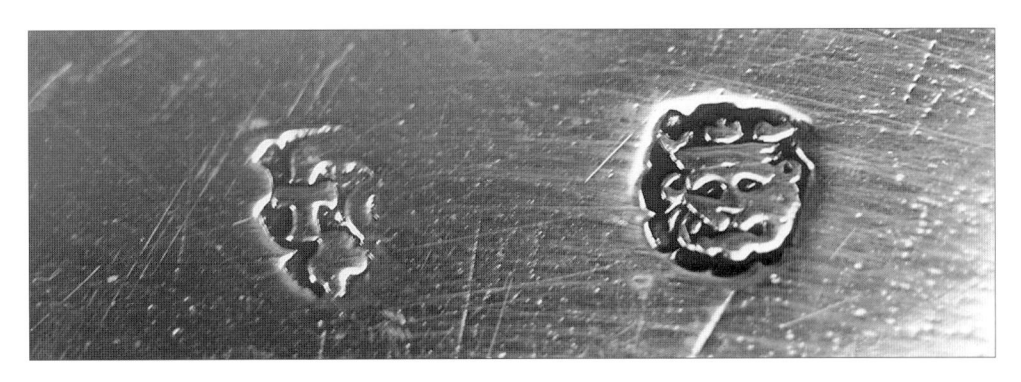

11. CHESTER CATHEDRAL: Maker's mark on alms dish. See page 3.

12. CHESTER CATHEDRAL: Pair of candlesticks, London 1678/79. See page 3.

13. CHESTER CATHEDRAL: Pair of alms plates, Chester 1737/38 with mark of Richard Richardson II. See page 4.

14. CHESTER CATHEDRAL: Communion cup, London 1685/86. See page 4.

15. CHESTER CATHEDRAL: Engraving on foot of communion cup. See page 4.

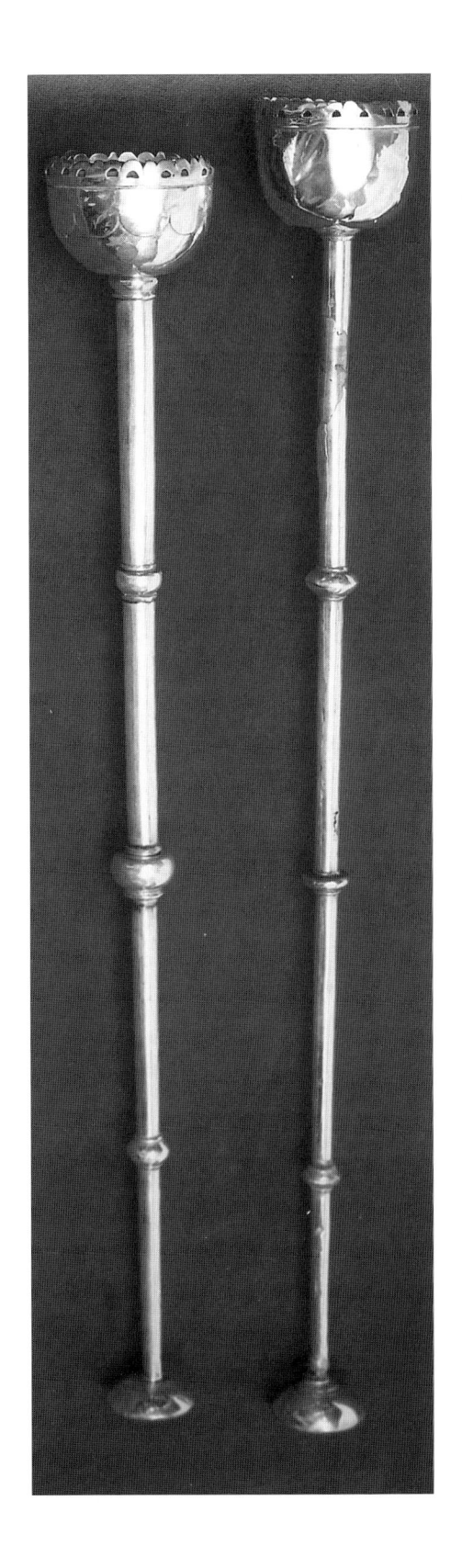

16. CHESTER CATHEDRAL: Dean's verge (*left*); Canon's verge (*right*). See page 4.

17. CHESTER CATHEDRAL: Engraving on top of Dean's verge. See page 5.

18. CHESTER CATHEDRAL: Engraving on top of Canon's verge. See page 5.

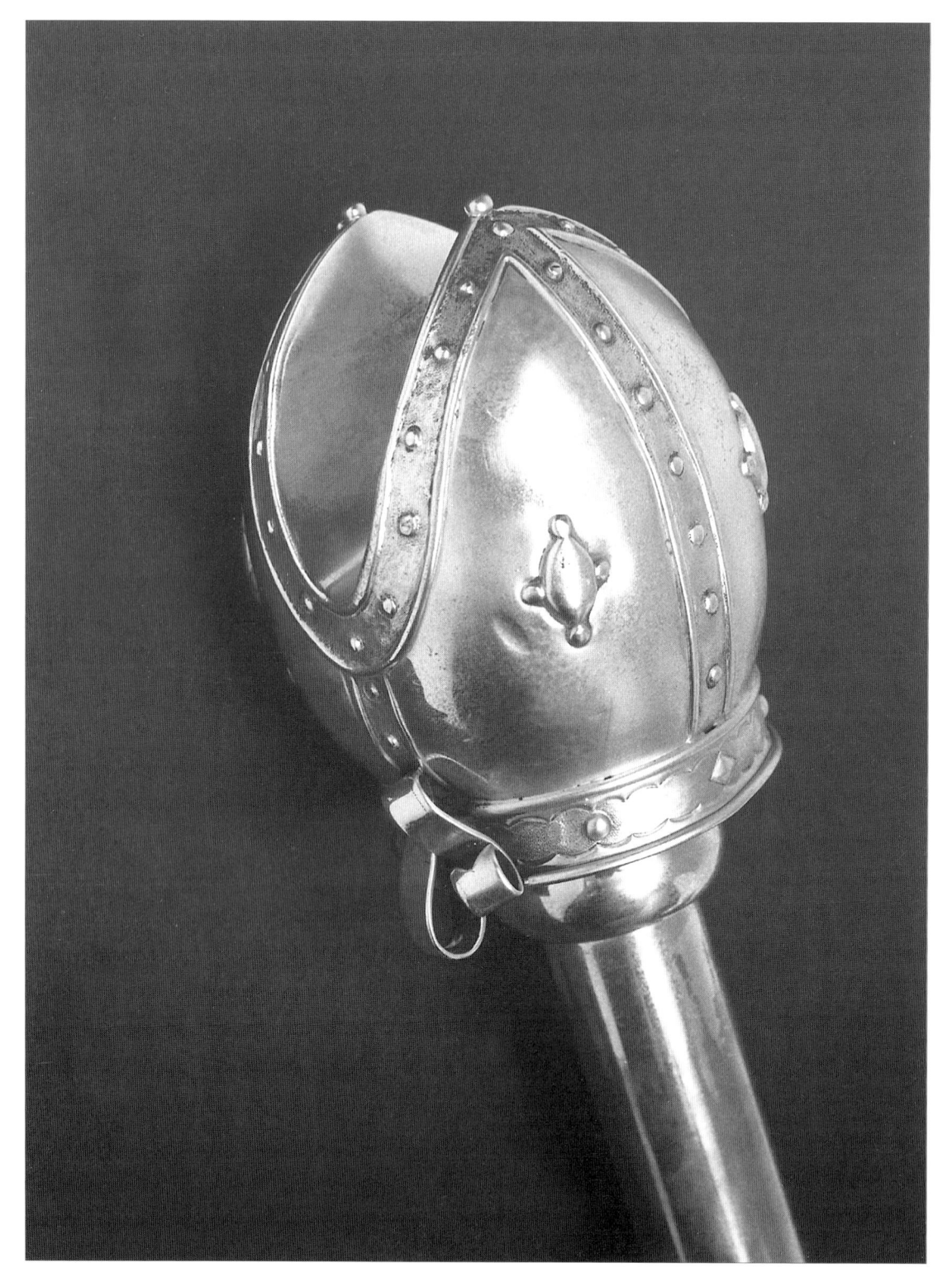

19. CHESTER CATHEDRAL: Head of mitred mace, London 1787/88. See page 6.

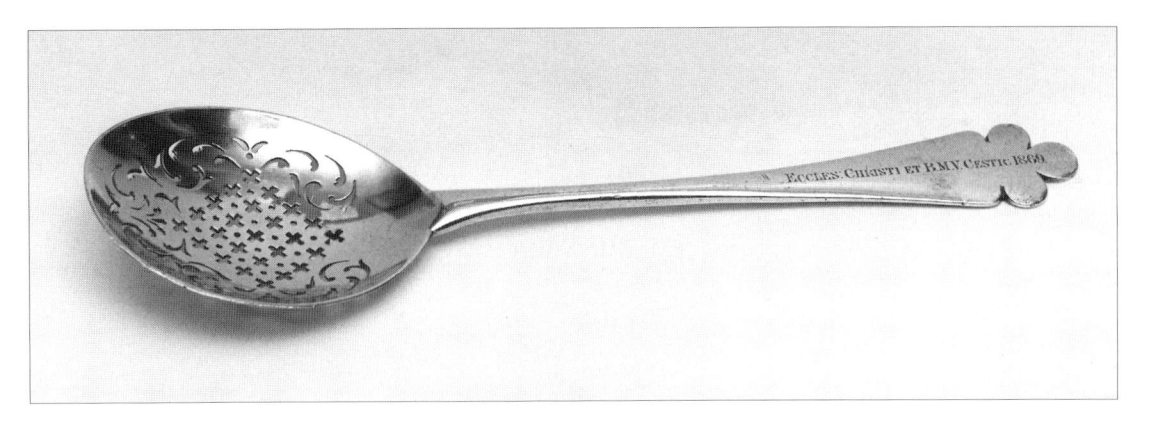

20. CHESTER CATHEDRAL: Strainer spoon, London 1691/92.
See page 6.

21. CHESTER CATHEDRAL: Communion cup, possibly Swiss.
See page 7.

22. CHESTER CATHEDRAL: Chalice and cover, possibly Dutch. See page 7.

23. CHESTER CATHEDRAL: Coat of arms engraved underneath chalice. See page 7.

24. CHESTER CATHEDRAL: Communion cup and cover, London 1678. See page 8.

25. CHESTER CATHEDRAL: Alms box, London 1677/78. See page 8.

26. (*Above*) Astbury: Mark of possibly William Faudrey on communion cup. See page 15.

27. (*Right*) Astbury: One of pair of flagons, London 1716/17. See page 16.

28. Aston: Medieval chalice. See page 17.

29. Aston: Engraving of St John on foot of medieval chalice. See page 17.

30. BOWDON: Alms dish, London 1775/76. See page 26.

31. BOWDON: One of pair of flagons, London 1775/76. See page 27.

32. BOWDON: Pair of communion cups and salver, London 1775/76. See page 27.

33. BUNBURY: Pair of flagons, London 1735/36; pair of alms plates, London 1747/48; stand paten, London 1716/17; communion cup, London 1632/33; paten, Chester late 16th/17th century. See pages 30-1.

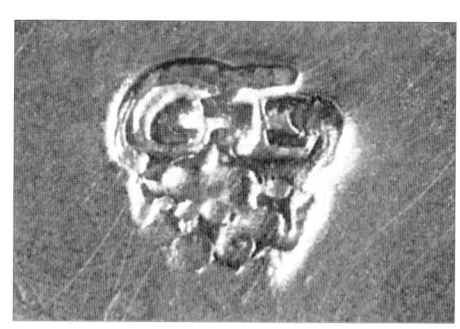

34. (*Above*) BUNBURY: Mark of Griffith Edwardes I on paten. See page 30.

35. (*Left*) CARRINGTON: Flagon, London 1688/89. See page 35.

36. (*Below*) CARRINGTON: Mark of Magdalen Feline on communion cup, London 1759/60. See page 35.

37. CHESTER: BISHOP OF CHESTER'S PRIVATE CHAPEL: Communion cup possibly by Richard Richardson I, Chester. See page 40.

38. CHESTER ST BRIDGET: Flagon, London 1697. See page 53.

39. CHESTER ST BRIDGET: Mark of Hugh Roberts, London 1697, on pair of plate patens. See page 54.

40. CHESTER ST MICHAEL: Communion cup, Chester c.1570, by William Mutton. See page 212.

41. CHESTER ST MICHAEL: Communion cup by Edward South, London 1635/36. See page 212.

42. CHESTER ST PETER: Flagon, London 1719/20; stand paten, London 1708/09; communion cup, Chester 1762/63. See pages 65-7.

43. CHURCH MINSHULL: Mark of John Bingley of Chester on communion cup. See page 75.

44. DARESBURY: Stand paten, London 1654/55. See page 80.

45. DARESBURY: Flagon, London 1731/32. See page 80.

46. DARESBURY: Mark of Richard Richardson II of Chester, and inscription under stand paten. See page 81.

47. DARESBURY: Communion cup, London 1773/74. See page 81.

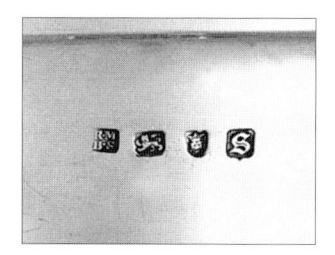

48. DARESBURY: Mark of Richard Morson and Benjamin Stephenson on communion cup. See page 81.

49. ECCLESTON: Communion cup, late 17th century. See page 86.

50. ECCLESTON: Flagon, London 1746/47. See page 87.

51. GREAT BARROW: Communion cup and paten cover. See pages 95-6.

52. GREAT BARROW: Flagon, London 1718/19. See page 96.

53. HARGRAVE: Maker's mark on beaker, possibly Dutch. See page 101.

54. HARGRAVE: Beaker, *c.*1700, possibly Dutch. See page 101.

55. HARGRAVE: Paten, *c.*1700, possibly Dutch. See page 101.

57. MALPAS: One of pair of flagons, London 1795/96. See page 117.

56. MALPAS: Communion cup and paten cover, York 1674/75. See page 115.

58, 59. MALPAS: Details of handle of flagon. See page 117.

60. MALPAS: One of pair of candlesticks, Sheffield 1809/10. See page 117.

61. MIDDLEWICH: Communion cup, London 1608/09. See page 121.

62. MIDDLEWICH: Flagon, London 1732/33 (*left*); communion cup, London 1667/68; flagon, London 1739/40 (*right*). See pages 121-2.

63. MOBBERLEY: Communion cup, London 1571/72. See page 123.

64. NANTWICH: Maker's mark on one of pair of flagons, London 1659/60. See page 126.

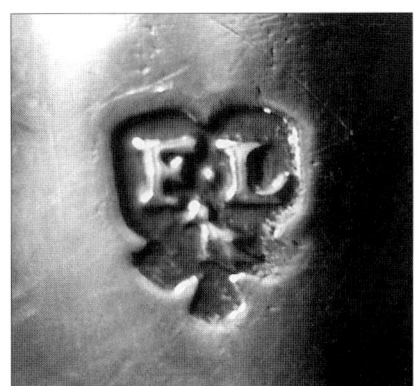

65. NANTWICH: Communion cup and paten cover, London 1604/05. See pages 125-6.

66. OVERCHURCH: Communion cup, London 1618/19. See page 133.

67. POTT SHRIGLEY: Flagon, London 1711/12. See page 135.

68. STOCKPORT ST MARY: Communion cup and paten cover, London 1580/81. See page 147.

69. SWETTENHAM: Communion cup, Chester 1704/05; stand paten, London 1713/14. See pages 152-3.

70. TARPORLEY: Communion cup, London 1711/12. See page 153.

71. TARPORLEY: Flagon, London 1711/12. See page 154.

72. TARPORLEY: Chalice, possibly Italian. See page 155.

73. TARPORLEY: Detail of stem of chalice. See page 155.

74. TARVIN: Flagon, London 1776/77. See page 157.

75. WINCLE: Communion cup, London 1645/46. See page 171.

HAZEL GROVE
St Thomas
Deanery of Chadkirk

(see **NORBURY**)

HESWALL
St Peter
Deanery of Wirral, North

Reference:
Budden, p.170ff.

1   STAND PATEN

A small stand paten, diameter 5¾ inches, having a moulded rim on a concave stem with a moulded base with shoulder and narrow flange. Overall height 2 inches. The diameter of the stem at its lowest point is 1¼ inches. Diameter of foot 2⅗ inches.

There is an inscription under the foot: 'The Gift of Wm Glegg Esqr to the Parish of Heswall in Cheshire 1740'.

There are four marks on the surface of the plate: (i) Maker's mark BA within a lobed rectangle, Richard Bayley (Grimwade 116); (ii) Britannia; (iii) Lion's head erased; (iv) Date letter C (cycle XIII), 1718/19, London.

2   COMMUNION CUP

A communion cup 8½ inches high, with a bell-shaped bowl and everted lip, depth 4¼ inches and diameter of rim 4 inches. The bowl rests upon a stem divided by a narrow moulded band, ¼ inch deep. The diameter at this point is 1¹/₁₆ inches. The foot has a shoulder moulding and a flange, diameter 4⅕ inches. Under the foot is an inscription: 'This was made new and enlarged at the expense of Mrs Glegg of Gayton 1739'.

In spite of this inscription it is clear that Mrs Glegg commissioned the cup in 1739 from the Richardsons, to replace an earlier cup (perhaps the one which accompanied the stand paten (no. 1).

There are five marks on the side of the bowl: (i) Maker's mark R midway pellet R within an angular shield – the top side imperfectly struck, Richard Richardson II Type 3c and William Richardson II Type 1; (ii) Lion passant guardant; (iii) Leopard's head crowned; (iv) Chester City coat (imperfectly struck); (v) Date letter script O (series 3), 1739/40, Chester.

Reference:
Ridgway 1985, p.189.

3   FLAGON

A flagon 13¼ inches high, having a moulded rim, diameter 4¾ inches. It has a domed cover and a broken scroll handle ending in a shield terminal and an open thumb. The sides of the flagon are tapered. A moulded band marks the bottom of the body below which the sides curve towards a step and shoulder and a moulded flange, diameter 8½ inches.

The body is engraved on the front with the sacred symbols surrounded by rays. Under the base is an inscription:

> The Gift of Phebe
> Wife of Richd Davenport
> of Calvely Esqr to the Parishioners
> of Heswall in the County of Chester
> in the year of our redemption
> MDCCXXXVI

Phebe Davenport also gave two flagons, by the same maker, to Bunbury Church (nos 4 and 5).

There are four marks: (i) Leopard's head crowned; (ii) Maker's mark TP in an oval, Thomas Parr II (Grimwade 2870); (iii) Lion passant guardant; (iv) Date letter a (cycle XIV), 1736/37, London.

4   CHALICE

Little is known of the origin of this chalice apart from the information inscribed upon the bowl that it was given to Heswall by Edward Rae in memory of his godchild Elsie Brocklebank in 1893 and that he, at any rate, believed it to be an old 'Danish Chalice'.

The chalice is 7¼ inches high with a tub-shaped bowl, diameter 4½ inches and 2 inches deep – the sides sloping inwards. The stem and knop are sexfoil as is the base which has six lobes. It has a large lobular knot, with six projecting lozenge bosses, each one set with a letter, forming I H E S V S. The base, which sweeps down to a moulded rim, overall diameter 5¾ inches, appears to be comparatively new, but the rest has evidently undergone considerable repair and is still in need of attention. There are no marks and its date is uncertain.

Reference: Budden, p.171 and plate 1.

HOLMES CHAPEL
ST LUKE
Deanery of Congleton

(see **CHURCH HULME**)

HUNTINGTON
St Luke
Deanery of Chester

(see **CHESTER** ST MARTIN)

1 COMMUNION CUPS

An identical pair of communion cups, each having a goblet-type bowl, plain stem and reeded foot. Each stands 6 inches in height, diameter of rim 3¼ inches and diameter of base 3 inches. Each weighs 6½ oz. On the bowl is the inscription:

> St MARTIN'S
> Thos Armitstead
> Rector
> Thos Jones
> Saml Bennett
> Churchwardens
> 1805

There are five marks: (i) Maker's mark (incorrectly recorded by Ball) is PB.AB. WB placed one above the other in a rectangle, entered in 1800 by Peter, Ann and William I Bateman (Grimwade 2141); (ii) Lion passant guardant; (iii) Leopard's head crowned; (iv) Date letter I (cycle XVII), 1804/05, London; (v) Duty mark.

    One of the cups was handed over on loan to the Bishop of Birkenhead on 5 May 1973 by the vicar and wardens of the newly proposed Parish of Chester and given to Huntington St Luke in 1985. The other cup was purchased by the Grosvenor Museum, Chester in 1988 and is on display in the Ridgway Gallery.

> Reference:
> Ball 1907, p.120.

2 STAND PATEN

A small stand paten, diameter 5⅜ inches, and 1⅞ inches high, formed of a single depression with incised lines around the rim. Diameter of foot 3 inches. Weight 5¾ oz. The inscription reads:

> S.Martin's Chester
> 1805
> Thos Armitstead, Rector
> Saml Bennett
> Chas King Ch Wardens

There are five marks: (i) PB above WB, Peter and William I Bateman (Grimwade 2143); (ii) Lion passant guardant; (iii) Leopard's head crowned; (iv) Date letter K (cycle XVII), 1806/07, London; (v) Duty mark.

Given to Huntington New Parish in October 1985.

The parish also has the use of a communion cup originally from Chester St Bridget.

INCE
St James
Deanery of Frodsham

COMMUNION CUP
A communion cup, 5¾ inches high, with a bell-shaped bowl, rim diameter 3½ inches, standing upon a trumpet-shaped stem with a narrow moulded band a little below the bowl. The base has a shoulder and very narrow flange. Diameter of foot 3 inches.

There are six marks on the side of the bowl: (i) Maker's mark RR in rectangle, Richard Richardson IV Type 2 (Compendium 7392); (ii) Lion passant guardant; (iii) Leopard's head crowned; (iv) Chester City coat; (v) Date letter n (series 5), 1788/89, Chester; (vi) Duty mark.

KNUTSFORD
St John the Evangelist
Deanery of Knutsford

The church at Knutsford was built on a new site in 1741-44 when the former church was demolished, and the plate was transferred.

1   COMMUNION CUP
The communion cup stands 7½ inches high and has a bucket-shaped bowl 5 inches deep with straight sides and everted lip – diameter 4⁹⁄₁₆ inches. The sides of the bowl turn sharply to a trumpet-shaped stem and the foot ends with a step and a shoulder, ending in a flange – diameter 4⁷⁄₁₀ inches. Weight 11 oz.

On the side of the bowl are four identical badly struck marks, of a five-petal rose within a circular frame.

The form of the communion cup shows it to belong to the latter part of the 17th century. Similar marks of five-petal roses are found at Henllan and Hope in the neighbouring Diocese of St Asaph, dated by inscription 1670.

Reference:
Ridgway 1997, pp.100, 106.

2   FLAGON

A flagon, overall height 13½ inches, with a domed lid and ribbed rim, diameter 5 inches. It has an S-scroll handle with a heart-shaped terminal and an oval collar at the junction of the scroll and body of the flagon. The thumb is open, with a ram's head twist on top. The moulded band marks the end of the body and beneath this drops down towards a small shoulder and a much larger one before the base, diameter 8¹/₁₀ inches. The inscription on the base reads: 'The Gift of Ann Hall of Nether Knutsford 1768'.

There are four marks on the inside of the domed lid and also on the side of the barrel: (i) Maker's mark F midway pellet C within a rectangle, Francis Crump (Grimwade 672); (ii) Lion passant guardant; (iii) Leopard's head crowned; (iv) Date letter Gothic N (cycle XV), 1768/69, London.

LITTLE BUDWORTH
ST PETER
Deanery of Middlewich

The will of Hugh Starkey of Oulton 1526 states: 'Also I bequeth to ye said church of Budworth a chales and a masse bok wt a vestmentt and all my clothes necessary for a p'est to say masse in …'

The three pieces of plate (1-3) have the same inscription: on the face of the paten and on the side of the cup and flagon:

>   The Gift of ye Honble Mrs Egerton
>   wife of John Egerton Esqr Eldest Son
>   Sr Philip Egerton of Egerton & Oulton
> Knight & only daughter of Robt Lord Cholmondeley
>   Visct Kells and Sister to the Right Honorable
>   Hugh Earl of Cholmondeley

References:
Brocklehurst, nos 36, 37.
RSLC, vol.XXXIII, p.11.

1   COMMUNION CUP (see no. 2)

A gilt communion cup 11 inches high with a 5-inch deep bell-shaped bowl, rim diameter 4⅗ inches with straight sides and slightly everted lip. The lower part of the bowl follows through to the stem, the sides of which are almost vertical and which is divided by a knop with two squarish collars – together 1⅖ inches deep. The base, diameter 4¾ inches, has a series of ogee shoulder mouldings, ending in a step.

There are four marks: (i) Maker's mark WA with an anchor between in a deckled shield frame, Joseph Ward (Grimwade 2989); (ii) Britannia; (iii) Lion's head erased; (iv) Date letter Q (cycle XII), 1711/12, London.

2   PATEN COVER (see no. 1)
A gilt paten cover to fit over the communion cup no.1. Diameter 7 inches, with incised lines on the up-sloping rim and with a sharp face to a single depression. It is 1⅞ inches high, the stem a cavetto, and the solid top diameter 3⅙ inches having the sacred symbols surrounded by rays and also three incised lines. The marks are the same as on the communion cup (no. 1).

3   FLAGON
A flagon 12¾ inches high with a flat moulded lid, including an inset with a set back cavetto moulding. The rim of the flagon is also moulded. There is no lip. The thumb, moulded with a corkscrew, is attached to the top of the lid and hinged to the top of the S-scroll handle which has a trefoil terminal. The barrel has a reeded band before dropping to a step, diameter 7¾ inches, and an ogee shoulder. Made in *c.*1710, it weighs 64½ oz.

There are four marks: (i) Maker's mark large capital G sheltering a small A in a shaped shield, Francis Garthorne (entered mark 1697), (Grimwade 736); (ii) Britannia; (iii) Lion's head erased; (iv) Date letter indecipherable.

These three pieces are on display in the Ridgway Gallery at the Grosvenor Museum, Chester, where they are on long-term loan.

LOWER PEOVER
ST OSWALD
Deanery of Knutsford

1   FLAGON
A flagon, overall height to top of the thumb 11¼ inches. The lid has a bun top above a moulded rim and flange and rests upon a moulded rim. The thumb, with an open heart-shape and open triangle with a double ogee head is attached to both the top of the bun top and the top of the handle, where it is hinged. The handle is S-shaped and the terminal a plain shield.

The barrel has straight sides and ends with a reeded band. Below this the foot splays outwards to a diameter of 6½ inches.

The arms of Leycester are engraved on the handle, and below this '1687 Nether Peover', and the sacred symbols and rays are inscribed on the front.

There are four marks on the side of the flagon and on the top of the lid, and the lion passant is also found under the base: (i) Maker's mark – conjoined I and

A script and in a square with rounded corners; (ii) Leopard's head crowned; (iii) Lion passant guardant; (iv) Date letter h (cycle XI), 1685/86, London.

2   COMMUNION CUP
The stem and foot have been damaged by compression, giving a present height of 6¾ inches. The diameter of the rim is 4 inches. The bowl is bell-shaped with an everted lip. It stands on a stem divided by a plain rounded knop. Originally the stem would have passed into a step followed by a shoulder and flange on which is an inscribed line.

There are five marks: (i) Maker's mark Ri within a square with rounded corners Richard Richardson I Type 4 (Compendium 6816); (ii) Britannia; (iii) Lion's head erased; (iv) Chester City coat; (v) Date letter capital P (series 2), 1715/16, Chester.

Reference: Ridgway 1968, p.171.

3 & 4   STAND PATENS
Two matching stand patens 8⁹⁄₁₀ inches diameter. Each has a narrow moulded rim which leads immediately to a sloping depression. Each stands upon a stem with a shoulder moulding below which the stem is vertical, turning slightly at the foot, diameter 1½ inches.

There are five marks: (i) Maker's mark Ri in a shaped shield, Richard Richardson I Type 3 (Compendium 6815); (ii) Britannia; (iii) Lion's head erased; (iv) Chester City coat; (v) Date letter capital P (series 2), 1715/16, Chester.

Reference: Ridgway 1968, p.169.

LOWER WHITLEY
ST LUKE
Deanery of Great Budworth

COMMUNION CUP
A communion cup with a deep beaker-type bowl. Total height 7 inches, having a rim diameter of 3½ inches. The bowl stands upon a trumpet-shaped stem divided by a deep knop having moulded collars. The stem leads to a shoulder followed by a moulding and a narrow flange and base, diameter 3 inches.

There are four marks on the side of the bowl: (i) Maker's mark IW with a midway pellet, John Watson, Sheffield; (ii) Lion passant guardant; (iii) Duty mark; (iv) Date letter a surmounted by a crown, 1824/25, Sheffield.

The paten provided with this cup is Victorian, and was supplied by Garrard's.

(Grateful thanks to the Revd David Johnson, Vicar, for his help.)

Lymm
St Mary the Virgin
Deanery of Great Budworth

Reference:
THSLC, vol. 52, 1902, pp.93-110.

1 Communion Cup

When Ball reported on the plate at Lymm 1900 he recorded 'a Paten also the gift of the Warburton family, older than the Chalice but supposed "locally" to be 1710' and that the marks were date letter P (1652/53), leopard's head crowned, lion passant guardant, and the maker's mark RC. Its whereabouts is unknown. Some time after Ball's survey the church lent to its daughter church in Statham a communion cup which, over the years, has been frequently mended. The accompanying paten is dated 1911.

The bowl of the cup at least is of the 17th century and probably earlier than the late 17th-century cup, paten cover and paten (nos 2, 3 and 4) at the parish church. The cup has no inscription or coat of arms and stands (though crushed) 6¼ inches high. The bowl, diameter 3⅞ inches and 3⅝ inches deep has straight sides and a slightly everted lip. The base turns to the step on the top of which are two inscribed lines. In its present state the stem is divided by a plain round knop and ends with a crushed shoulder and, after a flange and an inset followed by mouldings, a base, diameter 3⅝ inches. Much of the base has been blocked in some later repair.

The marks on the side of the bowl are indistinct, but appear to be: (i) Date letter F (cycle VIII), 1623/24, London; (ii) Lion passant guardant; (iii) Leopard's head crowned; (iv) Maker's mark (?)RC.

2 Communion Cup (see no. 3)

A communion cup 8¾ inches high with a rim diameter of 4½ inches, having a bowl 5 inches deep of straight sides with an everted lip and turning slightly at the base to meet the stem which is scribed beneath the junction with two lines. The stem is divided by a round knop ½ inch deep with an incised line at top and bottom. The stem ends with a step, shoulder and a flange on which is an incised line. The diameter of the base is 4 inches. On the side of the bowl the crest of Warburton of Arley.

There are four marks on the side of the bowl and the lion passant guardant is repeated under the foot: (i) Makers' mark I C above a five-point star or mullet within a shaped frame; (ii) Leopard's head crowned; (iii) Lion passant guardant; (iv) Date letter Gothic O (cycle XI), 1691/92, London.

3 Paten Cover (see no. 2)

A paten cover, diameter 5⅜ inches, to accompany the communion cup (no. 2). It has a wide rim on which is inscribed the crest of Warburton of Arley. It is edged with reeded mouldings. The overall height is 1¾ inches – the plate is domed and has a major step to fit over the rim of the cup, followed by a flange, and on this are incised lines and mouldings on both sides. The stand is 1⅛ inches diameter with a series of small mouldings at top and bottom. The marks are as on the communion cup (no. 2).

4 STAND PATEN
A stand paten, diameter 8⁵⁄₁₆ inches with a 1¼-inch-wide rim set at an angle, with a ½-inch moulded edge forming a single depression. The plate stands on a plain unblocked trumpet-shaped stem without mouldings and the diameter is 3 inches. On the centre of the plate the same crest as on nos 2 and 3.
    On the underside of the edge are four marks as on nos 2 and 3.

MACCLESFIELD
ST MICHAEL AND ALL SAINTS
Deanery of Macclesfield

The Chantry Returns of 1548 state that Macclesfield 'A Chapell of ease [of Prestbury] had Plate & Juells none'.

Earwaker's *East Cheshire*, vol. 2, p.490, quotes a memorandum 'of about 1665 or earlier':

> Item 2 Communion cupps of silver, whereof the one is a new one, the other made in the year 1572 hath a cover of silver according to the Booke of Articles.

Sir John Leigh is described in 1572 as 'late Curate of Macclesfield'. He remained as curate of Macclesfield until he died, in February 1609/10. He was succeeded by Thomas Short. He was evidently a reforming curate for the communion cup and cover paten of 1572 (now lost), referred to in the memo, were one of his introductions and were in use until after the Restoration in 1660.

1 & 3 TWO COMMUNION CUPS (see nos 2 & 4)
Apart from bearing a different coat of arms (also on the accompanying paten covers, with inscriptions as to the identity of the donors) both communion cups (and cover patens) are the same.
    Each is 9 inches high with a bell-shaped bowl 5 inches deep. The rim diameter is 4 inches and is very slightly everted. The bowl is separated from the spool-shaped stem by a cavetto moulding. The stem has a dividing knop with surface decoration and has both upper and lower collars. The stem ends in a step, followed by a large shoulder and an inset band of ovolos and a short flange. The foot diameter is 4 inches. Beneath the foot is inscribed the weight 18.5.

On one communion cup is the coat of arms of Snelson and on either side an inscription: 'The gift of Roger/Snelson Dier'. On the other communion cup, whose bowl is very pitted, is inscribed the coat of arms of Higginbothame and on either side an inscription: 'The gift of Phillip/Higginbothame Dier'.

There are four marks on the side of each bowl: (i) Maker's mark TH within a decorated shield; (ii) Date letter G (cycle VIII), 1624/25, London; (iii) Leopard's head crowned; (iv) Lion passant guardant.

2 & 4   PATEN COVERS (see nos 1 & 3)
Two paten covers to accompany communion cups (nos 1 and 3), each bearing a different coat of arms on the blocked base to correspond with those on the communion cups.

Each paten cover, made to fit over the cup rim with a bezel, is domed with a flange overriding the bezel. Diameter 4⅜ inches. Each has a spool-shaped stem to a circular top, diameter 1¾ inches, on which is the respective coat of arms and inscription.

On one paten cover is a coat of arms and the inscription: 'The gift of Roger Snelson', and on the other: a coat of arms and the inscription: 'The gift of Phillip Higginbothame Dier'.

There are four marks on the top side of the dome as on the communion cups (nos 1 & 3).

5   STAND PATEN
A large stand paten, 12 inches diameter, having a narrow moulded edge and a shallow depression. The plate has a spool-shaped stand 2³⁄₁₀ inches high, with a step and shoulder and a flange. Base diameter 4¾ inches. On the centre of the plate is a coat of arms surrounded by foliage within a circle. Total height 3½ inches.

There are four marks on the depression: (i) Maker's mark B A within two conjoined circles, closely resembling Richard Bayley (Grimwade 116); (ii) Lion's head erased; (iii) Britannia; (iv) Date letter D (cycle XIII), 1719/20, London.

6 & 7   TWO IDENTICAL FLAGONS
Two flagons, each 15¼ inches high, each having a domed lid attached to the top of an S-shaped handle – the thumb being open with a scroll top. The rim is 5 inches diameter. A narrow band of moulding marks the junction of the handle with the side, which terminates in a plain oval. Below the band the sides continue to a series of mouldings, and end in a shoulder and a step. The base diameter is 8¼ inches.

There is an inscription accompanied by the sacred monogram with rays on the side of each flagon: 'The gift of Thomas Heywood of Macclesfield, Alderman'.

There are four marks on the side of each flagon, which are repeated on the underside of the lid: (i) Maker's mark script EF with pellet above within a lobed frame, Edward Feline (Grimwade 587); (ii) Lion passant guardant; (iii) Leopard's head crowned; (iv) Date letter K (cycle XIV), 1745/46, London.

8 & 9   TWO ALMS PLATES
Two identical alms plates (almost dishes), diameter 11 inches, each having a wavy border with a gadrooned rim and a 1¼-inch curved edge leading to a deep depression.
   Each plate is inscribed:

> Hannae Eccles Ecclesiae Macclesfieldiensi Donum
> AD MDCCLVIII
> Hoc Pictatis Suae Testimonium
> Josephus Eccles Generosus
> A dieta Hanna Conjuge Clarissima
> moriturus expetivit

There are four marks on the underside of the rim: (i) Date letter Gothic C (cycle XV), 1758/59, London; (ii) Lion passant guardant; (iii) Leopard's head crowned; (iv) Maker's mark C midway pellet H within a rectangle, Charles Hollinshed (Grimwade 331).

MALPAS
ST OSWALD
Deanery of Malpas

1   COMMUNION CUP (see no. 2)
A York-made communion cup, 10 inches high, having a bucket-shaped bowl, diameter 5¼ inches and 5½ inches deep. It stands on a spindle-shaped stem divided by a large rounded knop 1¼ inches deep. The stem ends in a step and a flange, making the base diameter 4⁹⁄₁₀ inches.
   On the side of the bowl, in contemporary script, is inscribed:

> Donavit Ecclesiae de Malpas in Comit Cestr
> Guilielmus Holland Rector ibiden 1674

There are three marks on the side of the bowl: (i) Maker's mark TM above a five-point star in a heart-shaped frame, Thomas Mangy; (ii) The York mark; (iii) Date letter script R (table V), 1674/75, York. (Plate 56.)

2   PATEN COVER (see no. 1)
A paten cover to accompany the communion cup (no. 1), 6⅛ inches diameter. The cover, depth 2 inches, fits over the cup with a reeded bezel and the flange is ½ inch wide. The plate depression is ½ inch and the handle is formed by a cavetto rising to a blocked top, diameter 2½ inches.
   There are three marks on the top of the cover, as on no. 1. (Plate 56.)

3   COMMUNION CUP

A Chester-made communion cup, 7 inches high, with a bell-shaped bowl, depth 4½ inches, and everted lip, diameter 3¾ inches. The bowl turns to a stem divided by a very narrow band, having top and bottom collars. The stem leads to a slight step and shoulder and a flange, diameter 3¾ inches. Weight 18⅝ oz.

There are five marks on the side of the bowl: (i) Maker's mark Ri within a shaped frame, Richard Richardson I Type 3 (Compendium 6815); (ii) Britannia (repeated on the base); (iii) Lion's head erased; (iv) Chester City coat; (v) Date letter R (series 2), 1717/18, Chester.

4   PATEN or ALMS PLATE (see no. 9)

A plate, 9⅛ inches diameter, with a moulded rim 1½ inches wide, having a single depression in the centre of which is engraved the sacred symbols and rays. Weight 15½ oz.

There are three marks on the rim: (i) Lion's head erased; (ii) Britannia; (iii) Date letter C (cycle XIII), 1718/19, London.

5 & 6   ALMS PLATES

Two alms plates, diameter of each 9⅞ inches. Inscribed on the back of each plate:

> Ex dono Gulielmi Dod de Hampton Armigeri
> Ultimi Haeredis ijusdem Familiae 1742

Each has a plain border on which are four marks: (i) Leopard's head crowned; (ii) Date letter g (cycle XIV), 1742/43, London; (iii) Lion passant guardant; (iv) Maker's mark capital Gothic TM within a rectangle, Thomas Mann (Grimwade 2849).

7 & 8   TWO IDENTICAL COMMUNION CUPS

Two parcel gilt communion cups, each 9⅜ inches high, having a bell-shaped bowl. The rim, diameter, 4¼ inches, is strengthened, and each bowl, 4 inches deep, is engraved with the sacred symbols within rays, and the whole capped with a scroll on which is engraved in Roman capitals:

> ALL THINGS COME OF THEE O LORD AND OF THINE
> OWN HAVE WE GIVEN THEE

Each bowl stands upon a moulded baluster pedestal and the circular base has shoulder mouldings divided by a step, diameter 4½ inches. One of the cups has a paler gilt than the other. On the base of one cup is scratched 'No. 2', and on the base of the other 'No. 9'.

There are identical marks on the bases: (i) Lion passant guardant; (ii) Leopard's head crowned; (iii) Date letter Gothic capital K (cycle XV), 1765/66,

London; (iv) Maker's mark FC with midway pellet within a rectangle, Francis Crump (Grimwade 672).

9 PATEN or ALMS PLATE

A paten or alms plate, made to match no. 4, diameter 9⅛ inches, of the same design with the sacred symbols and rays on the centre of the plate. It was made some years later than no. 4.

There are four marks on the rim: (i) Maker's mark ID with a mid-way pellet and within a rectangle, John Dutton (Grimwade 1245); (ii) Lion passant guardant; (iii) Leopard's head crowned; (iv) Date letter capital Gothic R (cycle XV), 1772/73, London.

10 & 11 PAIR OF FLAGONS

These are two identical flagons, each 12¾ inches high, without spouts. Each has a high domed lid crowned with an urn finial. The lid overrides the body of the flagon with a flange. Rim diameter 3¹⁵⁄₁₆ inches. Each flagon has a cast thumb with a wavy top and on one side an acanthus leaf, hinged to the top of the handle.

Each flagon has an S-shaped handle ending in a shaped and ribbed terminal. Below this, on each flagon, is a reeded band and below this the sides spread out to a step followed by a shoulder and step. The diameter of each base is 7 inches. On the side of each flagon are the sacred symbols and rays. There is no inscription.

On the inside of the domed lids and on the side of the barrels are five marks: (i) Makers' mark PB over AB in a square frame, Peter and Ann Bateman (Grimwade 2140); (ii) Lion passant guardant; (iii) Leopard's head crowned; (iv) Date letter u (cycle XVI), 1795/96, London; (v) Duty mark. (Plates 57, 58, 59.)

12 & 13 CANDLESTICKS

A pair of candlesticks, made in Sheffield, 11½ inches high, with detachable nozzles 2¼ inches diameter with gadrooned edge. (One nozzle is a later replacement made in Birmingham.) A band of gadrooning before the base rises in an ogee to a slender tapered stem, having a final band of gadrooning leading to a baluster sconce into which the detachable nozzles fit. The circular base of each, diameter 5½ inches, is blocked with wood.

On the final step are five marks: (i) Maker's mark NS & Co within a rectangle, Nathaniel Smith & Co. (Jackson, p.442); (ii) Lion passant guardant; (iii) Crown; (iv) Date letter K (table II), 1809/10, Sheffield; (v) Duty mark.

The duty mark, lion passant guardant and maker's mark are repeated on the original sconce. (Plate 60.)

14 LADLE

A very small, badly damaged ladle without assay marks. Originally 4 inches in length, the fluted handle is detached from the small circular rat tail bowl, diameter 1¾ inches and ¾ inch deep. The rim has a pie crust edge and on the side, in contemporary script, is: 'The Gift is small/Respect is all'. It probably belongs to the late 18th or early 19th century.

MARBURY
St Michael
Deanery of Malpas

1 STAND PATEN

A stand paten, diameter 7 inches, having a narrow rim and a shallow depression. The plate stands upon a concave stem from which it is divided by a moulding. The open base, diameter 3⅛ inches, has a step and shoulder followed by a flange. Total height 2⅜ inches. The weight is inscribed 9=15.

There are four marks: (i) Lion passant guardant; (ii) Leopard's head crowned; (iii) Date letter inverted P (cycle VIII), 1632/3, London; (iv) Maker's mark, the first letter a W (rest obliterated) within a trefoil (unidentified).

2 COMMUNION CUP

A communion cup, 8 inches high, with a bell-shaped bowl with an everted moulded lip, rim diameter 3¾ inches. The bowl joins the stem with a simple moulding and is divided by a wide knop with moulded collars. The stem ends with a step and shoulder moulding and a narrow flange. The foot has been mended.

There are five marks on the side of the bowl: (i) A small script WP within a rectangle (unidentified; perhaps the mark of a repairer); (ii) Leopard's head crowned; (iii) Date letter g (cycle XIV), 1742/43, London; (iv) Lion passant guardant; (v) Maker's mark two letters, the second being a P above a five-point star within a frame – the star placed in a three-quarter circle (not in Grimwade).

MARPLE
All Saints
Deanery of Chadkirk

When the church here was demolished and a new building erected on a different site, the silver was transferred.

1 COMMUNION CUP

A communion cup, 9½ inches high, with a bell-shaped bowl; rim diameter 3¾ inches and depth of bowl 4½ inches. It stands upon a tall baluster stem and the base sweeps outwards to a 3¾-inch-diameter foot. There is a later inscription on the bowl and an elaborate coat of arms:

> Huic Templo Alicia Johannis
> Pimlott de Marple Armigeri Relictae Dono Dedit 1762

The Register states: 'Jan 3 1762 a Silver Chalice was given by Mad^m Pimlott relict of J^{no} Pimlott of Marple to this chapel for ever'.

It is clear that what Alice Pimlott gave to the church had been a domestic wine cup which may have belonged to her husband.

There are four marks on the side of the bowl: (i) Date letter M (cycle VIII), 1629/30, London; (ii) Lion passant guardant (repeated under the base); (iii) Leopard's head crowned; (iv) Maker's mark HS above a star within a shaped shield.

2. SALVER

A salver, 7 inches diameter, with a narrow moulded rim ¼ inch wide and curved depression and step. On the plate is an inscription in a cross-upon-rays border:

> Presented by
> James Bradshaw Isherwood
> A.M
> To Marple Church
> Decr 30th 1811

There are three feet, 1⅛ inches high with shell sides, and five marks on the underside: (i) Makers' mark PB above AB within a square, Peter and Ann Bateman (Grimwade 2140); (ii) Lion passant guardant; (iii) Leopard's head crowned; (iv) Date letter U (cycle XVI), 1795/96, London; (v) Duty mark.

3 FLAGON

A flagon, 11 inches high, having a high domed lid, rim diameter 3¾ inches, hinged, with an open ornate thumb to the top of an S-scroll handle capped with a reeded extension. The handle is attached to the side of the flagon by a circular collar and ends in a corkscrew and moulded terminal. The body end is marked by a reeded band. Below this the base spans out to a concave moulding and a reeded step – foot diameter 6½ inches. The same inscription as on the salver (no. 2) appears on the front of the flagon.

On the inside of the lid and on the side of the flagon are five marks: (i) Makers' mark PB over WB in a square frame, Peter and William I Bateman (Grimwade 2143); (ii) Lion passant guardant; (iii) Leopard's head crowned; (iv) Date letter Q (cycle XVII), 1811/12, London; (v) Duty mark.

MARTON
St James and St Paul
Deanery of Macclesfield

COMMUNION CUP
When the newly-appointed vicar arrived at Marton in 1945 he found this cup in a very dilapidated state and had it repaired, but it is not clear what the repairs entailed.

The cup is 7¼ inches high and has a bell-shaped bowl, 3⅜ inches deep, rim diameter 3¾ inches, which curves around to a series of small mouldings to an hour-glass stem divided by a round knop having reeded collars. The stem ends with similar mouldings, a shoulder leading to an offset, and an inset of small mouldings, a compressed shoulder and further mouldings to form the foot, diameter 3½ inches. There is an inscription on the side of the bowl in Roman capitals:

* THIS * CUP * AND * COVER * WAS * MADE * AT *

THE * CHARGES * OF * Y^E * TENANTS * OF *

MARTON * ∂ * WITHNTON * ∂ * TO * THEIR *

USE *

There are four marks on the side of the bowl: (i) Date letter V (cycle VI), 1597/98, London; (ii) Lion passant guardant; (iii) Leopard's head crowned; (iv) Maker's mark IG with a glove (hand) between in a shaped frame, (?)John Glover.

The paten which is used today was given in 1950 in memory of a member of the Bromley Davenport family who was killed in the Second World War in 1945. It has not been possible to discover what happened to the paten which was used before 1950.

MIDDLEWICH
St Michael and All Angels
Deanery of Middlewich

The Sheriff's Certificate in 1548 reads 'One Chales', and the churchwardens' Inventory of 1689:

> ... three pieces of Plate (viz) one Silver Salver,
> one large bowle, both the gift of Francis Leveson Esqr
> and one lesser Silver bowle, two Pewter Flaggons,

one communion cloth & one towell belonging to the
Parish Church of Middlewich 28 May 1689

Reference:
THSLC, vol. 27, 1875, pp.1-12.

1   COMMUNION CUP

A communion cup, 8¼ inches high with a goblet-shaped bowl, rim diameter 4⅛ inches. The bowl stands upon a baluster stem with a cavetto-formed base, diameter 3½ inches. There is an inscription under the spreading foot which has been partly erased, leaving: '[?] Langley obyt Jun 1ᶜ 1657', and on the top of the foot: 'Midle Wyche'

A crack on the rim was repaired in 1997.

There are four marks on the side of the bowl: (i) Date letter L (cycle VII), 1608/09, London; (ii) Lion passant guardant; (iii) Leopard's head crowned; (iv) Maker's mark IA within an ornamental shield. (Plate 61.)

2   COMMUNION CUP (see no. 3)

A communion cup 8¼ inches high with a bucket-shaped bowl, rim diameter 4¾ inches. The bowl, 5 inches deep, curves at a marked angle to a trumpet-shaped stem which has a marked step and a flange – the base diameter 5 inches. There is an elaborate coat of arms with crest surrounded by an ornate border beneath which is an inscription in contemporary script lettering:

> The Guift of Francis Leveson Esqʳ to ye Parish
> Church of Middlewich in Cheshire Aᵒ Dⁿⁱ 1666

There are four marks on the side of the bowl: (i) Maker's mark IN with a pellet; (ii) Leopard's head crowned: (iii) Lion passant guardant; (iv) Date letter Gothic K (cycle X), 1667/68, London. (Plate 62.)

3   STAND PATEN (see no. 2)

A stand paten 11½ inches diameter with a plain, slightly everted, rim 2⅝ inches wide forming a shallow depression on which are the same coat of arms and inscription as on the communion cup (no. 2). Opposite to this the four marks, as on the communion cup. The plate rests upon a trumpet-shaped stem, making an overall height of 2⅝ inches. The foot is open and 4¾ inches diameter.

4   FLAGON (1)

The smaller of two flagons, standing 12¼ inches high. It has a moulded 3⅞-inch rim. The cover is domed and moulded, with a baluster finial. There is an open moulded thumb with a well moulded hinge on the top of an S-scroll handle with an oval collar ending in a single shield with one moulding on the top. The barrel descends to a reeded band. Below this the lines of the barrel curve to a shoulder, an ogee moulding and then to a step. The foot is 6½ inches diameter.

On the side of the bowl is an inscription in script:

> The Gift of Mathew Vernon to the
> Parish Church of Middlewich Cheshire
> 1732

and also the coat of arms of the Vernons, with mantling.

There are three marks on the bezel of the cover and four on the side of the flagon: (i) Maker's mark ornate script N in a shaped frame, Francis Nelme (Grimwade 67) (repeated on the handle); (ii) Lion passant guardant; (iii) Leopard's head crowned; (iv) Date letter R (cycle XIII), 1732/33, London. (Plate 62.)

5 FLAGON (2)
This flagon stands 12¾ inches high. The cover is very similar to that on flagon no. 4, domed, and the ribbed and curving thumb is hinged to the S-scroll handle which terminates in a plain shield with top moulding. The rim is 3⅝ inches and moulded. There is a band moulding on the bottom of the body and beneath it the side continues to the base to a step and ogee shoulder and a step – foot diameter 6½ inches.

On the side of the barrel is an inscription:

> The Gift of Mrs Jane Vaudry
> to the Parish Church of Middlewich
> 1739

and below it a coat of arms in a lozenge with mantling, and the sacred symbols in rays.

There are four marks on the side of the barrel: (i) Maker's mark FN in ornamental shield, Francis Nelme (Grimwade 702); (ii) Lion passant guardant; (iii) Date letter d (cycle XIV), 1739/40, London; (iv) Leopard's head crowned. (Plate 62.)

6 COMMUNION CUP (for use when visiting the sick) (see no. 7)
A gilt communion cup, with paten cover, kept in a contemporary red-lined cylindrical case. The cup is 5 inches high, with a bell-shaped bowl with a moulded rim 2½ inches diameter. The bowl is separated from the baluster stem by a series of reed mouldings. The base has shoulder mouldings ending in a narrow step. Diameter 2¾ inches. There are no marks.

7   PATEN COVER (for use when visiting the sick) (see no. 6)
A gilt paten cover, 2¾ inches diameter, to fit over the cup. It has a plain depression and rests upon a short open-ended foot. Total height ⅜ inch. On the underside of the plate is an inscription:

> The Gift of Mr Robert Bridge to Middlewich
> Church at Easter 1755

There are no marks, but the date is assumed from the inscription.

MOBBERLEY
ST WILFRID
Deanery of Knutsford

1   COMMUNION CUP
The Elizabethan cup is 8¾ inches high and has a plain bell-shaped bowl with worked lip, diameter of rim 3⅝ inches, depth of bowl 3⅜ inches. The side of the bowl has a band of conventional foliage decoration between two bands of edging which cross over, and at the junctions are bound together by a lozenge of similar band which interweaves at the point of the cross-over. This occurs three times and begins an inch below the rim. The bowl curves down to a reeded offset and stands upon a stem interrupted by an egg-like knop 1⅝ inches deep with collars above and below and with a waist band. Below the knop, at the end of the stem, is another reeded inset followed by a shoulder and a band of ovolo and dart decoration as a flange. Diameter 3½ inches. The Churchwardens' accounts record: '1786 To Knutsford mending the Comm'n Cup 2/-'.

There are four marks on the side of the bowl: (i) Date letter O (cycle V), 1571/72, London; (ii) Lion passant guardant; (iii) Leopard's head crowned; (iv) Maker's mark motif within a shaped frame. The same mark, described as 'a pair of bellows', has been found at Evershot, Dorset (1570) (Jackson 1921, p.101, and at Malmesbury, Wiltshire (1575/76) (Jackson 1921, p.103). (Plate 63.)

2   COMMUNION CUP
A copy of the Elizabethan cup made in William IV's time and bearing these five marks: (i) Makers' mark of Edward, Edward Jnr, John and William Barnard (Grimwade 575); (ii) Lion passant; (iii) Leopard's head; (iv) Date letter u (cycle XVIII), 1835/36, London; (v) Duty Mark.

MOTTRAM
ST MICHAEL
Deanery of Mottram

The Sheriff's Certificate in 1548 stated that there remained: 'Chaleses Whyte ii'.

1 STAND PATEN

A stand or credence paten, diameter 8¾ inches, with a narrow moulded rim and a slight depression. The plate stands on a cavetto stem leading to a step, a shoulder and a small flange – diameter 3⅛ inches. Total height 2¼ inches.

On the surface of the plate are four marks: (i) Maker's mark Gothic capital S t, above Gothic capital P e in a shaped frame, John Martin Stockar and Edward Peacock (Grimwade 2646); (ii) Britannia; (iii) Lion's head erased; (iv) Date letter (cycle XII), 1709/10, London.

2 FLAGON (1)

The smaller of two flagons. Overall height 10¼ inches, with a high domed cover and a solid ram's head thumb hinged to the top of an S-scroll handle, ending in a shield with a moulded top side. The rim is moulded. A reeded band marks the bottom of the flagon beneath which the sides continue to a shoulder moulded base, diameter 6⅛ inches. On the side of the flagon is the inscription:

'The Gift of William Tatlow/To the Parish Church/of Mottram/1748'.

There are four marks on the side of the barrel: (i) Maker's mark HP with a pellet between over a five-point star and beneath a small heart within a quatrefoil, Humphrey Payne (Grimwade 1058) (repeated on the handle); (ii) Leopard's head crowned; (iii) Lion passant guardant; (iv) Date letter n (cycle XIV), 1748/49, London.

3 FLAGON (2)

This, the larger flagon, is 17 inches high, with a domed lid and cover hinged to the top of the S-shaped handle with an open scrolled thumb. The handle terminates in a scrolled terminal which is moulded. The body of the flagon is marked by a reeded band and below this the side sweeps down to a shoulder and a step, diameter of base 8¾ inches. There is an inscription on the side of the flagon:

The Gift of Thomas Heginbotham of
Mottram to the Parish Church July 25th 1768

There are four marks on the side of the flagon: (i) Maker's mark script FW within a rectangle, Fuller White (Grimwade 733) (repeated on the handle); (ii)

Lion passant guardant; (iii) Leopard's head crowned; (iv) Date letter Gothic H (cycle XV), 1763/64, London.

4 & 5   COMMUNION CUPS
Two identical communion cups, each 7⅜ inches high with a goblet-shaped bowl, 3½ inches rim diameter and 4 inches deep. It is divided from the stem by small mouldings and below them the stem sweeps down to a moulding, a shoulder, a band of ornament and a step, diameter 3⅝ inches. Inscribed along the step:

> JOHN LAWTON
> & JOHN WAGSTAFF
> Church Wardens
> Mottram 1780

There are four marks on the side of the bowl: (i) Maker's mark RM with a pellet between, within a rectangle, Richard Morton & Co. (Jackson, p.442); (ii) Lion passant guardant; (iii) Crown; (iv) Date letter Gothic A (cycle I), 1779/80, Sheffield.

NANTWICH
ST MARY
Deanery of Nantwich

1548 Namptwiche 'iiii Chalices whereof iii are gilt and the fourth ungilt
       On crosse of wood plated with silv'.

1   COMMUNION CUP (see no. 2)
A communion cup 7¾ inches high having a rim diameter of 3⅞ inches. The bowl is bell-shaped (almost bucket-shaped) with straight sides, 4⅝ inches deep. Immediately below the bowl is an offset containing a ladder decoration between mouldings. The stem is a cavetto without a knop, leading to another offset with ladder enrichment, a shoulder moulding and a band of ovolo decoration close to the foot, diameter 3¾ inches.
    There are four marks on the side of the bowl: (i) Date letter G (cycle VII), 1604/05, London; (ii) Lion passant guardant; (iii) Leopard's head crowned; (iv) Maker's mark I above W conjoined, within a shaped frame (?) John Wardlaw (Jackson, p.108). (Plate 65.)

2   PATEN COVER (see no. 1)
Paten cover to accompany communion cup no. 1, diameter of rim 4⅝ inches. The paten cover has a ⁷⁄₁₆-inch flange, which fits over the mouth of the cup. The cover is domed and has a cavetto stem separated from the domed cover by a step. The stand is blocked, diameter 1⅞ inches and is inscribed '1605'.

The overall height is 1¾ inches. On the dome the maker's mark is repeated and corresponds with that on the communion cup no. 1. (Plate 65.)

3   COMMUNION CUP
A communion cup 7¾ inches high with a bell-shaped bowl and everted lip, diameter 3¾ inches. The bowl is 4⅝ inches deep. The bowl curves round at the base to a plain inset and the hour-glass stem is divided by a substantial rounded knop without collars. There is a further inset leading to a shoulder, a flange on which is an inscribed line, a further inset and two small mouldings. The base diameter is 3½ inches. On the side of the bowl is an inscription, each word divided by ornate rose heads with either five or seven petals:

> (rose)Ex Dono(rose)Aliciae(rose)Wilbraham(rose)de Dorfould
>   1   6   3   3

the number inscribed beneath each rose giving the date 1633.

There are four marks on the side of the bowl: (i) Maker's mark VS above a fleur-de-lis within a plain shield, Valerius Sutton (Jackson, p.115) (see also Acton no. 2); (ii) Leopard's head crowned; (iii) Lion passant guardant; (iv) Date letter q (cycle VIII), 1633/34, London.

4 & 5   TWO FLAGONS
By a deed 6 May, 15 Charles 1 (1639) Elizabeth Davenport and Marg^t Woodnoth (widows)

> granted certain Tithes of Wich Malbanke, Willaston and Leighton to certain Trustees who were to receive the full sum of £26 and two flaggons and silver paten and deliver the same to the Church Wardens of the Parish Ch of Wich Malbanke and the rest of the money to the use of the preaching minister in and for the said town of Wich Malbanke for the time being so long as there be a preaching minister.

The flagons were not bought until 1659. The paten was not purchased until about the same time and it is not clear whether this is what is often referred to as a strawberry dish, see no. 6.

Each flagon is 13 inches high, having no spout. The lid is bun-shaped. The sides of the barrel are almost cylindrical. The rim 5 inches diameter. The thumb is pierced with a heart shape above a pierced triangle, and the S-scroll handle terminates in a shaped shield. A reeded band marks the end of the body and below this the foot is skirted and the base diameter 7¾ inches. On the side of the body are two coats of arms, Davenport and Woodnoth, each in a framework of scroll foliage, and an inscription:

> The guift of Eliz Davenport & Marg^t Woodnoth Widdowes
>   To ye Church of Namptwich 1659.

The marks on the side of the body are repeated in the top of the domed lid: (i) Maker's mark F L with a midway pellet above a small animal facing left, with a heart-shaped ornamental shield (similar to Jackson, p.123 which depicts a bird); (ii) Leopard's head crowned; (iii) Lion passant guardant; (iv) Date letter Gothic B (cycle X), 1659/60, London. (Plate 64.)

6   SWEETMEAT DISH (PATEN)

Although there is no record of any paten having been given by Elizabeth Davenport and Margaret Woodnoth it may be assumed that this dish is the one they provided in 1659. Atkinson comments in Glynne that this may be so, but is wrong in suggesting it is probably Flemish and that the only other one known is in the British Museum. A dish of similar type was often supplied at the beginning of the 17th century to act as a paten especially when, after the Civil War, plate had been lost. An example may be seen at Whittington, Shropshire.

The dish is scalloped, rim diameter 8 inches, and has two small shell handles. The dish is heavily repoussé with a shield and bands of geometrical ornament, the sides with radiating ribs, roundels and formal foliage.

There is a mark of W over M (?)William Maundy, c.1640.

References:
Brocklehurst, no. 18.
Glynne, pl. 7.

7 & 8   TWO ALMS DISHES

This pair of alms dishes, more like bowls, are each 8¼ inches diameter and are 1½ inches deep. They are plain except for a wavy shell and thread border. Each has the same clear inscription on the underside:

> The
> Gift of Mrs
> Eliz Wilbraham
> Relict of Stephen
> Wilbraham Esq[r]

They are of heavy gauge, and together weigh 28½ oz.

The four marks are very worn but appear to be London c.1740.

9   WINE STRAINER

A wine funnel of conventional form, in two parts, 5¼ inches long and the diameter of the head 3¾ inches. Both sections are fully hallmarked: (i) Maker's mark GK within a rectangle, George Knight (Grimwade 840); (ii) Lion passant; (iii) Leopard's head; (iv) Date letter g (cycle XVIII) 1822/23 London; (v) Duty mark.

10   APOSTLE SPOON

An Apostle spoon given in 1883. It is 7 inches in length and the oval bowl 2½ by 1¾ inches. It has a small rat-tail and the bowl is engraved with a thistle and a rose. The Apostle is gilded. The initials EE are engraved and there are two different marks, one of which is a motif followed by a capital B – a city mark used by Basle, Switzerland, in the 18th century and, in a rounded frame; the other, presumably the maker's mark, PS within a shaped frame.

NESTON
ST MARY AND ST HELEN
Deanery of Wirral, South

1   PLATE or ALMS DISH

A plate, sometimes used as an alms dish, diameter 10½ inches, having a reeded edge 1⅜ inches wide with a single depression. On the rim an inscription in script lettering: 'CORPUS CHRISTI IN SYMBOLO CREDE ET ECLE'.

In the centre of the plate is an inscribed woven crown of thorns in a circle surrounding a lily and a rose. Beneath is inscribed a Bible reference: '2 Cant.1 : 2' (I am the rose of Sharon and the lily of the valleys. As the lily among thorns so is my love among the daughters).

On the back of the plate an inscription:

>   This given to the Parish church of Great Neston for a
>   new year's gift by Mr Francis Green Vicar there 1683

There are four marks on the plate: (i) Maker's mark TC with a (?)fish above and a fleur-de-lis below, within a shaped frame (Jackson, p.133); (ii) Lion passant guardant; (iii) Leopard's head crowned; (iv) Date letter f (cycle XI), 1683/84, London.

2   COMMUNION CUP

A communion cup 10¾ inches high, diameter of rim 4½ inches, with a bell-shaped bowl 5¾ inches deep, having a pronounced everted lip, separated from the stem with a narrow band of reeding. The stem is divided by a rounded knop, having slight collars. The foot consists of a series of shoulder mouldings, ending in a flange. Diameter of base 4½ inches.

There is an inscription on the side of the bowl within an oval:

>   MDCCXVIII
>
>   In Usum Fidelium in
>   Ecclesia Parochiali de Neston
>   hunc Calicem Deo donavit
>   Richardus Foster Cler

> Qui MDCL in eadem Parochia
> natus, tandem Favente Deo
> ad Rectoriam de Crondal
> et Vicariam de East Church
> in Diaecesi Cantuariensi
> promotus erat

and an elaborate coat of arms, with mantling, showing a man holding in his right hand a longbow and in his left an arrow. The coat of arms has three arrows divided by a chevron.

There are four marks on the side of the bowl: (i) Maker's mark C L above a pellet within a heart-shaped frame, Joseph Clare I (Grimwade 353); (ii) Lion's head erased; (iii) Britannia (repeated under the foot); (iv) Date letter B (cycle XIII), 1717/18, London.

3   Paten

A plate paten, diameter 7½ inches, with a ½-inch rim with mouldings and a single depression. On the plate an inscription:

> C Calliso minoris Calicis Sacrati Operculo Patinam
> hanc propriis Sumptibus fieri facit Reverendus Johannes
> Urmson AM
>
> Mensaeque Dominicae in Ecclesia de Neston in hac nova
> Forma reddidit, dedicavit Anno dom 1753

which means that it was made from a smaller chalice lid by the Revd John Urmson who caused the paten to be made at his own expense and returned it and dedicated it in this new form to the Lord's Table in Neston Church in the year of Our Lord 1753.

On the back of the paten are four marks: (i) Leopard's head crowned; (ii) Date letter r (cycle XIV), 1752/53, London; (iii) Lion passant guardant; (iv) Maker's mark Script JB within a rectangle, John Bayley (Grimwade 1180).

4   Communion Cup

A communion cup 9¾ inches high with a rim diameter of 4½ inches. The bowl is bell-shaped and 5½ inches deep and curves to an hour-glass stem, having a very narrow knop. The foot is moulded, with a pronounced shoulder and ends with a moulded flange, diameter 4½ inches. On the side of the bowl is an inscription:

> In usum Ecclesiae Parochialis Nestoniae
> Abel Ward AM Vicarius D D D Anno Domini 1782

and also the sacred symbols of IHS, cross and nails, surrounded by rays.

On the side of the bowl are five marks: (i) Maker's mark RR in an indented rectangle, Richard Richardson IV, Type 3 (Compendium 7407); (ii) Lion passant guardant; (iii) Leopard's head crowned; (iv) Chester City coat; (v) Date letter e (series 5), 1780/81, Chester.

Nether Tabley

(see **Chester Cathedral**)

The gold communion cup and plate, alms box, and silver flagon were given to Chester Cathedral (nos 22-25) by the will of Lt.-Col. J.L.B. Leycester Warren.

Nether Whitley
Deanery of Great Budworth

(see **Lower Whitley**, St Luke)

Norbury
(Hazel Grove)
St Thomas
Deanery of Chadkirk

1   Communion Cup (see no. 2)

A communion cup $7^{7}/_{10}$ inches high, of goblet form, with slightly convex sides and accommodation for a cover which fits inside the rim (see no. 2). The rim has a diameter of $3^{3}/_{8}$ inches and the bowl is $3^{3}/_{8}$ inches deep and joins the stem with a narrow ribbed moulding. The stem has a concave moulding before a narrow string moulding, after which it sweeps down towards a reeded step followed by a wider plain step. Diameter of foot is $3^{1}/_{2}$ inches. Sacred symbols are inscribed on the side of the bowl. There is an inscription inside the foot:

> The Gift of Willm Maire Esqr Receiver of the Lyme
> Estate for the use of the Chapel of Norbury 1804

On the lower step of the stem are five marks: (i) Maker's mark imperfect, but recovered from the marks on the jug (no. 3) – T pellet H above R pellet S (unidentified); (ii) Lion passant guardant; (iii) Leopard's head crowned; (iv) Date letter I (cycle XVII), 1804/05, London; (v) Duty mark.

2   PATEN COVER (see no. 1)

A paten cover with a ribbed edge to fit inside the rim of the cup. It has a round stand with blocked top, on which is the same inscription as on no. 1. The edge of the stand is ribbed. Diameter of the plate is slightly under 3½ inches. The sacred symbols are found on the plate surface. Marked as on nos 1 and 3.

3   JUG (serving as a flagon)

A wine jug, serving as a flagon. Overall height 11 inches, of campana form, showing a high ribbed handle rising well above the rim, attached to the body at the rim and at the junction of the upper and lower parts of the body. At the top the ribbing extends around the rim and at the bottom ends in a small circle holding a conventional rose. On the side of the bowl are the conventional symbols of IHS, cross and nails within rays. The lid is piano hinged, has a ball-like finial, and is cut away for pouring. The body rests upon a short concave foot separated from the body by a narrow indent and the stem is concave, ending with a reeded step followed by a plain step on which are five marks (as on nos 1 and 2). There is an inscription beneath the foot as on nos 1 and 2. The marks are as on nos 1 and 2.

NORTHWICH (WITTON)
ST HELEN
Deanery of Middlewich

In the 1548 survey the Act of Parliament for making inventories of church plate, jewels and bells, the Commission under Sir Thomas Venables certified to the Court of Augmentations that the church had 'Two Chalices and one other in the hands of Sir John Deyne, priest'. Sir John was the founder of the Sir John Deane's Grammar School at Northwich.

In 1692 the churchwardens report that there were 'two pewter flaggons, and two plates. A Silver cupp … one Rundelet for Wine'.

In 1704 the wardens paid 2s. for 'the eschange of 2 flagons to buy two plates'.

In 1788 paid Mr Hadfield for a silver tankard for Communion £8 8s. 2d. By the end of the 20th century only one piece of early plate had survived, an 18th-century stand paten.

References:
Cox 1975, p.89.
Weston, p.37.

1   STAND PATEN

A stand paten, diameter 8⅛ inches, having a single depression and resting on a stem with concave sides. Overall height 2⅜ inches. The foot is blocked and is 2½ inches diameter. On the surface of the plate are the sacred symbols, and beneath the rim the words 'WITTON CHAPEL 1764'.

There are four marks: (i) Date letter capital Gothic I (cycle XV), 1764/65, London; (ii) Lion passant guardant; (iii) Leopard's head crowned; (iv) Maker's mark SW with pellet between in a rectangle, Samuel Wheatley (Grimwade 2664).

OVER
St Chad
Deanery of Middlewich

A churchwardens' inventory made 25 April 1769 includes: 'Two silver flagons, One silver challace, One silver salver, One small do salver'.

1 COMMUNION CUP

The cup is 8¾ inches high, with a bucket-shaped bowl, diameter 4¾ inches. It rests upon a stem having a large knop with collars. The foot has a shoulder moulding and a flange, base diameter 5 inches. On the side of the bowl are the coat of arms of the Purshall family and the inscription:

> The Chalice or Communion Cupp
> for the Parish of Over in Chesshire
> Anno Dom 1663

There are four marks: (i) Maker's mark M over a star within a heart-shaped frame (Jackson, p.121); (ii) Leopard's head crowned; (iii) Lion passant guardant; (iv) Date letter Gothic F (cycle X), 1663/64, London.

(There is also a Victorian stand paten, made in Sheffield, which is inscribed: 'Made from a paten belonging to St Chad's Church, Over', dated 1663.)

2 & 3 TWO FLAGONS (see no. 4)

A pair of identical flagons, each 1^{15}/$_{16}$ inches high having a bun-top or beefeater lid and pronounced inset moulding leading to a moulded rim and reeded top to the barrel which has no spout or lip. The sides of the barrel are vertical and terminate at a reeded girdle, then the foot splays out in a wide skirt ending in a narrow step. The sacred symbols within rays are engraved on the front of the barrel. The lid is attached to the rams' head thumb and hinged to the top of a scroll handle which terminates in a shield. On the top of the bun lid is an engraved crest of the Corbett family, and the inscription of the donor:

> 'The Gift of the Honble Wm Corbett of Darnhall Esqr to the
> Parish Church of Over 1747'

and a shorter inscription on the base.

There are four marks: (i) Maker's mark script capital GS in an oval frame, Gabriel Sleath (Grimwade 904); (ii) Lion passant guardant; (iii) Leopard's head crowned; (iv) Date letter m (cycle XIV), 1747/48, London.

4   STAND PATEN
Given at the same time as the two flagons, a stand paten, diameter 8⁵/₁₆ inches, with a wide border and moulded rim creating a curved depression, in the centre of which are the sacred symbols and around them an inscription:

> The Gift of the Honble Wm Corbett of Darnall Esqʳ
> to the Parish Church of Over 1747

and a slightly shorter version beneath the plate. The stand paten rests upon a stem with moulded base. Total height 1⁵/₁₆ inches.

There are four marks as on the flagons nos 2 and 3.

These four pieces are on display in the Ridgway Gallery, Grosvenor Museum, Chester, where they are on long-term loan.

OVERCHURCH
(sometimes referred to as **UPTON**)
ST MARY
Deanery of Macclesfield

1 COMMUNION CUP (see no. 2)
A communion cup 6⁷/₁₆ inches high, with a beaker-shaped body, diameter of rim 3³/₁₆ inches, having an everted lip. The bowl curves down to a rounded concave stand with a small inset before a large shoulder moulding and a small flange. The diameter of the foot is 3 inches. Weight 8 oz. On the side of the body is the coat of arms of Bold and an inscription:

> Carolus Bold filius Petri Bold de Upton armigeri
> dedit hunc Calicem ecclesie ibidem eodem
> tempore dedit illis Bibliam 1618

There are four marks on the side of the bowl: (i) Date letter a (cycle VIII), 1618/19, London; (ii) Lion passant guardant; (iii) Leopard's head crowned; (iv) Maker's mark CI imposed (Jackson, p.111). (Plate 66.)

References:
THSLC, vol. 64, 1913, pp.79-81, and
vol. 111, 1960, pp.77-92.

2   PATEN COVER (see no. 1)

A paten cover to go with the communion cup no. 1, of stand form, having a diameter of 3½ inches and consisting of a plate with a single depression. On the rim are two concentric lines. The cover stands on a spool-shaped stem, with a wide base diameter of 1¾ inches. Total height 1 inch. Weight 2½ oz.

On the solid base is a monogram of C B (Charles Bold) within limited scroll work.

The marks are the same as those found on the communion cup no. 1.

(Grateful thanks for the assistance of Dr Pullen, Churchwarden at the time.)

POTT SHRIGLEY
ST CHRISTOPHER
Deanery of Macclesfield

1   PATEN COVER

Only the paten cover has survived, but a cup of 1622/23 with London assay marks may indicate when the Elizabethan cup may have been lost. The paten cover stands 1¼ inches in height and the plate has a diameter of 3¾ inches. The stand is blocked and is inscribed with the date 1576 in large figures, ¾ of an inch in height. These are incised with double line and left plain against a background which is chased all over with a small engraving tool. The character of the figures is reminiscent of work found at Ruthin dated 1577. The shoulder has a ⅜-inch band of dots and is also stamped with the letters PC, once thought to be the maker's mark of Peter Conway (Compendium 6292), but now believed to stand for Pott Chapel.

References:
Ridgway 1968, p.35.
Ridgway 1997, p.243.

2   COMMUNION CUP

A James I communion cup supplied from a domestic source, perhaps when the Elizabethan cup which had accompanied the paten cover (no. 1) was lost. The cup is 8 inches high having a tumbler-shaped bowl, diameter 2¾ inches. The lower sides of the bowl are embossed with repoussé acanthus-type leaves which terminate in small chased trefoils. The stem is a narrow baluster form, ending in a foot diameter 2½ inches, engraved with chased conventional foliage.

There are four marks on the side of the bowl below the rim: (i) Date letter e (cycle VIII), 1622/23, London; (ii) Lion passant guardant; (iii) Leopard's head crowned; (iv) Maker's mark CB conjoined within a square frame.

The church also has a suite of silver comprising a communion cup and paten, a stand paten and a flagon made by Richard Bayley in 1711/12 (see nos 3, 4, 5 and 6).

Reference:
Brocklehurst, no. 10 and plate IV.

3   COMMUNION CUP (see nos 4, 5 & 6)
A communion cup 7½ inches high, having a bell-shaped bowl and everted and strengthened rim, diameter 3¾ inches. Slightly below half-way down the side the bowl has a narrow reeded strap, below which is a representation of the sacred symbols, the IHS surrounded by rays. The bowl curves round to a wide spool-shaped stem divided by a repeat of the narrow strap and the foot ends in a deep series of steps and shoulder mouldings, terminating in a narrow flange, diameter 3½ inches.

There are four marks on the side of the bowl: (i) Date letter Q (cycle XII), 1711/12, London; (ii) Lion's head erased; (iii) Britannia; (iv) Maker's mark BA in a lobed frame, Richard Bayley (Grimwade 116).

4   STAND PATEN (see nos 3, 5 & 6)
A stand or cover paten, diameter 4½ inches and height 1½ inches. The plate has a moulded rim and has the sacred symbols engraved in the centre. There are the London assay marks and the maker's mark of Richard Bayley.

5   STAND PATEN (see nos 3, 4 & 6)
A much larger paten, having a diameter of 7¾ inches and a height of 2 inches. The plate has a moulded rim and stands upon a stem with moulded foot. There are the same assay marks and maker's mark as on the other pieces in this suite.

6   FLAGON (see nos 3, 4 & 5)
A flagon made to complete the suite. It stands 10 inches high, having a lid with a flattened dome followed by a step and pronounced moulding overlapping a moulded instep. The rim is moulded and the thumb rises well above the lid and is of scroll form, one end hinged to the top of a broken scroll handle. The cylindrical tapered body has a narrow reeded band where the handle meets the side. Below this is a second narrow band leading to a bold moulding and further mouldings to the foot, diameter 5½ inches. On the side of the body and within the cover the marks as found on the rest of the suite, the sacred symbols on the front of the body. (Plate 67.)

PRESTBURY
ST PETER
Deanery of Macclesfield

1548	One Chalys	
1572	Item for a poke (bag) for the chalys	xiid
	Item for The archebishoppes Injunctions	xiid

	Item for the charges of the vycar and one of the churchwardens when the putte the Communyon Cuppe the makynge at Manchester	xiid
	Item on the makynge of the same Cuppe	xis iid
1573	Receipts	
	Item of the goldesmyth of Manchester wch he had owe for overweyghte of the Comunion cuppe belongynge to the parysh of Prestburye	iis viiid
1573	Item for a Comunyon cup to goe with in the paryshe	xiii
1576-1580	Receipts For an olde Tabernacle case	iis
1581-1584	Receipts For church stuffe solde to Sr Piers Leighe Mr Leighe of Adlington and Mr Warren	xviii iiiid

Inventory

1602	One Communyon Cupp of sylver and one pewter one A box to putte breade in & a bottell for wyne
1628	Paid to the old Churchwardens for the new Communion Cuppe and cover vii 1s vs.
1676	Paid for the carriage of two ould silver bowles and two chalices for the Comunion (wch were sent to London to be made bigger and hansomer after the mode and more Rich at the cost and charges of the Patron of this Parish) and their recarriage to Prestburie 00.01 ... 06
1680	When the Vicar's hoode, a plush pulpit cloath, two silver flagons, two surplishes and a green carpett cloath for the Comunion table were feloniously taken out of the chest standing in the Vestrie wch was locked and broken open. 00.06.00
1681	Paid for two new flagons for the Holy Communion 10-6
1682	Pd for a Mgr of Arts hood for the Vicar 1. 3.0
1684	Refers to John Grasson and his wife at London, who were conceived to have a hand in robbing Prestbury church

1692   Inventry.   It   2 silver chalices wth patents
                           2 Pewter flagons

1693   August ye 18 Spent then and att other times in goeing
        to Bramall and other places about ye Church Plate wch
        was stollen out of ye Parish Church in ye vestry in ye
        year of ouir Lord 1684 and this year found again (one of
        the flaggons) in a pitt in Cheadle Hulme. Paid for
        horse hire & other charges to sevrall men for searching
        ye pitt where ye said plate was found 3-18-10

What appears to be the oldest piece of silver remaining at Prestbury, the basin inscribed 'Prestbury Alms Basyn 1584', is, in fact, Victorian, 1883, though it may well have been remodelled from an earlier basin. As such it lies beyond the scope of this account.

Reference:
Earwaker 1880, p.217, which quotes extensively from
the records and Churchwardens' Accounts at Prestbury.

1   COMMUNION CUP
A communion cup, 7¾ inches high, having a bucket-shaped bowl, the lip slightly everted, diameter 4½ inches. The bowl rests upon a baluster stem and the base is spread out to a slightly domed foot, ending with a simple moulding. Diameter of foot 3⅜ inches.

On the side of the bowl an inscription: 'Prestbury + Communion Cup'.

There are four marks on the side of the bowl: (i) Date letter (very worn). If it is 'i' or 'l' (cycle VIII), 1626/27 or 1628/29 it could be the cup purchased about that time; (ii) Lion passant guardant; (iii) Leopard's head crowned; (iv) Maker's mark RF with three pellets above and a star below within a plain shield (not in Jackson). Beneath the foot, arranged in a triangle, are three identical marks which appear to be a rose within a sexfoil with concave sides.

2   FLAGON
A flagon, 10¾ inches high, with a bun-topped lid with a considerable overhang. The cylindrical body is divided from the base by mouldings and the base is skirted, diameter of foot 8 inches. There is an S-shaped handle ending in a small shield terminal. The thumb has a heart-shaped opening and moulded edges. There is an inscription on the side of the body: '+ This is the plate of presbary [*sic*] Church +'.

The marks are found on the side of the body, and the inside of the lid, and the lion passant guardant beneath the base: (i) Maker's mark WM with crown above and mullet below within a shaped shield; (ii) Leopard's head crowned; (iii) Lion passant guardant; (iv) Date letter L (cycle X), 1668/69, London.

3 & 4   Two Identical Cups
Each 9¾ inches high with a 5¹/₁₀-inch diameter rim. The body is bucket-shaped, with a slightly everted rim. The lower part of the bowl is decorated with a band of cut-card foliage above a row of ropework. The side is inscribed: 'Prestbury Communion Cupp'. The body rests upon an inverted trumpet-shaped stem, divided from the body by a simple moulding. The stem ends with a step then a large shoulder and a narrow moulding, diameter 4⅞ inches.

There are four marks on the side of the bowl: (i) Date letter T (cycle X), 1676/77, London; (ii) Lion passant guardant; (iii) Leopard's head crowned; (iv) Maker's mark (unclear), probably A P with pellet above and mullet below, within a shaped shield.

5 & 6   Two Identical Stand Patens
Two identical stand patens, diameter 8 inches, with a narrow edge having a narrow band of beads. Each plate has a single depression and stands upon a convex shaped stem with step and shoulder moulding and a narrow double step. Diameter of base 3¾ inches. There is an inscription in capitals: 'PRESTBURY CHURCH'.

There are four marks on the underside of the plate: (i) Date letter P (cycle XV), 1770/71, London; (ii) Lion passant guardant; (iii) Leopard's head crowned; (iv) Maker's mark I•C within a rectangle, Joseph Clare II (Grimwade 1208).

PULFORD
St Mary
Deanery of Chester

The Sheriff's Certificate of 1548 records that the church then had:

> 1 chalice, 1 paten and three bells

In the Eaton Accounts of 1762 there is an item:

> 1762 To Mr. Ald. Richardson for a silver waiter made
> a present to the Parish of Pulford.   5/-

That same year Richard Richardson II had supplied, and possibly made, the gold cup for Chester Races, costing £50. As the cup no longer exists, it is not possible to verify this. The church was entirely rebuilt in the late 19th century.

RINGWAY AND HALE BARNS
ALL SAINTS
Deanery of Bowdon

The church at Ringway was closed and the church at Hale Barns was rebuilt in the 1960s, and plate associated with these places has been moved to the new church. It is fortunate that any plate has survived, as the area was, at one time, the centre of considerable Nonconformist activity and suffered considerably.

In 1963 Canon Cox quotes from correspondence between Mr Lancaster and Bishop Gastrell, in which interesting reference is made to the church plate at Ringway.

> When Mr Whitaker came to Ringway [this would be Thomas Whitaker in 1785] the Communion Plate consisted of one Chalice or Cup of pure silver and one small Paten or Plate of silver also. The inscription on the chalice is 'Mark xiv. 23, Ryngey Chapel. 1726'. As the Communicants soon became very numerous Mr. Whitaker purchased, at his own expense, another Chalice or Cup of plated goods marked 'Ringway 1793'. About the year 1797 or 1798, Peter Davenport Finney Esquire, of Oversley Ford, made a present to the Chapel of a large Flaggon and a Plate or Paten of plated goods without any inscription.

Reference: Cox 1963.

1 COMMUNION CUP (see no. 2)
A communion cup 7¼ inches high with slightly everted rim, diameter 3½ inches, separated from the stem, which is almost vertical, by a row of small mouldings. The stem is divided by an almost flat knop having two small collars at each side. The foot is moulded, with a narrow shoulder ending in a moulded foot. Diameter 3½ inches.

On the side of the bowl an inscription: 'Ryngey Chap 1726 Mark xiv 23'.

There are four marks on the side of the bowl: (i) Maker's mark perhaps RO with motif below within a shield, (?)Gundry Roode (Grimwade 2394); (ii and iii) Lion passant guardant; (iv) Date letter E (cycle XIII), 1719/20, London.

2 STAND PATEN (see no. 1)
A small stand paten, diameter 5⅛ inches, having a very narrow reeded edge and a single depression separated from the stem with simple mouldings. The

stem is almost vertical, 1½ inches overall, showing signs of having once been damaged. Diameter of base 2⅜ inches. On the underside of the stand paten is an inscription: 'Ryngey Chapel 1726'.

There are four marks on the plate, clearer than those on the communion cup (no. 1) showing that the date letter here was K, 1725/26, London. The other three marks are lion passant guardant, a leopard's head crowned, and the maker's name which appears to be the same as on the cup.

ROSTHERNE
ST MARY
Deanery of Knutsford

Sheriff's Certificate 1549: Chales with paten white one
Church Wardens' Accounts 1735: Received for 2 old flaggons   0.4.8.

1 & 2   JUGS – FLAGONS
Two identical jugs used as flagons and forming a suite together with paten and salver. We may assume that the two communion cups made in 1770/71 may have been replacements for two stolen at that time, but made by a different goldsmith. Each jug is 9⅜ inches high, unlidded, with a rim diameter of 3⅜ inches with a spout, the rim overriding the spout. The body of the jug is pear-shaped, with a reeded girdle or band ⅛ inch deep half-way down the side of the body. The silver handle is broken at the top and is attached to the side of the body on the neck with a round collar, this is repeated below the reeded band. The body curves around to a narrow moulding which divides it from the base which is 1⅜ inches deep, of mouldings and step, ending in a step, base diameter 4⅜ inches.

There are four marks underneath the base, arranged in a circle: (i) Maker's mark script HP with star above and a star below in a quatrefoil, the spandrels containing a motif, Hymphrey Payne (Grimwade 1061); (ii) Lion passant guardant; (iii) Date letter V (cycle XIII), 1735/36, London; (iv) Leopard's head crowned.

Close to the marks is engraved 'Rosthern'.

3   PATEN
A plain paten, diameter 8¼ inches, having a reeded rim on an inch wide edge. This forms a depression 3¹/₁₆ inch deep; total height 1⁵/₁₆ inch. On the underside of the paten the word 'Rosthern'. There are four marks on the edge (as on the jugs nos 1 and 2).

4   SALVER
A salver with Chippendale border, moulded rim ³/₁₆ inch wide, diameter 9⁵/₁₆ inches and overall height 1¹/₁₆ inches. There are four hoof feet. Engraved on the underside 'Rosthern'. There are four marks on the border as on nos 1, 2 and 3.

5 & 6   Two Communion Cups

Two identical cups, each having a bucket-shaped bowl. Height 7¾ inches, depth of bowl 3¹⁵⁄₁₆ inches with slightly everted lip. Rim diameter 3⅞ inches. The bowl rests upon a stem with a deep moulded and tapered knop, leading to a deep moulded base having a foot diameter if 3½ inches. There is an inscription in script letters: 'ROSTHERN CHURCH 1771'. One cup has been damaged.

There are four marks on the bowls: (i) Maker's mark FC with pellet between in a rectangle, Francis Crump (Grimwade 672); (ii) Leopard's head crowned; (iii) Lion passant guardant; (iv) Date letter P (cycle XV), 1770/71, London.

(Grateful thanks to Mr Michael Sherratt for his considerable help in recording this silver.)

RUNCORN
ALL SAINTS
Deanery of Frodsham

1   Communion Cup

A communion cup 6⅞ inches high, having a well-formed beaker-shaped bowl 3⅞ inches deep, with sloping sides and a rim diameter of 4 inches. The bowl is plain but for a reeded band a third of the way down. Between the bowl and the stem is a band of ovolo and tassel enrichment. The stem is divided by a plain knop having collars, and joins the compressed shoulder with another band of ovolo and tassel decoration. The shoulder is plain and is separated from the edge of the foot by a further band of similar decoration. The diameter of the foot is 3⁹⁄₁₀ inches. Weight 9 oz. 15.

The cup is unmarked, but probably Elizabethan.

2   Flagon

A flagon, 9½ inches high, with lip, having a flat top lid and a series of rounds and shoulders. The lid is hinged to the top of an S-shaped scroll handle and a scroll thumb backed by an acanthus leaf. There is a band of reeding on the barrel beneath the rim. The handle joins the bottom of the band within a collar and ends in a plain shield terminal. The barrel joins the foot, diameter 6 inches, with a series of round mouldings. On the side of the barrel is an inscription with a coat of arms in a lozenge, surrounded with plumes:

> For Runckorn Church
> [Coat of Arms]
> The Gift of the Honourable the Lady
> Elizabeth Savage Daughter of Thomas late
> Earl Rivers for the use of the Parish Church
> of Runcorn Com: Cestr. 1704

There are four marks on the side of the bowl and on the lid: (i) Maker's mark EC within a shaped rectangle, John Eckfourd I (Grimwade 545); (ii) Britannia; (iii) Lion's head erased; (iv) Date letter H (cycle XII), 1703/04, London.

3   COMMUNION CUP (see no. 4)
A communion cup 9½ inches high with a bowl diameter 4¾ inches standing on a narrow baluster stem with a round base spreading out to a step and shoulder and narrow flange. Diameter 4⅞ inches. Weight 18 oz. There is an inscription on the side of the bowl:

>   The Lady Mary Brooke of Norton Her Legacy
>   to the Parish Church of Runcorn in Cheshire
>   for the Honour of Jesus Christ and the use
>   of those who have faith in his Blood   September 1670

There are no marks.

4   STAND PATEN (see no. 3)
A stand paten *c.*1670 to accompany the communion cup no. 3, 9½ inches diameter with a wide flat, 2-inch rim forming a single depression. On the edge of the rim is a script inscription identical to that on the communion cup except that the word 'for' is written 'ffor'. The plate rests upon a trumpet-shaped stand. There are no marks.

SANDBACH
ST MARY
Deanery of Congleton

The Sheriff's Certificate 1548 records: One Chales

Reference:
Earwaker 1890.

1 & 2   COMMUNION CUPS (see nos 3 & 4)
Two identical cups, each with a bucket-shaped bowl with slightly everted rim 7¼ inches high. The sides of each bowl, which are 4¼ inches deep with a 4-inch diameter rim, curve slightly round to a splayed stem, to a small step and a flange on which are three inscribed concentric lines. The base is 3⅞ inches diameter. There is an inscription on the side of each bowl:

>   The Guift of Lawrence Steele Sonne of Richard Steel of
>   Sandebach in Cheshire
>   to the use of the sayd Parish of Sandebach for ever

There are four marks on the side of the bowl: (i) Maker's mark HB conjoined above a five-point star in a shaped shield, (?)H. Babington; (ii) Leopard's head crowned; (iii) Lion passant guardant (repeated on the underside of the base); (iv) Date letter T (cycle IX), 1656/57, London.

3 & 4   PATEN COVERS (see nos 1 & 2)
Two identical paten covers, each 4¾ inches diameter. The plate has a depression 3⅝ inches diameter, considerably smaller than the rim diameter of the cup. The stand is blocked by a plain plate having a scribed line, diameter 2¼ inches.

There are four marks, as on the communion cups nos 1 and 2, and the same inscription and date.

4   ALMS DISH
A very large alms dish, diameter 18 inches, having a wide rim, 2⅝ inches wide. There is a moulded edge to the rim ¾ inch wide and a deep depression, 2¼ inches deep, with a central boss.

There are four marks: (i) Maker's mark (inverted) CL beneath a motif within a shaped frame, Jonah Clifton (Grimwade 348) or Richard Clarke (Grimwade 349); (ii) Britannia; (iii) Lion's head erased; (iv) Date letter O (cycle XII), 1709/10, London.

5 & 6   FLAGONS
Two spoutless flagons, overall height 13 inches, each having a domed cover divided by a small step, hinged to the top of a scroll handle with a cast ram's head scroll with acanthus leaf back, and the handle ending in a heart-shaped terminal. The sides of each flagon are tapered and the body marked by a reeded band. Below this the foot curves to a step and shoulder and moulded base, diameter 7½ inches. There is a long inscription on each. On one:

DEDICATED
To the Honour of CHRIST our GOD & SAVIOUR
For the more decent Celebration of the
H. COMMUNION in the Parish Church of
SANDBACH
By the equal contributions of the
following benefactors
Mrs Jane Hurst of Sandbach Spinster
Richard Maddock of Brickhouse ⎫
John Wilson of Sandbach   ⎬ Gent
Samuel Kent of Sandbach   ⎭
In the Year 1734

On the other the inscription is the same, apart from the benefactors' names:

> John Amson of Lees Esq
> John Jervis of Bradwell Esq
> Jeffrey Williams, Rector of Astbury
> Samuel Allon, Vicar of Sandbach
> In the Year 1734

There are four marks on the side of each flagon which are repeated on the inside of the cover: (i) Maker's mark GS above a wheatsheaf in ornamental shield, Gabriel Sleath (Grimwade 890); (ii) Date letter S (cycle XIII), 1733/34, London; (iii) Lion passant guardant; (iv) Leopard's head crowned.

7 ALMS PLATE

A small alms plate inscribed: 'The gift/of the Rev[d] Mr/ B. Baldwyn, Vicr, to the Parish of/Sandbach/1737'.

The only information available is from an inventory by John Lowe in 1963: that it was of George II period, was dated 1737 and by Robert Brown, and valued at £200. Robert Brown of London used two punches; as he did not enter his second mark until 1739 we must assume that the mark RB in a rectangular frame extant in 1736, is the one used here (Grimwade 2262). There were however many London goldsmiths who used the initials RB at this period and Richard Bayley (Grimwade 2262), Richard Burcombe (Grimwade 2264) and several others could also qualify. Richard Bayley provided silver at many churches in the Chester Diocese, and he is more likely to be the maker here.

SHOCKLACH
ST EDITH
Deanery of Malpas

Sheriff's Certificate 1548:

> Shokle Churche   Chalis and Patten i

Churchwardens' Accounts:

1731	For a new tankard and cleaning the Coop (cup)	5/-
1850	Mr Mayer, silversmith, for a Communion cup and plate	£8.0.0
	Engraving the plate etc.	7/6

Reference:
Bennett, p.219.

1 Stand Paten

A stand paten, presumably purchased from Mr Mayer in 1850 which he engraved with a cross as it was for ecclesiastical use.

The stand paten, 9 inches in diameter, is decorated with gadrooned edge, and stands on a stem with an open base, which also has a gadrooned edge, diameter 3¾ inches.

There are four marks: (i) Maker's mark (indistinct) but apparently RO with three pellets above and three below within an oval frame, Phillip Rollos I (Grimwade 2383); (ii) Lion passant guardant; (iii) Leopard's head crowned; (iv) Date letter O (cycle XII), 1691/92, London.

2 Communion Cup

A communion cup also purchased from Mr Mayer in 1850. The cup is of goblet form, 6¾ inches high, with a rim diameter 3¾ inches. The bowl stands upon a stem of trumpet form with a moulded foot, diameter 3¼ inches.

There are four marks on the cup: (i) Maker's mark worn; (ii) Hibernia; (iii) Harp; (iv) Date letter C (table XX), 1799, Dublin.

SHOTWICK
St Edwin
Deanery of Wirral, South

Communion Cup

A communion cup 5⅘ inches high. The bowl, 3⅖ inches deep, is straight-sided but with a slightly everted lip, rim diameter 3½ inches. The bottom of the bowl turns sharply to a trumpet-shaped stem ending with a step and a flattened shoulder and a moulded splay, diameter 3⅗ inches.

On the side of the bowl an inscription:

| John Hale | Church Wardens of the Parish |
| William Briscoe | of Shotwick 1685 |

The cup was made before the use of date letters at Chester, and on the side of the bowl are the marks of Peter Pemberton in his early days as a goldsmith: (i) Maker's mark PP crowned within an ornate frame, Peter Pemberton I Type 1 (Compendium 6460); (ii) Sterling in two lines; (iii) Wheatsheaf as used by Peter Pemberton I (Compendium 4).

There is also a pewter flagon at Shotwick engraved with the date 1685 as on the communion cup. There is, in the Visitation Book for 1665, a record which states that the Churchwardens at Shotwick were to provide 'a Cup C'lice and Flagon for the Sacrament which were lost in the late Warrs'.

References:
Ball 1905b, p.5.
Ridgway 1968, p.150 and plates 42, 43.

SIDDINGTON
ALL SAINTS
Deanery of Macclesfield

The earlier silver at Siddington was stolen on 28 October 1792 and never recovered. An advertisement appeared in the *Manchester Mercury* (6 November 1792) which gives the following list of the plate lost: Silver quart tankard 1.45. Silver salver 'The Gift of John Ward Esq'. Cup and Cover. 1596 on cover.

STOCKPORT
ST MARY
Deanery of Stockport

Commission 1548:
 'One White Chales'

Churchwardens' Accounts:
Sept 11 1683

What goods or utinsels to the Pish Church of Stockport,
and were delivered by Thomas Armatryding, John Collier,
John Henshall and John Cooke unto William Lowe,
John Jefferson and Henry Wyld the present Churchwardens.

> Imprimis.   One silver Cupp and Patten, guilt with gold
>
> Two Flaggons of Pewter for the service of the Sacram^t (etc)

Churchwardens' Accounts
    1719   £1.12.0 for a new oake chest to keepe the plate in

Inventry of Contents in 1722 May 4
    In the Chest with 3 locks on in the Vestrey in Stockport Church

    Two Pewter Flaggons
    One large Pewter Dish
    One Silver Flagon and a black case for the same
    One silver Plate with AWS upon and a coate of Arms on
    One silver Decanter
    One Silver Cup or Challish gilt with gould
    One silver cover for the sd Challish gilt with gould

> One Silver Salvor with ye words A gift for the use
> of the Communion att Stockport
> Anno 1716

Churchwardens' Accounts 1790
An Account of the Communion Plate belonging to the Parish Church of Stockport

		oz	dwts
Flagon	The gift of Ann Arden widdow of John Arden Esqr Da^r of William Ingleby of Ripley in Yorkshire	59	18
Jug	A gift for the use of the Communion atte Stockport An 1716	22	19
Chalice & Cover	No inscription	18	19
Chalice & Cover	Ex dono Gul^{mi} Wright Arm^{ri} in usum Ecclesiae Stae Mariae de Stockport	20	14
*Small Plate	No inscription	9	17
Salver	A gift for the use of the Communion at Stockport An 1716	10	3
Dish	W Wardens Arms H S	22	9
		164	19

*A later note records 'On underside "St Mary's Church Stockport 1801 9oz 11dwts 21 gr" '.

1   COMMUNION CUP (see no. 2)
A communion cup 8½ inches high with a bell-shaped bowl and everted lip, diameter 4⅜ inches. On the side of the bowl a band of chased formal foliage 1⅝ inches below the rim and ⅝ inch wide. The bowl is 4⅝ inches deep and turns abruptly to an inset with ladder decoration between mouldings – the lower one prominent. The stem is convex, divided by a round knop with collars. Below the stem is an inset repeating the ladder decoration, followed by a shoulder moulding, a plain inset and the base has a band of ovolo and dart enrichment – foot diameter 3¼ inches.

There are four marks on the bowl: (i) Date letter C (cycle VI), 1580/81, London; (ii) Lion passant guardant; (iii) Leopard's head crowned; (iv) Maker's mark I S imposed within a shaped frame, (?)Isaac Sutton. The I resembles a cross. (Plate 68.)

References:
Brocklehurst, no. 8 and plate III.
Heginbotham, vol. 1, p.207ff.

2   PATEN COVER (see no. 1)

A paten cover to fit over the communion cup (no. 1). Overall diameter 4½ inches. The slightly domed cover has a spool-shaped stand and a blocked foot, diameter 2 inches. There is a band of foliage on the cover. The four marks are as on the cup (no. 1). (Plate 68.)

3   ALMS DISH

An alms dish, diameter 11½ inches, having a 2-inch edge with moulded rim. It forms a single depression. There is a coat of arms on the edge (identified by Ball as Warren of Poynton) also the initials within a wreath W above H•S for Humphrey and Susann Warren. Humphrey was the son of the Revd Henry Warren, Rector, 1663-74.

There are four marks: (i) Maker's mark G G above a fleur-de-lis within a shaped shield, (?)George Garthorne (Jackson, p.132); (ii) Leopard's head crowned; (iii) Lion passant guardant; (iv) Date letter Gothic R (cycle X), 1674/75, London.

Reference:
Brocklehurst, no. 31.

4   STAND PATEN

A stand paten, diameter 7½ inches, with a narrow moulded edge and a single depression. The paten stands on an almost vertical stem, which sweeps down to a shoulder and narrow flange. Diameter of base 3 inches. There is an inscription on the plate surface within a foliage frame:

The Gift for the use
of the Communion
at Stockport
Anno 1716

There are four marks: (i) Maker's mark (indistinct); (ii) Lion's head erased; (iii) Britannia; (iv) Date letter V (cycle XII), 1715/16, London.

5   EWER

A gilt jug, overall height 7½ inches, used as a flagon, but of a form of a large cup with handle and spout, standing upon a short stand. The overall width is 9½ inches and the rim diameter 5 inches. The spout rises slightly above the

STOCKPORT: ST MARY   149

rim and ends in a drop. The bowl has a plain moulded edge, the handle is S-shaped but broken at the top, joining the bowl below the rim, 1¾ inches below which is a further moulding. The total depth of the bowl is 6 inches. The foot is 1 inch, consisting of a moulding and a shoulder. The base diameter is 3 inches.

On the side of the bowl, within an oval, an inscription:

> A Gift
> for the use of
> the Communion
> att Stockport
> An 1716

There are four marks under the foot: (i) Lion's head erased; (ii) Britannia; (iii) Maker's mark DA under a six-point star within a shaped rectangle, Josiah Daniel (Grimwade 440); (iv) Date letter A (cycle XIII), 1716/17, London.

Reference:
Brocklehurst, no. 38.

6   FLAGON

A silver flagon, overall height 13¾ inches, having a domed lid hinged to the S-shaped handle with a scroll and thumb. The handle ends in a scrolled and barred terminal. The flagon's body ends in a narrow ribbing and the foot splays out to a ribbed base, diameter 8¾ inches. There is an inscription on the side of the barrel and a coat of arms in a lozenge placed between – Arms of Arderne of Harden:

> The Gift of Ann Arden   Widdow of John Arden Esqr
> Da^r of Sr William Ingelby   of Ripley in Yorkshire

There are four marks on the side of the barrel, which are also on the inside of the domed lid: (i) Maker's mark Ma and five-point star below, in a shaped rectangle, Thomas Mason (Grimwade 1971); (ii) Lion's head erased; (iii) Britannia; (iv) Date letter C (cycle XIII), 1718/19, London.

7   COMMUNION CUP (see nos 8 & 9)

A communion cup with bell-shaped bowl, and an everted lip, 9¼ inches high. Rim diameter 4⅜ inches. The bowl sweeps round to a single moulding and continues to an almost vertical stem 3½ inches deep, divided by a narrow knop having collars. The base, diameter 4⅜ inches, has two shoulder mouldings, the second much larger. There is an inscription on the side of the bowl:

> Ex dono Gul^{mi} Wright Arm^{ri} in usum
> Ecclesiae S^{tae} Mariae de Stockport 1760

There are four marks: (i) Date letter Gothic C (cycle XV), 1758/59, London; (ii) Lion passant guardant; (iii) Leopard's head crowned; (iv) Maker's mark (inverted) Script FW within a rectangle, Fuller White (Grimwade 733).

8   PATEN COVER (see nos 7 & 9)
A paten cover to accompany the communion cup (no. 7). Diameter 5½ inches. It stands on a blocked base, 2¼ inches diameter with inscribed lines and a spool-shaped stem 1 inch deep. The plate is flat and part of a single depression with an edge ⅜-inch-wide with mouldings. There are four marks on the underside of the plate, the same as on nos 7 and 9.

9   PLATE PATEN
A plate paten 7¾ inches diameter, having an edge 1⅛ inches wide and a moulded rim. There is a single depression and under the plate is later inscribed:

ST. MARY'S CHURCH
STOCKPORT
1801

There are four marks, as on nos 7 and 8.

STOCKPORT

ST PETER

Deanery of Stockport

1   COMMUNION CUP
A parcel-gilt communion cup 8¼ inches high, rim diameter 3¾ inches, with a bell-shaped bowl, the rim with strengthened moulding and slightly everted. The bowl curves round to a narrow cavetto moulding at the top of the stem which has vertical sides divided by a narrow knop with collars. The base of the stem is a large shoulder with inscribed lines, and ends with a short lined flange. Base diameter 3¾ inches.

   On the side of the bowl in large Roman capitals is the name of the church.

   There are four marks on the side of the bowl: (i) Maker's mark double struck but may have been I•K in a rectangle (upside down), John King (Grimwade 1446); (ii) Lion passant guardant; (iii) Leopard's head crowned; (iv) Date letter Gothic M (cycle XV), 1767/68, London.

(There was a plate paten to go with this cup. It was stolen about 1990 before a record could be made. It would presumably have confirmed the maker's mark.)

STOCKPORT
St Thomas

Deanery of Stockport

The church retains two pieces of silver given to the church about the time of the consecration, and a communion cup and a flagon, the latter given by Viscountess Warren Bulkeley in 1825.

1   COMMUNION CUP (see no. 2)
A communion cup 8½ inches high, having a bell-shaped bowl, 4⅜ inches deep, with an everted lip. The bowl curves round to a stem divided from it by two mouldings. The stem is divided by a narrow knop with collars, and sweeps down to a moulded foot, the third member having gadrooned decoration. Below this is a plain step. The base is 4 inches diameter. (The stem and base appear to be silver plate.)

There are four marks on the side of the bowl: (i) Maker's mark RG within a shaped shield, Robert Gainsford, Sheffield; (ii) Lion passant guardant; (iii) Duty mark; (iv) Date letter a with crown above (series III), 1824/25, Sheffield.

2   FLAGON (see no. 1)
The ornate flagon – overall height 11 inches – has a domed lid with a band of gadrooned enrichment before a flange, beneath which is a bezel on which an additional set of markings has been made – diameter 4¼ inches. There is an ornate thumb, having an acanthus leaf on the outside and ribs over a plain round blocked arch on the inside. The lid is hinged to the top of an S-shaped handle surmounted by a leaf and the top resting upon a ribbed shell pattern against the body of the flagon. The handle is attached to the body of the flagon by a series of oval collars and ends in a heart-shaped terminal.

The flagon has a pronounced lip with a leaf on top creating a spout. The top of the body has the inscription recording its gift to the church, surrounding the sacred symbols with rays:

> The gift of the Right Honourable Elizth Harriet
> Viscountess Warren Bulkeley to the Church
> of St. Thomas Stockport County of Chester 1825

It is divided by a narrow reeded band. The body has a moulded foot and a bold band of gadrooning. Diameter 6¼ inches.

There are five marks on the side of the body: (i) Maker's mark RG within a shaped shield, Robert Gainsford, Sheffield; (ii) Lion passant guardant; (iii) Duty mark; (iv) Crown; (v) Date letter a in plain frame (series III) 1824/25, Sheffield.

On the bezel of the lid: (i) Maker's mark RG; (ii) Lion passant guardant; (iii) Duty mark; (iv) Date letter a beneath a crown (series III), 1824/25, Sheffield.

STRETTON
St Matthew
Deanery of Great Budworth

Lancashire and Cheshire Wills. Chetham Society, vol. xxxiii, p.20.

Will of Richard Starkey of Stretton 1527/28:

> Also I bequeth towards the maynteynyng of devyne service off the chapell or orotorye of Saynt Savyo^{ir} off Stretton a chalice gylt w^t these words graven in the upper pte of the said chalice on the owte syde Exdono Rici Starky

> Itm I gyff to the use of the said chapell a sylv pece pcell gylt they to p'y for my sowle my Ffader sowle my brod Thomas Byron sowle and all christen sowles

There is now no early plate at Stretton.

SWETTENHAM
St Peter
Deanery of Congleton

Reference:
Ridgway 1968, p.154.

1 COMMUNION CUP

A communion cup 7⅞ inches high, with a bell-shaped bowl, diameter 4 inches, resting on a spool-shaped stem divided by a knop ⅝ inches deep with slight collars. After a slight moulding is a shoulder, followed by a flange, diameter 3⅞ inches.

There is an inscription on the side of the bowl:

> The Gift of
> Roger Manwaring Junr Esqr of Kermincham
> to the Parish Church of Swettenham 1705

There are five marks on the side of the bowl: (i) Maker's mark Pe within a rectangle for Peter Pemberton I Type 4 (Compendium 6314); (ii) Chester City coat; (iii) Britannia; (iv) Leopard's head erased; (v) Date letter D (series 2), 1704/05, Chester. (Plate 69.)

2   STAND PATEN
A stand paten, diameter 9 inches, with shallow depression and reeded rim. The paten stands upon a stem with deep mouldings including a shoulder moulding. An inscription on the back of the plate records the gift by John Shaw (1677-1715): 'Given to the Church of Swettenham by J.S. Rector 1713'.

There are four marks: (i) Maker's mark LO a key above and a device below in a shaped shield, Nathaniel Lock (Grimwade 1948); (ii) Lion's head erased; (iii) Britannia; (iv) Date letter S (cycle XII), 1713/14, London. (Plate 69.)

TABLEY HALL
ST PETER

(see **CHESTER CATHEDRAL**)

The gold communion cup and plate, the alms box, and the silver flagon were given to Chester Cathedral (nos 22-25) by the will of Lt.-Col. J.L.B. Leycester Warren.

TARPORLEY
ST HELEN
Deanery of Malpas

1   COMMUNION CUP (see nos 2 & 3)
A communion cup 9¼ inches high, rim diameter 4⅜ inches, having a bell-shaped bowl 5½ inches deep with an everted rim. The bowl has almost vertical sides which curve to the wide spool-shaped stem divided by a round knop. The foot is moulded, including at the bottom of the bowl, in Roman capitals written in a motto scroll the date 1711: 'THE GIFT OF Sr JOHN CREW OF UTKINTON 1711' beneath a full coat of arms of Crew.

There are four marks on the side of the bowl: (i) Maker's mark LO with a key above and a device below in a shaped shield, Nathaniel Lock (Grimwade 1948); (ii) Britannia; (iii) Lion's head erased; (iv) Date letter Q (cycle XII), 1711/12, London. (Plate 70.)

2   STAND PATEN (see nos 1 & 3)
A stand paten, diameter 8½ inches, having a narrow reeded rim and a single depression. The paten stands upon a spool-shaped stem with a base of mouldings including a narrow shoulder and a flange. Base diameter 2½ inches. The plate is inscribed: 'Torpurley Jan^{ry} 18 1711'. There are four marks as found on the cup (no.1) and flagon (no.3).

3   FLAGON (see nos 1 & 2)
A partly gilt flagon given by Sir John Crew(e) along with a communion cup (no. 1) and a stand paten (no. 2) made by Nathaniel Lock in 1711/12. The flagon is 13½ inches high overall. The domed lid has a step below the dome, a half-round moulding and a flange. The barrel has almost vertical sides and has a rim diameter of 4¾ inches. There is no spout. The lid is attached to the top of an S-shaped handle and a ram's head thumb and is capped on the top of the handle with a graded moulding with a pear-shaped end. The handle ends with a heart-shaped terminal meeting the body of the flagon above the narrow reeded girdle. Below the girdle the sides continue a little then turn outwards to a step and shoulder and a rounded base, diameter 7 inches. The flagon carries the same inscription and coat of arms as found on the communion cup.

There are four marks (as on nos 1 and 2) found on top of the dome and repeated on the side of the flagon. (Plate 71.)

4   COMMUNION CUP (for use when visiting the sick) (see no. 5)
A small communion cup, 4⅕ inches high with a bell-shaped bowl. The rim diameter 2⅕ inches. The bowl has an everted lip and the sides curve to the stem which is divided by a narrow knop with small collars. The base has a well pronounced shoulder with a hair line on the top of the flange. The base has a diameter of 2³⁄₁₀ inches. There is an inscription:

> The Gift of R M Rector of Torpurley
> for the use of ye sick of ye Parish

Ralph Mark was Rector of Tarporley from 1716 to 1732.

There are five marks on the side of the bowl: (i) Lion passant guardant; (ii) Leopard's head crowned; (iii) Chester City coat; (iv) Maker's mark Ri within a circular frame, Richard Richardson I Type 4 (Compendium 6815); (v) Date letter Y (series 2), 1724/25, Chester.

> Reference:
> Ridgway 1968, p.170.

5   STAND PATEN (for use when visiting the sick) (see no. 4)
This Dublin-made stand paten was given to accompany the communion cup (no. 4). Of domestic origin it bears a cypher of RJS and an added inscription 'For the use of the Parish'. On the top of the plate the sacred symbols within rays. The inscribed weight 4.18 seems to be contemporary.

The stand paten is 5½ inches diameter and stands 2¼ inches high. The plate has a narrow rim and a single depression and stands on a spool-shaped stem, with a narrow moulded step and a base diameter of 1¾ inches.

There are three marks on the underside of the plate: (i) Harp; (ii) Date letter Gothic capital E (table VIII), 1724/25, Dublin; (iii) Maker's mark, script HD conjoined, Henry Daniell.

6 & 7 Two Alms Plates

Each plate is 10⅛ inches in diameter and has an edge 1¼ inches wide, the rim moulded on the underside with a simple moulding. There is a single depression. Engraved on the rim an inscription: 'For the offertory at the Parish Church of Torpurley'.

There are four marks: (i) R ... within a rectangle with rounded corners – the second letter not clear; (ii) Lion passant guardant; (iii) Leopard's head crowned; (iv) Date letter probably b (cycle XIV), 1737/38, London.

There are two interesting pieces of foreign plate at Tarporley. Their origin has not been traced, nor when they came to the church:

8 Chalice

A gilt chalice, 6½ inches high, having a plain straight-sided bowl 2 inches deep and rim diameter 3⅛ inches, with a cut-card decoration embracing the bowl – probably of copper. The stem has six sides and the large knop has six round projections housing base metal circular enamel discs, each ornamented differently with cinquefoils. Below the projections the stem continues, leading with six panels edged with copper and each having different treatment of inscribed decoration, two of which have enamel medallions let in. One panel contains an inscription:

> PIE
> TRAN
> GNERV
> E BATTI
> ST A 1618
> + IHS

Below the panels the round base, diameter 4½ inches, is approached by a steep step culminating in a flange. There is what might have been a single mark on the underside of the flange – but this could be a fault. The chalice is an extraordinary confection and its origin, and further interpretation, awaits an answer.

The inscription seems to link the gift to some Order of John the Baptist and the form of the numerals at first could be seen as 1518 but are probably 1618. This date would also be more in keeping with the shape and decoration if its provenance proved to be Italy. (Plates 72, 73.)

9 Paten

The second piece of foreign plate at Tarporley is a plain gilded paten which may not be silver. It is a plain disc-like paten 5¾ inches diameter with a 1½-inch edge forming a single depression. Its origin is not known.

There are two marks on the underside: (i) A shield containing what might be a motif with small motif on either side; (ii) An oblong – poorly struck, containing three motifs. This might be a shield with three horizontal motifs.

TARVIN
St Andrew
Deanery of Chester

Inventory of church goods by the King's Commissioners 1548 reported at Tarvin Church and St Michael's chapel:

> three chalices and patens, given in charge of the Rector with an injunction that 'he presumes not to alyen, sell or otherways put awaye or give theyre assets, to any suche sale alreanac'on or puttinge awaye but that the same be safely kepte and p's'ved as he wille answere for the contrary at his uttermoste p'ell.

Reference:
Ball 1905a.

1   Loving Cup

The two-handled cup stands, with cover, 13 inches high. The cover has a high dome with an acorn finial, the edge having a gadrooned border. The rim is 6 inches diameter. On either side of the bowl are broken scroll handles, capped with a leaf, attached to the bottom with a circular collar. The bowl rests upon a stand, the stem having a step and a gadrooned border, and ending with a narrow shoulder, the base diameter 12½ inches. The overall width 10½ inches. Weight of lid 9 oz., weight of cup 42 oz.

On one side of the bowl a finely engraved coat of arms. Below the arms is the motto 'Je me fie en Dieu'. There is an inscription on the opposite side to the coat of arms:

> The Earl of
> Plymouth
> to the Parish of
> TARVIN
> 1775

The cover is unmarked, but the cup has four marks: (i) Maker's mark I D within a rectangle, John Deacon (Grimwade 1246); (ii) Lion passant guardant; (iii) Leopard's head crowned; (iv) Date letter T (cycle XV), 1774/75, London.

This piece is on display in the Ridgway Gallery, Grosvenor Museum, Chester, where it is on long-term loan.

2 & 3   Communion Cups

Two identical communion cups, each 8 inches high. Each bowl is bell-shaped with a rim diameter of 4 inches and stands on a stem divided by a moulded knop. The base is moulded, including a gadrooned enrichment. On each bowl is an inscription:

Richard Wilbraham Bootle Esqr

to

The Parish of Tarvin

Scratched below the base of each is the weight, 12.4.

There are four marks: (i) Maker's mark (worn and illegible); (ii) Lion passant guardant; (iii) Leopard's head crowned; (iv) Date letter U (cycle XV), 1775/76, London.

4   STAND PATEN

In 1905 Ball recorded two identical stand patens, but by 1999 there was only one.

The stand paten which survives stands 3 inches high, has a diameter of 11 inches, and is formed with a single depression with a gadrooned edge to the rim. This is repeated on the base of the foot. In the centre of the plate are inscribed the sacred symbols surrounded by rays. Below this are the arms of the family of Brock (Azure on a chief argent, a lion passant guardant gules). These are placed in an heraldic shield around which is the inscription: 'Thos Brock Esquire to Tarvin Parish 1775'.

There are four marks: (i) Maker's mark RR midway pellet in a two-lobed frame, Richard Rugg (Grimwade 2421); (ii) Lion passant guardant; (iii) Leopard's head crowned; (iv) Date letter U (cycle XV), 1775/76, London.

5   STAND PATEN

A small stand paten which was not recorded by Ball in 1905. The diameter is 5 inches and has a single depression after a narrow rim. The plate rests upon an hour-glass stem and has an overlapping flange.

There are only two marks, which are struck on the underside of the rim: (i) Maker's mark RR in a deckled frame, Richard Richardson III Type 1 which is also found on plate by Richard Richardson II Type 6 (Compendium 7405) (see also Church Hulme (no. 5) and Bebington (no. 3)); (ii) Lion passant guardant.

6   FLAGON

A flagon, 12½ inches high with a domed lid and rim diameter of 4½ inches. The curved spout rises above the rim and narrows towards the body with a series of flattened beads. The thumb is pierced. The flagon has an S-scroll handle ending in a heart-shaped terminal. Overall width 9½ inches. Around the body is a reeded girdle and beneath this the sides continue vertically before sweeping outwards to form a double shoulder and a narrow flange. Diameter of base 7½ inches. On the side of the flagon the sacred symbols with rays and beneath this an inscription:

> the GIFT of
> Henry Jeffs and Thomas Edwards Gent[n] Natives of Tarvin
> &
> Thomas Patten and Charles Goodwin of Chester Gent[n]
> to
> the Parish of TARVIN 1777

There are four marks on the flange of the lid and four beneath the base: (i) Maker's mark I R in a rectangle, John Robins (Grimwade 1623); (ii) Lion passant guardant; (iii) Leopard's head crowned; (iv) Date letter A (cycle XVI), 1776/77, London.

This piece is on display in the Ridgway Gallery, Grosvenor Museum, Chester, where it is on long-term loan. (Plate 74.)

TATTENHALL
ST ALBAN
Deanery of Malpas

1 FLAGON
A flagon 12½ inches high having a domed lid attached to an open cartouche thumb with scallop shell. There is an S-shaped handle ending in a heart-shaped terminal. Inside the base, which is well moulded and has a 7⅗-inch diameter, is an inscription: 'The Gift of the Rev[d] Samuel Peploe LLB Rector 1762'.

On the side, the sacred monogram of IHS surrounded by rays and an inscription:

> Sacrum
> Ecclesiae Parochiali
> de Tattenhall
> 1762

There are four marks inside the lid and on the side of the barrel: (i) Maker's mark script FW within a rectangle, Fuller White (Grimwade 733); (ii) Lion passant guardant; (iii) Leopard's head crowned; (iv) Date letter Gothic F (cycle XV), 1761/62, London.

2 COMMUNION CUP
A communion cup 7½ inches high with a bell-shaped bowl with everted rim, diameter 3⅞ inches. The base of the bowl sweeps round towards a stem

divided by a band knop with collars and the foot has a step and a moulding, followed by a shoulder and a flange, beneath which is inscribed: 'The Gift of the Rev[d] Samuel Peploe LLB Rector 1762'.

On the side of the bowl, the sacred symbols and an inscription:

Sacrum
Ecclesiae Parochiali
de Tattenhall
1762

There are five marks on the side of the bowl: (i) Maker's mark RR within a rectangle, Richard Richardson II Type 5b (Compendium 7386); (ii) Lion passant guardant; (iii) Leopard's head crowned; (iv) Chester City coat; (v) Date letter m (series 4), 1762/63, Chester.

References:
Croston, vol. 5, p.325.
Ridgway 1985, p.158.

3 SALVER

A salver, diameter 9¹/₁₀ inches, with reeded rim and single depression, having in the centre the sacred symbols of IHS with cross and nails surrounded by rays and an inscription: 'Sacrum Ecclesiae Parochiali de Tattenhall 1767'. It stands on three feet, having broken legs and five toes. It is inscribed: 'The Gift of the Rev[d] Samuel Peploe LLD Rector 1767'.

There are four marks: (i) Maker's mark (incuse) WF with I above and K below, not identified (Grimwade 3878). Compare mark on flagon at Mold; (ii) Lion passant guardant; (iii) Leopard's head crowned; (iv) Date letter Gothic m (cycle XV), 1767/68, London.

Reference:
Ridgway 1997, p.214.

4 STAND PATEN OR PATEN COVER

A stand paten 6⅜ inches diameter and an overall height of 1¾ inches. The stand has a blocked base on which is an inscription: 'The Gift of the Rev[d] Samuel Peploe LLD 1767'. The base is 2 inches diameter and meets the paten plate with a plain curve. The paten has a single depression with a reeded border a little over ¼ inch wide.

There are five marks on the underside of the plate: (i) Maker's mark RR with pellets above and below within a deckled rectangular frame, Richard Richardson II Type 7 (Compendium 7404); (ii) Lion passant guardant; (iii) Leopard's head crowned; (iv) Chester City coat; (v) Date letter R in deckle-edged square (series 4), 1767/68, Chester.

THORNTON-LE-MOORS
St Mary
(anciently St Helen)
Deanery of Frodsham

1   COMMUNION CUP (see no. 2)
A communion cup (dated by the accompanying paten cover 1567), height 7⅜ inches. The rim, diameter 3⅞ inches, is much wider than the bottom of the bowl which is bell-shaped with straight sides. On the side of the bowl, 1⅜ inches below the rim, is a band of conventional foliage – the borders crossing over five times with small sprigs of leafy conventional foliage rising on either side. The depth of the bowl is 3⅝ inches. There is a band of ovolo and dart enrichment immediately below the bowl and the stem is divided by a round knop with collars. After a band of the same decoration there is a shoulder moulding and a third band of the ovolo and dart pattern, leading to a small flange. The diameter of the foot is 3½ inches.

This is one of the earliest Elizabethan cups and should be compared with that at Runcorn and another formerly at Chester Holy and Undivided Trinity. There are no marks.

2   PATEN COVER (see no. 1)
A paten cover to accompany the communion cup (no. 1). It fits inside the rim of the cup by means of a bezel which has three ribs and a very small flange. The diameter is 4⅛ inches. The plate is slightly domed and is divided from the spool-shaped stem by a narrow band of ovolo and dart enrichment. The stand, diameter 1⅜ inches, is blocked and is inscribed 'ANO 1567'. There are no marks (see no. 1).

3   STAND PATEN
A stand paten 9¼ inches diameter with single depression, upon a stem which is splayed. The foot is moulded. The plate is engraved: 'Thornton Church 1731'.

There are five marks: (i) Maker's mark RR adorsed within a shaped frame Richard Richardson II Type 1 (also Richard Richardson I Type 6) (Compendium 7376); (ii) Lion passant guardant; (iii) Leopard's head crowned; (iv) Chester City coat; (v) Date letter script F (series 3), 1731/32, Chester.

Reference:
Ridgway 1985, p.141.

THREAPWOOD
St John
Deanery of Malpas

The silver is contemporary with the building of the church shortly after the Battle of Waterloo and comprises four individual pieces, all engraved:

S^t. JOHN'S CHAPEL
THREAPWOOD
1817

All pieces were made by Richard Sibley I of London in 1816/17. Nos 1 and 2 are kept in an oak box, and nos 3 and 4 in a large oak box which has been lined with a printed military document and covered by a felt lining. There is also a supplier's card attached to this which reads:

Makepeace & Harker
Goldsmiths and Jewellers
Terle Street, Lincolns Inn Fields.

1   COMMUNION CUP (see no. 2)
A communion cup 6¾ inches high, having a bell-shaped bowl with everted lip, diameter 3¹/₁₀ inches. The bowl stands on a narrow pedestal stem divided by a narrow band of reeding. The stem sweeps outward to a very simple drop and a step. The sacred symbols IHS surrounded by rays are on one side of the bowl and the inscription on the other.
   There are four marks on the side of the bowl: (i) Lion passant guardant; (ii) Leopard's head crowned; (iii) Date letter a (cycle XVIII), 1816/17, London; (iv) Duty mark. The maker's mark, script RS in a rectangle is found under the base, Richard Sibley I (Grimwade 2440).

2   PATEN COVER (see nos 1, 3 & 4)
A cover to accompany no. 1, diameter 4¼ inches. It was not intended as a paten. The top is slightly curved and has two steps before reaching the spool-shaped handle on which are engraved the sacred symbols within rays in a circle. These are repeated on the underside, where are also the five marks as found on the communion cup.

3   STAND PATEN (see nos 1, 2 & 4)

A stand paten 8⅛ inches diameter, having a moulded rim and a slight depression. The sacred symbols are engraved on the surface of the stand and show knife cuts. The plate stands on a splayed foot 3¾ inches diameter which is blocked, and inscribed as on the other silver. On the underside of the stand paten are the five marks (as on nos 1, 2 and 4).

4   FLAGON (see nos 1, 2 & 3)

A flagon 10¾ inches high, with a high domed lid in two sections with a flange upon a moulded top, diameter 3¾ inches. The barrel is divided from the base by a reeded band and below this the foot spreads out towards a plain shoulder and a step, base diameter 6½ inches. The thumb is moulded and is hinged to the top of an S-shaped handle which is attached to the side of the barrel with an oval collar and has a heart-shaped terminal.

There is an inscription on the barrel below the sacred symbols and rays.

There are five marks on the side of the flagon: (i) Maker's mark script RS within a rectangle, Richard Sibley I (Grimwade 2440); (ii) Date letter a (cycle XVIII), 1816/17, London; (iii) Lion passant guardant; (iv) Duty mark; (v) Leopard's head crowned. The first three marks are repeated on the inside of the cover.

THURSTASTON
ST BARTHOLOMEW
Deanery of Wirral, North

It is fortunate that Beazley referred to the plate at Thurstaston, as about half a century later it was stolen and has not been recovered.

The flagon mentioned by Beazley appears to be of plate. He reported that it had neither assay marks nor inscription, but that it was made by Elkington & Co. The flagon was 9½ inches high with a hinged lid 'surmounted by a cross motive'. The rim diameter was 3½ inches and the base diameter 5½ inches.

This seems to be the only surviving record and, though inadequate in some detail, the account which follows is based upon it.

Reference:
Beazley, pp.100-03.

1   COMMUNION CUP (see no. 2)

A communion cup, 5½ inches high, rim diameter 3 inches and base diameter 2½ inches. There is an inscription on the side of the bowl:

Presented by Mrs Browne
of Thurstaston Hall
to the Parish of Thurstaston
A.D. 1827

There are five marks: (i) Maker's mark script J.H., Jonathan Hayne (Grimwade 1408); (ii) Lion passant; (iii) Leopard's head uncrowned; (iv) Date letter l (cycle XVIII), 1826/27, London; (v) Duty mark.

Under the base in 'old figures' is the date 1706, so that it may have been remodelled.

2   PATEN (see no. 1)
A paten made by the same goldsmith as no. 1, having the same marks and inscription, also the added date 1706.

TILSTON
ST MARY
Deanery of Malpas

1   COMMUNION CUP (see no. 2)
A communion cup, 7⅛ inches high, having a rim diameter of 4¼ inches. It has a bucket-shaped bowl with straight sides 3⅞ inches deep. It turns abruptly at the base towards a stem which has a rounded knop, and the foot has a step and a moulding followed by a flange. Base diameter 4⅜ inches.

There are four marks on the bowl: (i) Maker's mark TL above (?)a wheatsheaf in a plain shield; (ii) Leopard's head crowned; (iii) Lion passant guardant; (iv) Date letter Gothic F (cycle X), 1666/67, London.

2   PATEN COVER (see no. 1)
A paten cover to accompany the communion cup no. 1. Diameter of plate 4⅞ inches. The paten is squat, only ⁹⁄₁₆ inches high and the stand is 2⅜ inches diameter and is blocked, on which is a lion passant mark. The stem is narrow and the base 4 inches, having a wide flange. On the plate side of the flange the four marks as found on the communion cup.

TUSHINGHAM
ST CHAD
Deanery of Malpas

The church, which was rebuilt between 1689 and 1691 still stands, but another church was built on a new site in 1862, and the plate was removed to the new church.

1   COMMUNION CUP
A parcel gilt communion cup 6⅜ inches high, with a bell-shaped bowl and moulded rim, diameter 3⅜ inches, standing on a tall stem divided by a very narrow reeded band and sweeping down towards a shoulder and a narrow flange. Base diameter 2⅞ inches. Beneath the base are a later monogram and the date 1862, which coincides with the date of the two small silver plates (1863/64).

There are four marks on the side of the bowl: (i) Maker's mark FG within a rectangle (unidentified); (ii) Lion passant guardant; (iii) Leopard's head crowned; (iv) Date letter N (cycle XV), 1768/69, London.

2 JUG
A parcel gilt lidded jug, 8 inches high, serving as a flagon, having a domed lid and a scroll handle. The proportions are those of a coffee pot. The spout curves over and is moulded, with a drop on the side of the inverted pear-shaped body (sometimes referred to as swag bellied). This stands on a moulded pedestal stem which is moulded with a shoulder and narrow flange. There are four marks, as on the communion cup no. 1.

WARBURTON
ST WERBURGH
Deanery of Bowdon

The old church, once in the possession of the monks of the Premonstratensian Order, was closed and its plate removed to a church on a new site.

The Warburton family of Arley, who had supplied silver to Lymm church in about 1691 also provided silver for Warburton church about the same time; it bore the Warburton coat of arms. Unfortunately it was sold in 1870 and apparently no record was kept. It has not been located. There is now no old plate at Warburton.

WARMINGHAM
ST LEONARD
Deanery of Congleton

Sheriff's Certificate 1548

One Chales

Terrier of Church Property and Land, kept among the church records, includes:

One gilt Chalice the Gift of Daniel Apelford Rector Anno 1685		27oz	0dwts
A small Salver gilt the gift of – do –		5	10
A silver salver the gift of Samuel Kent of Sandbach		16	0

A small salver bought by the Parishioners	4	0
A silver Chalice bought by " "	13	15
A silver Decanter the gift of William Vernon Anno 1729	34	0

    Syned by Offley Crewe   Rector
    Thomas Lowe
    John Edwards   } Church Wardens

    (and two others)

A Benefactions Board under the tower reads:

Mr William Vernon gave a silver Decanter for the use of the Communion	£11
Mr Samuel Kent gave a silver salver for the use of the Communion	£ 5
Mr Thomas Hall, Ironmaster, gave the second bell value	£30

1   COMMUNION CUP (see no. 2)
A communion cup 7¼ inches high, rim diameter 4 inches. It has a bell-shaped bowl with slightly everted lip. The bowl is 3½ inches deep and curves round towards a baluster stem ending in a splayed foot, diameter 4 inches. Around the top of the bowl is the inscription: 'William Gibbons Thomas Moore Churchwardens of Warmingham 1663'.

    To the left of the names, four marks: (i) Maker's mark TP with crescent above, in a plain shield; (ii) Leopard's head crowned; (iii) Lion passant guardant (repeated below the foot); (iv) Date letter Gothic F (cycle X), 1663/64, London.

2   PATEN
A paten, diameter 6⅖ inches, with very pale gilt, having a slightly sloping border one inch wide including a narrow band of three incised lines on the edge. Under the border, which forms a very slight depression, is a one-line inscription: 'Daniel Apelford Rector Ecclesiae de Warmingham Anno 1685 hane etiam patinam deo dicavit'.

    There are four marks under the border: (i) Date letter Gothic G (cycle X), 1664/65, London; (ii) Lion passant guardant; (iii) Leopard's head crowned; (iv) Maker's mark TL above a star and an inverted crescent within a shaped frame.

3   Jug

A jug, serving as a flagon. Overall height 8 inches with a bulbous body – the spout and scroll handle rising slightly above the rim – diameter 4¾ inches. The spout has a midway moulding and terminates with a series of graded mouldings. There is, in line with these, a plain waist-band. The handle ends in a simple shield attached by an oval collar. The body of the jug stands on a truncated stand with a shoulder moulding and a narrow step, diameter 4½ inches.

There is a coat of arms beneath the spout and an inscription:

> Deo op^t Max
> D.D
> Gul Vernon Gener^s
> Tu ne despice Christe
> 1729

There are four marks arranged haphazardly on the bottom of the body: (i) Maker's mark WD beneath a three-leaf sprig and with a trefoil frame, William Darker (Grimwade 3078); (ii) Date letter O (cycle XIII), 1729/30, London; (iii) Lion passant guardant; (iv) Leopard's head crowned.

4   Stand Paten

A stand paten, diameter 9 inches, having a narrow moulded border ⅖ inch wide forming a slight depression. The stand is cavetto, separated from the plate by a simple moulding, and ends with a drop and moulding to an ogee shoulder and a moulded foot, diameter 2¹/₁₀ inches. On the face of the plate is the inscription:

> The Gift
> of Samuel Kent of
> Sandbach Mercer
> for the use of the
> Communion Service in
> The Parish Church of
> Warmingham
> 1740

Under the stand, which is 2¼ inches high, is an inscription: 'He was born at the house called Lane End in Ecton in this Parish July 12th 1679'.

There are four marks on the top side of the plate: (i) Lion passant guardant; (ii) Maker's mark script RB within a deckled frame, Richard Bayley (Grimwade 2279); (iii) Leopard's head crowned; (iv) Date letter e (cycle XIV), 1740/41, London.

5 ALMS DISH

An alms dish 9 inches in diameter, having a 1³/₁₀-inch border which includes a ²/₅-inch moulded edge. The depression is curved to ½ inch. There is an inscription on the border in one line with divisions where indicated: 'Warmington Parish ÷ Charles Crewe Rector ÷ Samuel Kettle ÷ Daniel Jackson ÷ Church Wardens ÷ 1787 ÷'.

There are five marks on the underside of the border: (i) Maker's mark TL with a rectangle, Thomas Lamborn (Grimwade 2824); (ii) Lion passant guardant; (iii) Leopard's head crowned; (iv) Date letter L (cycle XVI), 1786/87, London; (v) Duty mark.

WAVERTON
ST PETER
Deanery of Malpas

COMMUNION CUP

A communion cup with a rim of 4 inches and a bowl, engraved 'Waverton', with steep sides and slightly everted lip, 3¼ inches deep. The bowl curves round to a short stem which is divided by a plain knop ⁹/₁₀ inches deep. The foot has simple mouldings and terminates rather abruptly. The diameter of the foot is 3³/₅ inches.

On the side of the bowl and a little below the rim are five marks: (i) Maker's mark Bu, Nathaniel Bullen Type 4 (Compendium 982); (ii) Chester City coat; (iii) Britannia; (iv) Lion's head erased; (v) Date letter L (series 2), 1711/12, Chester.

Reference:
Ridgway 1968, p.130.

WEAVERHAM
ST MARY THE VIRGIN
Deanery of Middlewich

Sheriff's Certificate 1548   Chalis and Patten   1 Gyld
Churchwardens' Acounts 1745
    Spent hiding the Church Plate   6d.

STAND PATTEN

A stand paten, diameter 10¾ inches. A narrow border creating a depression. It stands upon a cavetto stem with a moulded foot. There is an inscription:

Weaverham Church
Bernard Pickering   Peter Dutton
Church Wardens
1715

There are four marks: (i) Maker's mark LO with a key placed above within a shaped shield, Nathaniel Lock (Grimwade 1948); (ii) Lion's head erased; (iii) Britannia; (iv) Date letter Gothic U/V (cycle XII), 1714/15, London.

WHITEGATE
ST MARY
Deanery of Middlewich

Extracts from the Churchwardens' Accounts:

In 1633 a new 'fflagon' was purchased for the use of the church at a cost of 4 shillings, showing that it was made of pewter and not of silver.
1646   For a christening bason   £1 2s. 8d.
1657   Paid for a warrant to search for the communion cup   0 0 6
         Payd to Mr Edwardes in Chester the 17th day of December for the Communion Cup   1 1 5

(The cup having been taken it was redeemed from Edwardes for £ 1 1s. 5d.)

The church has a splendid suite of silver given by Essex Cholmondley in 1832. It comprises a communion cup and large paten, a jug and a large flagon, made by William Bateman II in 1832/33.

Reference:
Cheshire Sheaf, New series, vol. 1, 1891, p.133, no.226.

1   COMMUNION CUP (see nos 2, 3 & 4)
A communion cup 8¾ inches high with a bell-shaped bowl and everted lip. The rim is moulded and 4¼ inches diameter. The bottom third is embossed with a skirt of large acanthus leaves and the sides curve round to the ornate stem containing a moulded knop, below which the base curves outwards to a step. Diameter of foot 3½ inches. There are the sacred symbols and rays on the bowl. Inscribed 'The gift of Essex Cholmondley 1832'.
   There are five marks: (i) Maker's mark WB within a rectangle, William Bateman II (Grimwade 3038); (ii) Lion passant; (iii) Leopard's head; (iv) Date letter lower case r (cycle XVIII), 1832/33, London; (v) Duty mark.

2   PATEN (see nos 1, 3 & 4)
A large plate paten, diameter 9¾ inches, to accompany the communion cup (no. 1). The edge is decorated and borders a wide rim creating a single

depression, in the centre of which are the sacred monogram IHS within rays and the inscription. Marks and inscription as on the communion cup (no. 1).

3   EWER (see nos 1, 2 & 4)
A highly ornamental ewer, 8¾ inches high, with a bell-shaped bowl, rim diameter 4¾ inches, broken through by a large curved lip rising above the rim, continuing the moulding enrichment on the bowl, and with an acanthus support beneath it. In line with the lip, and continuing around the bowl, is a band of vine leaves. The ewer has a broken leaf capped scroll handle which rises in a curve above the rim. The handle joins the bowl at the widest part of the bowl, around which is a reeded girdle. The bottom third of the bowl is enriched with a cup of acanthus leaves. The ewer rests upon a stem divided by an ornate knop and the base has a band of leaves above a shoulder on which is the inscription.
 There are five marks: (i) Maker's mark WB within a rectangle, William Bateman II (Grimwade 3038); (ii) Lion passant; (iii) Leopard's head; (iv) Date letter r (cycle XVIII), 1832/33, London; (v) Duty mark.

4   FLAGON
A flagon belonging to the suite (nos 1, 2 and 3). Overall height 18 inches. The domed lid has a baluster terminal, is decorated, and rests upon a decorated rim. Like the ewer this is broken into by a large lip rising above the rim – moulded and resting upon an acanthus leaf. The broken scroll is leaf-capped. The barrel has a base reeded girdle below which the sides continue to a shoulder, an indent and a deep step. Marked and inscribed as the other pieces of this suite.

WHITEWELL
ST MARY
Deanery of Malpas

The communion cup, paten, alms dish and flagon were given in 1821, but the pieces, though forming a suite, have different assay marks. Each piece is inscribed: 'Whitewell Chapel Parish of Malpas 1821', and carries the same sacred symbols surrounded by rays.

1   COMMUNION CUP (see nos 2, 3 & 4)
A parcel gilt communion cup, 8 inches high, with a tulip-shaped bowl resting upon a form of gadrooning which is repeated on a projecting flange at the top of the stem. The stem has a wide knop with narrow collars, the foot has a band of gadrooning leading to a step.
 There are five marks on the side of the bowl: (i) Maker's mark WE within a rectangle, William Elliot (Grimwade 3107); (ii) Lion passant guardant; (iii) Leopard's head crowned; (iv) Date letter b (cycle XVIII), 1817/18, London; (v) Duty mark.

2   PATEN (see nos 1, 3 & 4)
A paten, diameter 8½ inches, with a narrow type of gadrooning and a deeply formed edge forming a pronounced depression. The same assay and maker's marks as on nos 1, 3 and 4, but with the date letter i (cycle XVIII), 1824/25, London.

3   ALMS DISH (see nos 1, 2 & 4)
An alms dish, an enlargement of the paten (no. 2), 11 inches diameter and with the date letter d (cycle XVIII), 1819/20, London.

4   FLAGON (see nos 1, 2 & 3)
A flagon to match the rest of the suite, 8½ inches high with a slightly tapering barrel and a curved spout. The low-domed lid is hinged, and is surrounded by a band of gadrooning. The thumb is cast and the S-scroll handle capped with a leaf. The barrel has a waist of reeding and the sides continue to a shoulder moulding of gadrooning, and end in a reeded step.

The marks are the same as nos 1-3 but the date letter f (cycle XVIII), 1821/22, London, and the lid has only two of these marks on the inside.

WILMSLOW
ST BARTHOLOMEW
Deanery of Knutsford

There is now no plate earlier than 1837, but the record of what was once in the church is interesting:

Sheriff's Certificate 1548

> Chaleses gilt   i
> Chaleses Whyte   ii

Churchwardens' accounts (which begin in 1585)

Apr 1638 List of Church Property

> … one silver cupp with a cover on, one pewter cupp one pewter bottle, two pewter flagons …

1619	Payde for a Communion Cuppe	1s visd
1628	Payde for two new Flagons	ixs
1666	Paid for a new fflagon for the Communion	3s 10d
1678	Paid in exchange with the old flagon for 2 new ones 2 plates and one Cup	7s 6d
1733	Repairs to the Candlesticks	
1839	Old Chalice sold for £3/9/-	

WINCLE
St Michael
Deanery of Macclesfield

1 COMMUNION CUP (see no. 2)
A communion cup 9 inches high with a bucket-shaped bowl and everted rim, diameter 4½ inches and 4½ inches deep. The bowl turns abruptly to a spool-shaped stem divided by a considerable knop. Below the stem is a flat and acute shoulder leading to a flange edged by a moulding. The base diameter is 4½ inches. On the side of the bowl is a flowered circle containing a contemporary engraving of a coat of arms (Snelson) beneath which is an inscription: 'The Guift of Roger Snelson'.

There are four marks on the side of the bowl: (i) Maker's mark DW with a mullet below and motif above (? mitre) within a heart-shaped frame; (ii) Leopard's head crowned; (iii) Lion passant guardant; (iv) Date letter h (cycle IX), 1645/46, London. (Plate 75.)

2 PATEN (see no. 1)
A partly gilt paten cover, total height 3½ inches, made to fit over the communion cup (no. 1) and having a single depression. It stands on a spool-shaped handle which extends as a flange, base 4 inches. The plate is hallmarked as on the communion cup. Weight 6 oz. Tr.

(I am grateful to the Revd Canon D.W. Moir for his help.)

WISTASTON
St Mary
Deanery of Nantwich

Sheriff's Certificate:

> On^e Chalice

1 STAND PATEN
A stand paten, diameter 6¾ inches, having a narrow moulded edge ¼ inch wide forming a depression. It rests on a stand 1⅗ inches wide at the top and has a cavetto side. The piece has been very badly crushed but the base could be of a step and shoulder leading to a narrow flange, diameter 2⅗ inches.

On the surface of the plate are four marks: (i) Maker's mark TL with a five-petal rose above and a five-petal rose beneath. On either side of the initials are three pellets (not in Grimwade); (ii) Lion passant guardant (also under the base); (iii) Leopard's head crowned; (iv) Date letter E (cycle XIII), 1720/21, London.

2 FLAGON

A flagon, 12½ inches high, having a domed lid attached to which is an open scroll thumb hinged to the top of the broken scroll handle, with a moulded attachment ending in a flattened pellet. The broken scroll ends in a heart-shaped shield attached to the barrel with an oval collar. The barrel is moulded at the rim, diameter 4⅗ inches. There is a reeded band to mark the bottom of the flagon and below this the sides turn outwards to a moulding, a shoulder and a flange. Diameter of base 7¹/₁₀ inches.

There is an elaborate coat of arms on the side of the flagon, and an inscription:

> The Gift of Rebecca Walthall
> Relict of Richard Walthall Esqr
> 1732

There are four marks on the top of the dome and on the side of the flagon, and the maker's mark is repeated on the bottom of the broken-scroll handle: (i) Lion passant guardant; (ii) Maker's mark R midway pellet B within a rectangle, Richard Bayley (Grimwade 2262); (iii) Leopard's head crowned; (iv) Date letter R (cycle XIII), 1732/33, London.

3 & 4 COMMUNION CUPS

Two identical communion cups 7¹/₁₀ inches high, each with a goblet-shaped bowl with a slightly everted lip, diameter 4 inches. Each bowl stands upon a thin stem, at the junction a ¾-inch-wide reeded band. Below this a trumpet-shaped stand ending in a reeded step continued by a plain step – diameter 3¼ inches.

On the side of each cup an inscription:

> The Gift of
> Peter Walthall Esqr
> and Ann his Wife
> 1791

Under the foot are four marks: (i) Maker's mark PB over AB in a square, Peter and Ann Bateman (Grimwade 2140); (ii) Lion passant guardant; (iii) Leopard's head crowned; (iv) Date letter q (cycle XVI), 1791/92, London.

WITTON
Deanery of Middlewich

(see **NORTHWICH**)

WOODCHURCH
HOLY CROSS
Deanery of Birkenhead

Exchequer Deposition by Commission, Chester 8 Elizabeth
Easter No. 2, Dated at Westminster 12 Feb 8 Eliz.(1566)

> … about 2 years ago Robert Lenott and John Coventry, being churchwardens of the said parish, sold the chalice, vestment, albe and cope mentioned in the 5 interr., but for what sum he cannot say.
>
> Ales Rabow widow dec'ed gave the said chalice &c., to the inhabitants of the said parish the year before the insurrection in the north, about 30 years ago.
>
> Deponent has heard that the said John Hocknell bought the said chalice, &c., of the churchwardens of Woodbridge for 40s.'whereof he paid 4d. in earnest,' but whether he ever paid the said 40s. witness does not know.
>
> The said 'Challice and other clothes' were given to the whole parish of Woodchurch, for the better maintenance of God's service, and not for the maintenance of a priest.
>
> Raphe Robinsonne of Prenton, aged about 62, deposes that he brought 4 pieces of gold, of 10s. the piece, to John Coventry, then churchwarden for the said chalice and clothes, but he refused to take it, because his fellow-churchwarden was not present.
>
> John Coventry, of Knocktorom, in co. Chester, aged about 60 years, deposes that he and Rob.t Lennarden being the churchwardens of Woodchurch, sold the said chalice, &c., for 40s.

Reference:
Cheshire Sheaf, 3rd series, vol. I, 1896, pp.5-6, no. 6.

1   COMMUNION CUP

A communion cup 7¼ inches high having a 4-inch-deep beaker-shaped bowl with a rim diameter of 3¾ inches. Encircling the bowl and a little above half way is a band of conventional foliage between plain borders. Half an inch below the rim is an inscription:

The Communion Cupp of Woodchurche
William Balle   Thomas Coventrie
Churchwardens 1625

Below the bowl and dividing it from the stem is a series of well defined mouldings. The stem is divided by a fairly large moulded knop, 1¼ inches in diameter, having a narrow belt and collars above and below. The stem splays out towards the shoulder and a well-splayed moulded foot, 3⅘ inches diameter.

There is only one mark, struck twice, IL within an ornate frame, John Lingley of Chester (Compendium 4195 or 4196).

Reference:
Ridgway 1968, p.42f.

WRENBURY
ST MARGARET
Deanery of Nantwich

1   SWEETMEAT DISH

A sweetmeat dish sometimes called a strawberry dish, used as a paten, 5½ inches diameter, with two shell-like handles projecting 1¼ inches beyond the rim. The whole decorated with pressed out decoration rising in the centre with a convex boss on which is a circular band of six-petal flower heads. On the base is engraved S.B., indicating the domestic origin of this piece and the communion cup (no. 2), which were probably given to refurnish the church with communion plate after the Civil War.

There is one imperfect mark on the outside of the dish, presumably that of the maker – H with tiny circles top and bottom and on either side. There is also a line making the H look as though it could be HN or NH imposed, but this could equally well be a flaw. The mark has not been traced. The form of sweetmeat dish indicates a mid-17th-century date.

(See also **NANTWICH**)

2   COMMUNION CUP

A communion cup 6¼ inches high with a bell-shaped bowl with everted lip, diameter 3¾ inches, standing on a moulded baluster stem on a spreading foot with inscribed line near edge, foot diameter 3⅝ inches. Scratched beneath the base the letters S.B. as on the sweetmeat dish (no. 1).

There are four marks on the side of the cup: (i) Maker's mark W with two crescents above and a five-point star below within a shaped shield; (ii) Lion passant guardant; (iii) Leopard's head crowned; (iv) Date letter Gothic capital G (cycle X), 1664/65, London.

3 Flagon

> 'Mrs Hannah Jones of Namptwich gave the sum
> of £50 to be disposed of as followeth
> viz £10 towards buying a silver flagon for the use
> of ye Sacrament in ye Parish Church of Wrenbury'

A flagon 11 inches high, having a high domed lid hinged to the top of a scroll handle with a scroll thumb. The rim is 3¾ inches diameter and moulded. The sides of the flagon are almost vertical. The end of the body is marked by a narrow moulded band, below which the sides spread towards a step and shoulder, and end in a step, diameter 6 inches.

There are four marks on the side of the body, which are repeated under the base, and the maker's mark is repeated on the underside of the lid: (i) Maker's mark Gothic Pa with a five-point star above within a shaped frame, very like Humphrey Payne (Grimwade 2118); (ii) Lion's head erased; (iii) Britannia; (iv) Date letter M (cycle XII), 1707/08, London.

Reference:
Hall, p.342 (footnote).

4 Jug

A jug serving as a flagon. Overall height 11¼ inches with a pear-shaped baluster body and moulded rim, diameter 2¾ inches. The cover is reel-shaped with a baluster finial to which is hinged an open voluted thumb. The spout rises from a half pear motif which is lidded. The jug has a double scroll broken handle. It rests upon a moulded pedestal foot, diameter 4¼ inches. Under the foot is a later inscription:

> Richard Stapleton Cotton Colonel in Queen Victoria's
> Army this cup is the inalienable property of
> Wrenbury Parish Church. Jubilee Year

There are four marks on the side of the jug: (i) Maker's mark Li above a pellet within a shaped frame, John Lingard (Grimwade 1933); (ii) Lion's head erased; (iii) Britannia; (iv) Date letter D (cycle XIII), 1719/20, London.

5 Communion Cup

A communion cup 8 inches high, with a bell-shaped bowl and slightly everted moulded lip, diameter 3¾ inches. The bowl is 4½ inches deep, sweeping down towards the broad stem and separated from it by a simple mould. The stem is divided by a round knop, diameter 1½ inches, with collars. The foot is moulded by a step and spread collar and a step – diameter 4 inches.

There is a one-line inscription on the side of the bowl: 'The Gift of John Mafsie of Namptwich to the Church of Wrenburey 1727'.

There are five marks on the side of the body: (i) Maker's mark RR adorsed within an oval with indented sides, Richard Richardson I Type 7 (Compendium 7377); (ii) Lion passant guardant; (iii) Leopard's head crowned; (iv) Chester City coat; (v) Date letter script B (series 3), 1727/28, Chester.

References:
Ridgway 1968, p.172.
Ridgway 1985, p.137.

WYBUNBURY
ST CHAD
Deanery of Nantwich

Richards, p.373:

'In 1464 Wybunbury church was broken into by two thieves (later ordered to be hanged) who were local. They took:

Cross worth five marks
a Shrine with relics and other jewels
2 Chalices worth £10
2 Silver phials worth 13s.4d.'

Nicholas Daryngton (Vicar of Wybunbury 1542) presented, among other bequests:

a chalice of 40s to accompany masses

Sheriff's Certificate 1548:

'On challice'

In 1969 the Vicar of Wybunbury, the Revd Stanley Jones and his son, Mr Peter Jones, found under the tower of the church an old iron safe. It was about to be thrown out, but was fortunately saved, as it contained several pieces of plate:

1 COMMUNION CUP
A communion cup 6¾ inches high, with a beaker-shaped bowl 2¼ inches deep and a rim diameter of 4 inches. The bowl stands upon a baluster stem which spreads outwards to a base diameter of 3¾ inches, beneath which is a sterling mark.
There are four marks on the side of the bowl: (i) Maker's mark TD with a five-point mullet above and below with tiny rings on either side of each mullet, within a square frame with clipped corners (see Chester Cathedral no. 2 and Great Barrow no.1); (ii) Leopard's head crowned; (iii) Lion passant guardant; (iv) Date letter u (cycle X), 1677/78, London.

2   STAND PATEN

A stand paten, diameter 10⅝ inches. The plate has a moulded edge which curves down to a depression and together is 1½ inches wide. The depression is half an inch deep. The plate stands upon a stem of cavetto, leading to a shoulder and reeded flange, diameter 3⅝ inches. Overall height 3¾ inches. Weight 2 lb. 1¼ oz. (avdp).

There are four marks on the edge: (i) Maker's mark indistinct (?)mitre above, (?)Samuel Smith I who entered his mark in 1700 (Grimwade 2578); (ii) Britannia; (iii) Lion's head erased; (iv) Date letter G (cycle XII), 1702/03, London.

3   SPOON

A Hanoverian spoon, 9½ inches in length, with a very pronounced rib and well-developed drop on the bowl, which measures 3⅜ inches by 2 inches. Its use as an ecclesiastical piece is unknown except perhaps as a spoon for administration.

There is only one mark, repeated three times: RW with midway pellet within an ornamental rectangle. The spoon is probably provincial, *c.*1720, and weighs 3¼ oz. (avdp).

4   COMMUNION CUP

A communion cup 8¾ inches high, with a bell-shaped bowl with almost vertical sides and a double moulded rim, diameter 4 inches. The bowl, which is inscribed, is 4⅝ inches deep and curves around towards a wide stem divided by a round knop with collars. The stem splays towards a step and shoulder and a slight flange, diameter 4⅜ inches. Weight 15½ oz. (avdp).

There are five marks on the side of the bowl: (i) Maker's mark RR adorsed within a shaped shield, Richard Richardson I Type 6 (also Richard Richardson II Type 1) (Compendium 7376); (ii) Lion passant guardant; (iii) Date letter script C (series 3), 1728/29, Chester; (iv) Chester City coat; (v) Leopard's head crowned.

Reference:
Ridgway 1985, p.135.

5   FLAGON

A flagon, 13 inches high overall, having a high domed lid and, after a step, a pronounced convex moulding followed by lesser mouldings which are continued on the rim of the flagon. The lid is attached to the top of an S-scroll handle and has a ram's head thumb. The handle is attached to the bottom of the body by an oval collar. The bottom of the flagon is marked by a ribbed girdle and the foot below this spreads to a step, a shoulder, and a slight step. Diameter of base 7⅜ inches. Weight 4 lb. 3 oz. (avdp). The side of the body is inscribed:

Inter
Innumera ejus
Munificentiae Specimina
Parochiae Wybunburienci
Hocce ex dono dedit Anophorum
RHODÆ DELVES THOMÆ DELVES
de Doddington in Comitatu
Cestrensi Baronetti Uxor
quarta Anno Domini
1726[7]

There are four marks on the underside of the lid and on the side of the flagon. The maker's mark is also repeated on the handle: (i) Maker's mark (?)script JP imposed within a shaped shield, probably John Penfold (Grimwade 3674); (ii) Lion passant guardant; (iii) Leopard's head crowned; (iv) Date letter L (cycle XIII), 1726/27, London.

6 COMMUNION CUP (for use when visiting the sick) (see no. 7)

A communion cup used for administration to the sick, 3¼ inches high, of goblet form, with rim diameter of 2 inches. The sides of the bowl sweep down with a break between goblet and stem of a narrow band of reeding. The depth of the bowl is 2 inches. The stem ends with a band of reeding and a step. The diameter of the foot is 2 inches.

There is an inscription on the side of the bowl:

This cup and plate
were presented by
the late Mrs Jane Birch
to
the Rev^d J A Hayes
for the private use of the Parish
of Wybunbury
and his successors for ever

There are five marks on the foot: (i) Maker's mark HC within a rectangle, Henry Chawner (Grimwade 971); (ii) Lion passant; (iii) Leopard's head; (iv) Date letter p (cycle XVIII), 1830/31, London; (v) Duty mark.

7 PATEN (see no. 6)

A paten to accompany the communion cup no. 6, having a wide rim edged with reeding and forming a single depression. In the centre of the plate, surrounded by a circle of leaves, a script B and the inscription as found on the communion cup no. 6.

Tankard

It would be remiss to exclude from this survey reference to this tankard which was also found in the safe, and became the subject of a meeting under Chancellor Gower Jones at a Consistory Court assembled at Chester in December 1976 (referred to in the *Daily Telegraph*, 30 March 1977).

In spite of strong opposition by members of the Chester Advisory Committee, the Ancient Monuments Society and descendants of the Delves family, the orginal donors of the tankard, all of whom recommended that it should not be sold, the Chancellor agreed it should be sold to help provide money for the building of a new church. It was eventually sold in 1977 to a London dealer.

A tapered cylindrical tankard, 7¼ inches high, having a flat-topped cover which is hinged to the top of a scroll handle with a thumb of intertwined dolphins. The handle is attached to the side of the bowl with a tapered support 3¼ inches in length. The handle terminates in a serrated rectangular shield. The flange oversteps the rim.

The tankard has a moulded base formed of a step and shoulder and a flange – diameter 7¼ inches, above this is a repoussé and chased band of palm and acanthus foliage.

Beneath the foot are inscribed the letters D above T and R (standing for Thomas and Rhoda Delves). Weight 4 lb. 9 oz. (avdp).

There are four marks on the cover and on the side of the tankard: (i) Date mark Gothic M (cycle X), 1677/78, London; (ii) Lion passant guardant; (iii) Leopard's head crowned; (iv) Maker's mark TK with mullet below within a plain shield (repeated on the handle).

Appendix 1

Abbreviations

A	Alms Basin
AB	Alms Box
AD	Alms Dish
AP	Alms Plate
B	Baptismal Basin
BK	Beaker
BM	Book Mount
Ca	Candlestick
CC	Communion Cup
CCC	Chalice/Ciborium
Ci	Ciborium
Co	Cover
Cr	Cruet
D	Dish
E	Ewer
F	Flagon
FR	Flagon Ring
J	Jug
L	Ladle
LC	Loving Cup
M	Mace
Mus	Museum
P	Paten
PC	Paten Cover
PP	Plate Paten
S	Salver/Salver Paten
(S)	Denotes for use when visiting the sick
SD	Sweetmeat Dish
SN	Spoon
SP	Stand Paten
T	Tankard
Tz	Tazza
V	Verge
WB	Wafer Box
WS	Wine Strainer

Appendix 2

Makers' Marks 1697-1837

Recorded in:
Arthur G. Grimwade, FSA, *London Goldsmiths 1697-1837 – Their Marks & Lives*, London, Faber & Faber, 1976. (Number is the reference from Grimwade.)

No.	Maker	Parish	Item	Date
57	Augustin Le Sage	Burleydam	CC P SP F	1769/70
67	Francis Nelme	Middlewich	F 1 of 2	1732/33
68	Anthony Nelme	Acton	SP 2	1706/07
			F	1705/06
		Alderley Edge	CC(S) PP(S)	?18th century
116	Richard Bayley	Astbury	PC 2	1712/13
			F 2	1716/17
		Church Hulme	F	1719/20
		Heswall	P	1718/19
		Macclesfield	P	1719/20
		Pott Shrigley	CC SP 2 F	1711/12
249	Abraham Buteux	Chester Holy and Undivided Trinity	SP	1694/95
331	Charles Hollinshead	Macclesfield	A 2	1758/59
341	Charles Kandler I	Great Budworth	SP	1743/44
348 or 349	Jonah Clifton Richard Clarke	Sandbach	AD	1709/10
353	Joseph Clare I	Christleton	F	1722/23
		Congleton	F	1718/19
		Great Budworth	F 2	1719/20
		Neston	CC	1717/18
440	Josiah Daniel	Stockport St Mary	E	1716/17
493	Daniel Piers	Barthomley	F 2	1749/50
545	John Eckfourd I	Runcorn	F	1703/04

APPENDIX 2: MAKERS' MARKS 1697-1837

550	Ebenezer Coker	Delamere	S	1768/69
575	Edward, Edward Jnr, John and William Barnard	Mobberley	CC	1835/36
576	Edward Feline	Forest Chapel	CC PC	c.1720
587	Edward Feline	Macclesfield	F 2	1745/46
591	Elizabeth Godfrey	Audlem	B	1744/45
604	George Ellis	Chester St Peter	F	1719/20
662	John Fawdery I	Astbury	CC 2 SP	1707/08
		Congleton	SP	1699/1700
672	Francis Crump	Grappenhall	F	1766/67
		Knutsford	F	1768/69
		Malpas	CC 2	1765/66
		Rostherne	CC 2	1770/71
674	Francis Crump	Harthill	F	1774/75
702	Francis Nelme	Middlewich	F 1 of 2	1739/40
733	Fuller White	Goostrey	CC F	1759/60
		Mottram	F 1 of 2	1763/64
		Stockport St Mary	CC PC PP	1758/59
		Tattenhall	F	1761/62
736	Francis Garthorne	Little Budworth	F	c.1710
738	William Gamble	Eaton	F	1711/12
823	John Gibbons	Chelford	A P 1 of 2	1709/10
840	George Knight	Nantwich	WS	1822/23
890	Gabriel Sleath	Sandbach	F 2	1733/34
904	Gabriel Sleath	Over	SP F 2	1747/48
971	Henry Chawner	Wybunbury	CC(S) P(S)	1830/31
977	Henry Chawner and John Emes	Great Budworth	CC 2	1796/97
1005	Hyam Hyams	Grappenhall	CC(S) PC(S)	1825/26
1058	Humphrey Payne	Mottram	F 1 of 2	1748/49
1061	Humphrey Payne	Bunbury	SP	1716/17
		Chester St Thomas of Canterbury	CC 2 SP AD F	1725/26
		Coddington	SP	1725/26
		Chester St Olave/ Grosvenor Museum	E	1728/29
		Rostherne	F/J 2 P S	1735/36

1092	John Jackson I	Great Barrow	F/J	1718/19
1179	John Berthellot	Eccleston	F/J	1746/47
1180	John Bayley	Neston	P	1752/53
1208	Joseph Clare II	Prestbury	SP 2	1770/71
1214	John Carter II	Bowdon	CC 2 P 2 F 2	1775/76
		Harthill	AD	1775/76
1220	John Clarke II	Haslington	CC PC F AD	1811/12
1244	John Dare	Stoak/Grosvenor Museum	E	1771/72
1245	John Dutton	Malpas	P (or AP)	1772/73
1246	John Deacon	Tarvin	LC	1774/75
1343	John Gorham	Harthill	CC	1773/74
1408	Jonathan Hayne	Thurstaston	CC P	c.1827
		Guilden Sutton	CC	1821/22
1446	John King	Stockport St Peter	CC	1767/68
1492	Joseph Lock	Cheadle	CC 2	1804/05
1616	John Rowe	Alsager	CC P SP F	1789/90
1623	John Robins	Chester St John without the Northgate	CCC	1781/82
		Tarvin	F	1776/77
1643	James Smith I	Church Hulme	SP	1722/23
1746	John Whittingham	Chester St Mary without the Walls	AD	1822/23
1894	Thomas Langford I	Cheadle	SP	1718/19
1933	John Lingard	Wrenbury	J	1719/20
1945	Seth Lofthouse	Bowdon	AD	1705/06
		Church Hulme	SP	1700/01
		Chester St Michael/Grosvenor Museum	F 2	1701/02
1948	Nathaniel Lock	Tarporley	CC SP F	1711/12
		Chester St Mary without the Walls	F	1712/13
		Swettenham	SP	1713/14
		Weaverham	SP	1714/15
1971	Thomas Mason	Stockport St Mary	F	1718/19
1981	Willoughby Masham	Chester St Peter	SP	1708/09
2028	Magdalen Feline	Carrington (Partington)	CC	1759/60
2087	Jonathan Newton	Alderley Edge	SP	1713/14

APPENDIX 2: MAKERS' MARKS 1697-1837

2118	Humphrey Payne	Brereton	CC SP AD	1722/23
		Wrenbury	F	1707/08
2120	Thomas Parr I	Congleton	CC	1709/10
2140	Peter and Ann Bateman	Calveley	CC	1796/97
		Dodleston	E	1796/97
		Malpas	F 2	1795/96
		Marple	S	1795/96
		Wistaston	CC 2	1791/92
2141	Peter, Ann and William I Bateman	Huntington	CC	1804/05
		Chester St Martin/ Grosvenor Museum	CC	1804/05
2143	Peter and William I Bateman	Dodleston	SP	1805/06
		Huntington	SP	1805/06
		Marple	F	1811/12
2237 or 2239	Peter Tabart or Peter Taylor	Eaton	CC2	1748/49
2262	Richard Bayley	Bunbury	AP 2	1747/48
		Chester St Peter	AP	1736/37
		Chester St John the Baptist	AP 2	1735/36
		Handley	J	1734/35
		Sandbach	AP	c.1737
		Wistaston	F	1732/33
2279	Richard Bayley	Warmingham	SP	1740/41
2309	Rebecca Emes and Edward Barnard I	Birkenhead	CC2 PP F	1827/28
2374	Richard Morson and Benjamin Stephenson	Daresbury	CC	1773/74
2382	Hugh Roberts	Birkenhead	SP	1698/99
		Chester St Bridget/ Grosvenor Museum	PP 2 F	1697/98 1697
2383	Phillip Rollos I	Shocklach	SP	1691/92
2394	?Gundry Roode	Ringway and Hale Barns	CC SP	1719/20 1725/26
2420	Richard Rugg	Great Budworth	S	1766/67

2421	Richard Rugg	Stoak/ Grosvenor Museum	P	1764/65
		Tarvin	SP	1775/76
2440	Richard Sibley I	Threapwood	CC PC SP F	1816/17
2536	Solomon Hougham	Burton	CC AP E	1809/10
2578	Samuel Smith I	Wybunbury	SP	1702/03
2646	John Martin Stockar and Edward Peacock	Mottram	SP	1709/10
2661	Samuel Whitford I	Gawsworth	CC	1763/64
2664	Samuel Wheatley	Northwich	SP	1764/65
2749	Thomas Farren	Cheadle	F	1731/32
2824	Thomas Lamborn	Warmingham	AD	1786/87
2849	Thomas Mann	Malpas	AP 2	1742/43
2870	Thomas Parr II	Bunbury	F 2	1735/36
		Heswall	F	1736/37
2938	Thomas Tearle	Church Hulme	CC	1723/24
		Halton	CC SP F	1731/32
2976	Thomas Whipham II and Charles Wright	Acton	CC	1764/65
		Chelford	F	1759/60
2989	Joseph Ward	Little Budworth	CC PC	1711/12
2990 or 2991	Samuel Wastell	Goostrey	SP	1705/06
2997	William Allen I	Chester Christ Church	SP	1725/26
3037	William Bateman I	Church Lawton	CC P F	1817/18
		Chester Christ Church	CC 2	1821/22
3038	William Bateman II	Whitegate	CC P E F	1832/33
		Bunbury	CC	1834/35
3051	Walter Crisp	Frodsham	CC 2 D A 2 F 2	1763/64
3055 or 3059	William Cowley or William Caldecott	Hargrave	J	1784/85
3078	William Darker	Warmingham	J	1729/30
		Chester Holy and Undivided Trinity	F 2	1727/28
3079	William Darker	Chester St John the Baptist	F2	1729/30
		Daresbury	F	1731/32

3107	William Elliot	Whitewell	CC P AD F	1817/18
3146 or 3147	William Grundy	Alderley Edge	F	1752/53
3163	William Hall	Grappenhall	CC PC AD 2	1766/67
3213	William Kingdom	Christleton	CC(S) PC(S) CR(S)	1833/34
3357	William Vincent	Farndon	F	1781/82
3381	Edward Yorke	Astbury	Tz	1709/10

Unregistered Marks in Grimwade

3561	Edmund Vincent	Disley	CC Co P 2 E 2	c.1769
3582	?George Cowles	Frodsham	SP 2	1766/67
3674	?John Penfold	Wybunbury	F	1726/27
3838	Unidentified	Norbury	CC PC J	1804/05
3878	Unidentified	Tattenhall	S	1767/68

Appendix 3

Makers' Marks 1570-1962

recorded in

Maurice H. Ridgway, FSA and Philip T. Priestley, FSA, *The Compendium of Chester Gold & Silver Marks 1570-1962,* Woodbridge, Antique Collectors' Club Ltd, 2004. (Numbers given are the Compendium numbers – all makers are Chester Goldsmiths unless shown otherwise.)

No.	Maker	Parish	Item	Date
1	William Mutton sheep's head in a shaped shield. Earliest known mark	Chester Holy and Undivided Trinity	CC P	*c.*1570-5
		Chester St Mary without the walls	CC PC	*c.*1570-75
		Great Budworth	CC PC	*c.*1570-75
		Stoak/Grosvenor Museum	CC P	*c.*1570-78
		Chester St Michael/ Grosvenor Museum	CC	*c.*1570
4 and 6460	Peter Pemberton Type 1 PP with crown above in an ornamental frame (associated with a sheaf in ornamental frame)	Shotwick	CC	Inscribed 1685
789	John Bingley Bi with pheon above, in rounded frame	Church Minshull	CC	1704/05
982	Nathaniel Bullen Bu in plain frame	Waverton	CC	1711/12
2773	Griffith Edwardes I GE with a large	Bunbury	P	*c.*1600

188

Appendix 3: Makers' Marks 1570-1962

	unidentified motif below in a trefoil frame			
4137	Joseph Duke I ID with star between in a square	Harthill	SP	Between 1769-80
4195	John Lingley IL in an ornate frame	Baddiley	P	Late 16th century
		Woodchurch	CC	Late 16th century
6147	Nathanial Bullen Type 1 NB Script conjoined in a shaped frame	Chester St Mary without the Walls	P	c.1683
6314	Peter Pemberton Type 4 script Pe in a square surround	Swettenham	CC	1704/05
6460	Peter Pemberton I Type 1 PP in a shaped shield	Shotwick	CC	c.1685
6815	Richard Richardson I Type 3 Ri in ornamental shield with pointed base	Chester St John the Baptist	P CC(S) PC(S)	1717/18 1725/26
		Lower Peover	SP 2	1715/16
		Chester St Peter	CC F	1713/14
		Chester St Thomas of Canterbury	CC(S) PC(S)	1724/25
		Malpas	CC	1717/18
		Chester St Michael/ Grosvenor Museum	CC SP PP	1723/24 1723/24 1724/25
		Chester St Bridget/ Grosvenor Museum	CC	1718/19
		Christleton	CC SP	1722/23
6816	Richard Richardson I Type 4 Ri within a rounded frame	Chester St John without the Northgate	SP	1716/17
		Lower Peover	CC	1715/16
		Tarporley	CC(S)	1724/25

6956	Thomas Robinson Type 2 Ro in a shaped frame	Chester St Mary without the Walls	FR	1711/12
7375	Richard Richardson II Type 1 RR adorsed within a shaped shield (see Ri I, Type 3)	Bebington	CC	1736/37
		Thornton-le-Moors	SP	1731/32
7376	Richard Richardson I Type 6 RR adorsed in a shield with rounded base	Coddington	E	1727/28
		Wybunbury	CC	1728/29
		Chester Cathedral	AP 2	1737/38
7377	Richard Richardson I Type 7 RR adorsed in a small oval frame with indented sides	Coddington	CC P	1727/28
		Wrenbury	CC	1727/28
7385	Richard Richardson II Type 5A RR in a rectangle	Chester Holy and Undivided Trinity	CC	1752/53
		Chester St Peter	CC	1762/63
		Chester St Mary without the Walls	CC PC	1759/60
7386	Richard Richardson II Type 5B RR in a rectangle	Tattenhall	CC	1762/63
		Christleton	AD	1763/64
		Great Budworth	CC(S) P(S)	1763/64
7392	Richard Richardson IV Type 2a RR in a rectangular frame having wavy edges at top and bottom. Sometimes with a midway pellet	Ince	CC	1788/89
7399	William Richardson II Type 3c and William Richardson II Type 1c RR with a midway pellet	Daresbury	SP	1746/47

APPENDIX 3: MAKERS' MARKS 1570-1962

	within a shaped shield which has an angular base			
		Heswall	CC	1739/40
7403	Richard Richardson II Type 6 RR within a rectangle with deckled edges	Bebington	CC	1769/70
7404	Richard Richardson II Type 7 RR in a rectangle with deckled sides with pellets above and below the letters	Tattenhall	SP (or PC)	1767/68
7405	Richard Richardson III Type 1 RR very small punch with deckled top, bottom and sides	Church Hulme	CC SP	1776/77
		Tarvin	SP	No date
7407	Richard Richardson IV Type 3 RR in a very small rectangle	Neston	CC	1780/81
7502	Robert Welshman Manchester RW with a pellet or motif in heart-shaped shield	Cheadle	CC	Early 17th century
7503	Ralph Walley RW within an ornamental shield	Chester St John the Baptist	AD	Inscribed 1683
9571	William Richardson WR conjoined in a rectangle with clipped corners	Dodleston	CC	1732/33

Appendix 4

Makers' Marks, Provincial, Unascribed, Foreign and Indistinct

Items with London Hallmarks

Maker's Mark	Parish	Item	Date
Glove (see IG)	Marton	CC	1597/98
?Grasshopper	Chester Cathedral	CCC	1496/97
Beaked Bassinet or Bird's head erased (Jackson, p.97, 1567)	Davenham	CC	1570/71
'Bellows'	Mobberley	CC	1571/72
An animal in a shield	Brereton	CC	1653/54
AP with pellet above and a mullet below within a shaped shield	Prestbury	CC 2	1676/77
CB conjoined in a square frame	Pott Shrigley	CC	1622/23
CI imposed (see IC)			
DB with star above and inverted crescent below in a square frame	Chelford	SP	1693/94
DW with a mullet below and a motif (?mitre) within a heart-shaped frame (?Jackson, p.116)	Wincle	CC P	1645/46
E-? script letters in an oval	Congleton	CC SP	1696/97
ES in a dotted circle (Jackson, p.116)	Chester St Michael/ Grosvenor Museum	CC	1635/36
FL with midway pellet above a bird in heart-shaped ornamental shield (Jackson, p.123)	Nantwich	F2	1659/60
FG in rectangular frame	Tushingham	CC J	1768/69
GG above a fleur-de-lis within a shaped frame	Stockport St Mary	AD	1674/75
GG star and mullet between (Ball	Chester	CC	1672/73

APPENDIX 4: MAKERS' MARKS, PROVINCIAL, UNASCRIBED, FOREIGN AND INDISTINCT 193

says 'fleur-de-lys') in shaped shield	St John the Baptist		
HB conjoined above a five-point star in a shaped shield	Sandbach	CC 2 PC 2	1656/57
HI above -D in square frame	Eccleston	S	1786/87
HS above a star within a shaped shield	Marple	CC	1629/30
IA within an ornamental shield	Middlewich	CC	1608/09
IA script conjoined in a rectangular frame	Lower Peover	F	1685/86
IC imposed in a shield (or CI) (Jackson, p.111)	Overchurch	CC PC	1618/19
IC above a five-point star or mullet in shaped frame	Lymm	CC PC SP	1691/92
IC (or IO) in oval frame	Bruera	CC	1695/96
IG with a glove between in a shaped frame	Marton	CC	1597/98
IH above a five-point star within an ornamental shield	Baddiley	CC	1624/25
IN above a five-point star in a heart-shaped frame (Jackson, p.125)	Chester Cathedral (one no maker's mark)	F 2	1662/63
IN with pellet between	Middlewich	CC SP	1667/68
IO (see IC)	Bruera	CC	1695/96
IS imposed in shaped frame	Stockport St Mary	CC PC	1580/81
IS a crown above in a shaped frame John Singleton	Chester Cathedral	SN	1691/92
IT above a mullet or pellet in a double-edged heart-shaped frame	Chester St John the Baptist	CC	1633/34
	Chester St John without the Northgate	CC	1641/42
J conjoined in a W-shaped frame	Nantwich	CC PC	1604/05
JB above a crescent within a lozenge frame	Alderley Edge	CC	1696/97
M above a star in a heart-shaped frame (Jackson, p.121)	Over	CC	1663/64
PP above a motif (?fleur-de-lis) in a trefoil frame	Brereton	F	1660/61
PR cypher script with pellet below in shaped shield	Carrington	F SP	1688/89

P- with pellets above and a crescent below within a shaped frame	Audlem	CC	1635/36
R- within rectangular frame	Tarporley	AP 2	1737/38
?RC	Lymm	CC	1623/24
RC above a pheon surmounted by pellets within a heart-shaped frame	Bunbury	CC	1632/33
RC above a fleur-de-lis within a shaped frame	Christleton	AB	1595/96
RF with three pellets above and a star below in a plain shield	Prestbury	CC	1626/27 or 1628/29
RF above a five-point star in a heart-shaped frame	Chelford	CC	1652/53
RH over a star (or mullet) in a plain shield	Chester St John the Baptist	P	1664/65
RL above a fleur-de-lis within a plain shield	Aston	SP	1675/76
	Audlem	SP	1683/84
		AD	1684/85
	Barthomley	SP	1681/82
RM above a motif (?heart) in a shaped frame	Farndon	PC	1622/23
RN with a pellet between above a five-point star within a shaped frame	Chester Cathedral	SP 2	1662/63
S.H above a fleur-de-lis within a heart-shaped frame	Barthomley	CC	1669/70
SL with motif above and below in a shaped frame	Daresbury	SP	1654/55
TC, a fish above and a fleur-de-lis below, in a shaped frame	Chester Cathedral	CC P F AB	1677/78
	Chester Cathedral	AD	1673/74
	Neston	AD	1683/84
TC, a fish above and a five-point star below in a deckled shield	Barthomley	CC PC	1676/77
TD with five-point mullet above and below with tiny rings on either side of each mullet within a square frame with clipped corners	Chester Cathedral	CC PC 2	c.1662
	Great Barrow	C PC	c.1662
	Wybunbury	CC	1677/78

APPENDIX 4: MAKERS' MARKS, PROVINCIAL, UNASCRIBED, FOREIGN AND INDISTINCT

TH within a decorated shield	Macclesfield	CC 2 PC 2	1624/25
TK with mullet below within a plain shield	Wybunbury	T	1677/78
TL above a ?wheat-sheaf in a plain shield	Tilston	CC PC	1666/67
TL above a star and an inverted crescent within a shaped frame	Warmingham	P	1664/65
TP with crescent above in a plain shield	Warmingham	CC P	1663/64 1664/65
T above R- within lobes	Eccleston	P	1736/37
VS above a fleur-de-lis within a plain shield (Jackson, p.115)	Acton	CC	1633/34
	Nantwich	CC	1633/34
WA with a two-handled vase above in a shaped shield	Chester Christ Church	SP	1725/26
W- within a trefoil frame	Marbury	SP	1632/33
W with two crescents above and a five-point star below in a shaped shield	Wrenbury	CC	1664/65
W over M ?William Maundy	Nantwich	SD	c.1640
WM with crown above and mullet below within a shaped shield	Prestbury	F	1668/69
WM above a five-point star in a simple shield (imperfectly struck)	Cheadle	P (or AD)	1666/67
WS within a rectangle	Davenham	CC	1633/34

PROVINCIAL MARKS OTHER THAN CHESTER

MAKER'S MARK	PARISH	ITEM	DATE
	BIRMINGHAM		
MB IF both within rectangles Matthew Boulton & James Fothergill	Frodsham	E	1774/75
	DUBLIN		
Harp	Chester St John without the Northgate	SP	No date
	Shocklach	CC	1799 (worn marks)
HD, Henry Daniell	Tarporley	SPs	1726/27

Maker's Mark	Parish	Item	Date
	EDINBURGH		
Mark rubbed	Eaton	SP	c.1781
	MANCHESTER		
RW Compendium 7502 Robert Welshman	Cheadle	CC	Early 17th century
	SHEFFIELD		
D&S within a rectangular cameo Dixon & Son	Chester Christ Church	AP	1838/39
IW with a midway pellet in a rectangle John Watson	Lower Whitley	CC	1824/25
NS & Co within a rectangle Nathaniel Smith & Company	Malpas	Ca 2	1809/10
RG within a shaped shield Robert Gainsford & Company	Stockport St Thomas	CC F	1824/25
RM pellet between in a rectangle Richard Morton & Company	Mottram	CC 2	1779/80
	YORK		
TM above a five-point star in a heart-shaped frame Thomas Mangy	Malpas	CC P	1674/75

FOREIGN PLATE

Maker's Mark	Parish	Item	Date
Payenne, Switzerland	Chester Cathedral	CC	
?Dutch	Chester Cathedral	Ci	
Very worn, perhaps an animal or bird head within ornamental shield German	Audlem	CCC	Inscribed 1725
Indistinct, but perhaps an animal in an irregular frame German	Audlem	WB	
European	Chelford	Tz	
?Dutch	Hargrave	BK P	
?Danish	Heswall	CCC	
Basle, Switzerland	Nantwich	SN	
?Italian	Tarporley	CCC	

APPENDIX 4: MAKERS' MARKS, PROVINCIAL, UNASCRIBED, FOREIGN AND INDISTINCT   197

UNKNOWN OR INCOMPLETE MARKS

MAKER'S MARK	PARISH	ITEM	DATE
(No mark)	Aston	CCC PP	14th century
?Le in round frame	Alderley Edge	PP	?Provincial
RW with a midway pellet in ornamental rectangle	Wybunbury	SN	c.1700 (provincial)
Tudor Rose	Knutsford	CC	Late 17th century ?Provincial
Unrecorded mark	Wistaston	SP	1720/21 London?
-H	Wrenbury	SD	
-W	Wrenbury	CC	1664/65 London?
5-pointed star above rubbed letters	Davenham	SP	1707/08
Unrecorded mark	Marbury	CC	1742/43
Indistinct mark	Chester Cathedral	Ca 2	1678/79
Indistinct mark		CC	1685/86
Indistinct mark		M	1787/88
Indistinct mark	Bebington	SP	1704/05
Indistinct mark	Chester St Mary without the Walls	P SN	1638/39 18th century
Indistinct mark	Farndon	CC	
Indistinct mark	Nantwich	AD 2	c.1740
Indistinct mark	Stockport St Mary	SP	1715/16
Indistinct mark	Tarvin	CC 2	1775/76
No maker's mark	Malpas	AP	1718/19

PLATE WITHOUT MARKS

PARISH	ITEM	DATE
Chester Cathedral	V 2	?16th century
Acton	PP	17th century
Alderley Edge	PP	Late 17th century
Aston	CCC P	Late 14th century
Chester Bishop's Private Chapel	CC(S)	c.1730
Congleton	AD	Early 18th century

Cotebrook	CC P SP	16th century *c.*1684
Eccleston	CC	*c.*1683
Gawsworth	CC P	16th century
Handley	CC	16th century
Malpas	L	Late 17th/early 18th century
Middlewich	CC(S) PC(S)	*c.*1755
Pott Shrigley	PC	?16th century
Runcorn	CC	Elizabethan *c.*1670
	CC SP	
Thornton-le-Moors	CC PC	Elizabethan

Appendix 5

List of Plate in Parishes

ALMS BASIN
1595/96   Christleton

ALMS BOX
1677/78   Chester Cathedral – part of the Leycester
                     Warren bequest

ALMS DISHES
?   Congleton – no marks
?   Frodsham – WC in rectangle only
1666/67   Cheadle – alms dish or paten
1673/74   Chester Cathedral
1674/75   Stockport St Mary
1683   Chester St John the Baptist – date in inscription
1683/84   Audlem
1683/84   Neston – plate/alms dish
1705/06   Bowdon
1709/10   Sandbach
1722/23   Brereton
1725/26   Chester St Thomas of Canterbury
c.1740   2   Nantwich
1763/64   Christleton
1775/76   Harthill
1786/87   Warmingham
1797/98   2   Grappenhall
1811/12   Haslington
1819/20   Whitewell
1822/23   Chester St Mary without the Walls

ALMS PLATES
1709/10   2   Chelford
1735/36   2   Chester St John the Baptist
1736/37   Chester St Peter
c.1737   Sandbach
1737/38   2   Chester Cathedral

1737/38	2	Tarporley
1742/43	2	Malpas
1747/48	2	Bunbury
1758/59	2	Macclesfield
1772/73		Malpas – alms plate or paten
1809/10		Burton – stolen 1995 – not recovered
1838/39		Chester Christ Church

CHALICES/CIBORIUM

Unidentified	Tarporley – no date – Italian?
?late 14th century	Aston
1496/97	Chester Cathedral
?	Heswall – no marks – Danish?
1661	Chester Cathedral – chalice and cover (or ciborium) – 1661 on inscription – Dutch? unidentified
1725	Audlem – date given in inscription of German origin
1781	Chester St John without the Northgate – missing

COMMUNION CUPS

No marks		Middlewich – c.1755
No marks		Great Budworth – William Mutton
No marks		Stoak – William Mutton – Grosvenor Museum
16th century		Gawsworth – no marks
16th century		Handley – no marks
Elizabethan		Cotebrook
Elizabethan		Runcorn
1567		Thornton-le-Moors
1570		Chester Holy and Undivided Trinity – William Mutton – transferred to Blacon
c.1570		Chester St Mary without the Walls
c.1570		Chester St Michael – Grosvenor Museum, 1988
1570/71		Davenham
1571/72		Mobberley
1580/81		Stockport St Mary
1597/98		Marton
Early 17th century		Cheadle
1604/05		Nantwich
1608/09		Middlewich
1618/19		Overchurch
1622/23		Pott Shrigley
1623/24		Lymm – indistinct, but appears to be 1623/24
1624/25		Baddiley
1624/25	2	Macclesfield

APPENDIX 5: LIST OF PLATE IN PARISHES

1625		Woodchurch – John Lingley – inscribed 1625
1626/27 or ?1628/29		Prestbury
1629/30		Marple
1630/31		Chester Cathedral, similar to recusant chalices of 1630/31 – ?Swiss
1632/33		Bunbury
1633/34		Chester St John the Baptist
1633/34		Nantwich
1633/34		Davenham
1633/34		Acton
1635/36		Chester St Michael – Grosvenor Museum, 1988
1635/36		Audlem
1641/42		Chester St John's without the Northgate – at Chester St Thomas of Canterbury
1645/46		Wincle
1652/53		Chelford
1653/54		Brereton
1656/57	2	Sandbach
c.1662		Great Barrow – marks as Bridgman silver at Chester Cathedral
1662/63		Chester Cathedral
1663/64		Over – on loan to Grosvenor Museum, Chester
1663/64		Warmingham
1664/65		Wrenbury
1666/67		Tilston
1667/68		Middlewich
1669/70		Barthomley
c.1670		Runcorn – no marks, but inscription includes date 1670
1672/73		Chester St John the Baptist
1674/75		Malpas
1676/77	2	Prestbury
1676/77		Barthomley
1677/78		Chester Cathedral – part of the Leycester Warren bequest
1677/78		Wybunbury
1683		Eccleston – date engraved on cup
c.1685		Shotwick – no mark, but 1685 included in inscription
1685/86		Chester Cathedral
1691/92		Lymm
1695/96		Bruera
1696/97		Alderley Edge

1696/97		Congleton
c.1697		Alderley Edge – maker's mark entered 1697
Late 17th century		Knutsford
1704/05		Church Minshull
1704/05		Swettenham
1707/08	2	Astbury
1709/10		Congleton
1711/12		Tarporley
1711/12		Pott Shrigley
1711/12		Little Budworth
1711/12		Waverton
1713/14		Chester St Peter
1715/16		Lower Peover
1717/18		Malpas
1717/18		Neston
1718/19		Chester St Bridget – Grosvenor Museum, 1988
1719/20		Ringway and Hale Barns
c.1720		Forest Chapel – bowl inscribed 1732
1722/23		Brereton
1722/23		Christleton
1723/24		Chester St Michael – Grosvenor Museum, 1988
1723/24		Church Hulme
1724/25		Chester St Thomas of Canterbury – from Chester Cathedral
1724/25		Tarporley
1725/26		Chester St John the Baptist
1725/26	2	Chester St Thomas of Canterbury – from Chester Cathedral
1727/28		Coddington
1727/28		Wrenbury
1728/29		Wybunbury
c.1731		Bishop of Chester's Private Chapel, inscribed 1731, see also Chester St Martin
1731/32		Halton
1732/33		Dodleston
1736/37		Bebington
1739/40		Heswall
1742/43		Marbury
1748/49	2	Eaton
1752/53		Chester Holy and Undivided Trinity – transferred to Blacon
1758/59		Stockport St Mary
1759/60		Carrington – transferred to Partington
1759/60		Goostrey
1759/60		Chester St Mary without the Walls

APPENDIX 5: LIST OF PLATE IN PARISHES

1762/63		Tattenhall
1762/63		Chester St Peter
1763/64		Great Budworth
1763/64	2	Frodsham
1763/64		Gawsworth
1764/65		Acton
1765/66	2	Malpas
1767/68		Stockport St Peter
1768/69		Tushingham
c.1765		Disley – marked EV only
1769/70		Bebington
1769/70		Burleydam
1770/71	2	Rostherne
1773/74		Daresbury
1773/74		Harthill
1775/76	2	Bowdon
1775/76	2	Tarvin
1776/77		Church Hulme
1779/80	2	Mottram
1780/81		Neston
1783/84		Chester St Bridget – on loan to Huntington, 1985
1789/90		Alsager
1788/89		Ince
1791/92	2	Wistaston
1792/93		Farndon
1796/97	2	Great Budworth
1796/97		Calveley
1797/98		Grappenhall
1799		Shocklach – Dublin mark
1804/05	2	Chester St Martin – 1 to Huntington, 1 to Grosvenor Museum
1804/05	2	Cheadle
1804/05		Norbury
1804/05	2	Huntington – 1 to Grosvenor Museum, 1988
1804/05		Chester St Paul
1809/10		Burton – stolen 1995 – not recovered
1811/12		Haslington
1816/17		Threapwood
1817/18		Church Lawton
1817/18		Whitewell
1821/22		Guilden Sutton
1821/22	2	Chester Christ Church
1824/25		Stockport St Thomas – side of bowl only marked

1824/25		Lower Whitley
1825/26		Grappenhall
1826/27		Thurstaston – + 1706 in old figures remodelled? – stolen 1974
1827/28	2	Birkenhead – 1 on loan to Barnston
1830/31		Wybunbury
1830/31		Chester St Paul
1832/33		Whitegate
1833/34		Christleton
1834/35		Bunbury
1835/36		Church Lawton
1835/36		Mobberley

PATENS

Unidentified	Tarporley – no date – ?Italian
Elizabethan	Cotebrook
No date	Great Budworth – William Mutton
16th century	Gawsworth – no marks
?	Burleydam – date illegible
1570	Chester Holy and Undivided Trinity – William Mutton – transferred to Blacon
c.1600	Bunbury – Griffith Edwardes I
1638/39	Chester St Mary without the Walls
1645/46	Wincle
1664/65	Warmingham
1664/65	Chester St John the Baptist
1666/67	Cheadle – paten or alms dish
1677/78	Chester Cathedral – part of the Leycester Warren bequest
c.1700	Hargrave – inscription shows 1700
1717/18	Chester St John the Baptist
1718/19	Malpas – paten/alms plate
1727/28	Coddington
1735/36	Rostherne
1736/37	Eccleston
1752/53	Neston
1763/64	Great Budworth – for use when visiting the sick
1772/73	Malpas – paten or alms plate
1817/18	Church Lawton
1824/25	Whitewell
1826/27	Thurstaston – 1706 shown in old figures – remodelled? – stolen in 1974

APPENDIX 5: LIST OF PLATE IN PARISHES

?1830/31		Wybunbury – for use when visiting the sick
1832/33		Whitegate
Victorian		Handley

PATEN COVERS

*c.*1567		Thornton-le-Moors – no date, but 1567 in inscription
*c.*1570		Chester St Mary without the Walls
*c.*1576		Pott Shrigley – no date, but 1576 in inscription
1580/81		Stockport St Mary
1604/05		Nantwich
1618/19		Overchurch
1622/23		Farndon – imperfect mark, but seems to be 1622/23
1624/25	2	Macclesfield
1656/57	2	Sandbach
*c.*1662		Great Barrow – marked as Bridgman silver in Chester Cathedral
1662/63	2	Chester Cathedral
1666/67		Tilston
1674/75		Malpas
1676/77		Barthomley
1691/92		Lymm
1711/12		Little Budworth
1712/13	2	Astbury
*c.*1720		Forest Chapel – slight ?EF
1725		Chester St Thomas of Canterbury – no date, but 1725 in inscription
1725/26		Chester St John the Baptist – for use when visiting the sick
*c.*1755		Middlewich – no date mark, but 1755 in inscription
1758/59		Stockport St Mary
1759/60		Chester St Mary without the Walls
1776/77		Church Hulme
1797/98		Grappenhall
1804/05		Norbury
1811/12		Haslington
1816/17		Threapwood
1825/26		Grappenhall – for use when visiting the sick
1833/34		Christleton – for use when visiting the sick

COVER

| ? | | Disley – no marks |

PLATE PATENS

?	Alderley Edge – goes with 1697 communion cup but seems later – no marks
?late 14th century	Aston
Late 16th century	Alderley Edge
Late 16th century	Baddiley
17th century	Acton
1697/98 2	Chester St Bridget – Grosvenor Museum, 1988
1724/25	Chester St Michael – Grosvenor Museum, 1988
1758/59	Stockport St Mary
1789/90	Alsager
1827/28	Birkenhead – on loan to Barnston, 1984

SALVER PATENS

1764/65	Stoak – paten/salver
1775/76 2	Bowdon

STAND PATENS

?	Tarvin – no date mark, but Richard Richardson II/III
?	Eaton – date letter B, Thistle?
1632/33	Marbury
1654/55	Daresbury – with later additions
1660/61	Brereton
1662/63 2	Chester Cathedral
1667/68	Middlewich
c.1670	Runcorn – no marks – inscription includes date 1670
1675/76	Aston
1681/82	Barthomley
c.1683	Chester St Mary without the Walls – no date mark, but inscribed 1683 – paten/stand paten
1683/84	Audlem – stand paten or alms dish
c.1684	Cotebrook
1688/89	Carrington – transferred to Partington
1691/92	Lymm
1691/92	Shocklach
1693/94	Chelford
1694/95	Chester Holy and Undivided Trinity – transferred to Blacon
1696/97	Congleton
1698/99	Birkenhead
1699/1700	Congleton
1700/01	Church Hulme
1702/03	Wybunbury

Appendix 5: List of Plate in Parishes

1704/05		Bebington
1705/06		Goostrey
1706/07	2	Acton
1707/08		Astbury
1707/08		Davenham
1708/09		Chester St Peter
1709/10		Mottram
1711/12	2	Pott Shrigley
1711/12		Tarporley
1713/14		Swettenham
1713/14		Alderley Edge
1714/15		Weaverham
1715/16		Stockport St Mary
1715/16	2	Lower Peover
1716/17		Bunbury
1716/17		Chester St John without the Northgate – redundant
1718/19		Cheadle
1718/19		Heswall
1719/20		Macclesfield
1720/21		Wistaston
1722/23		Brereton
1722/23		Church Hulme
1722/23		Christleton
1725/26		Ringway and Hale Barns
1725/26		Chester Christ Church
1725/26		Coddington
1725/26		Chester St Michael – Grosvenor Museum, 1988
1725/26	2	Chester St Thomas of Canterbury – from Chester Cathedral
1726/27		Tarporley – Dublin mark
1731/32		Halton
1731/32		Thornton-le-Moors
1740/41		Warmingham
1743/44		Great Budworth
1746/47		Daresbury
1747/48		Over – on loan to Grosvenor Museum, Chester
1764/65		Northwich
c.1764		Chester St John without the Northgate – form of Hibernia mark appears to confirm the date
1766/67	2	Frodsham
1767/68		Tattenhall – stand paten/paten cover
1769/70		Burleydam
1769-1780		Harthill – Joseph Duke I

1770/71	2	Prestbury
1775/76	2	Tarvin
1789/90		Alsager
1805/06		Dodleston
1805/06		Huntington from Chester St Martin
1816/17		Threapwood

Over has a Victorian stand paten made from a paten dated 1663

(Sweetmeat) Dishes

c.1640		Nantwich – sweetmeat dish (paten)
Mid 17th century		Wrenbury – sweetmeat dish
c.1765	2	Disley – dishes – patens – EV in rectangle

Salvers

1735/36	Rostherne
1766/67	Great Budworth
1767/68	Tattenhall
1768/69	Delamere
1786/87	Eccleston
1795/96	Marple

Tazze

1709/10	Astbury
No date	Chelford

Cruet

1833/34	Christleton

Ewers

1716/17		Stockport St Mary
1727/28		Coddington
1728/29		Chester St Olave – ewer/flagon – Grosvenor Museum, 1988
?1765	2	Disley – no marks – EV in rectangle
1771/72		Stoak
1774/75	2	Frodsham
1796/97		Dodleston
1809/10		Burton – stolen 1995 – not recovered
1832/33		Whitegate

Flagons

1659/60	2	Nantwich
1660/61		Brereton
1662/63	2	Chester Cathedral (one unmarked)
1668/69		Prestbury
1677/78		Chester Cathedral – part of the Leycester Warren bequest

APPENDIX 5: LIST OF PLATE IN PARISHES

1685/86		Lower Peover
1688/89		Carrington – transferred to Partington
1697		Chester St Bridget – transferred to Chester St Mary on the Hill – Grosvenor Museum, 1988
1701/02	2	Chester St Michael – Grosvenor Museum, 1988
1703/04		Runcorn
1705/06		Acton
1707/08		Wrenbury
c.1710		Little Budworth – Francis Garthorne – mark entered 1697
1711/12		Eaton
1711/12		Pott Shrigley
1711/12		Tarporley
1712/13		Chester St Mary without the Walls
1713/14		Chester St Peter
1716/17	2	Astbury
1718/19		Congleton
1718/19		Great Barrow – flagon/jug
1718/19		Stockport St Mary
1719/20		Church Hulme
1719/20	2	Great Budworth
1719/20		Chester St Peter
1722/23		Christleton
1725/26		Chester St Thomas of Canterbury – transferred from Chester Cathedral
1726/27		Wybunbury
1727/28	2	Chester Holy and Undivided Trinity – transferred to Blacon
1729/30	2	Chester St John the Baptist
1731/32		Cheadle
1731/32		Daresbury
1731/32		Halton
1732/33		Middlewich
1732/33		Wistaston
1733/34	2	Sandbach
1735/36	2	Bunbury
1736/37		Heswall
1739/40		Middlewich
1745/46	2	Macclesfield
1746/47		Eccleston – flagon/jug
1747/48	2	Over – on loan to Grosvenor Museum, Chester
1748/49		Mottram
1749/50	2	Barthomley
1752/53		Alderley Edge

1759/60		Chelford
1759/60		Goostrey
1761/62		Tattenhall
1763/64	2	Frodsham
1763/64		Mottram
1766/67		Grappenhall
1768/69		Knutsford
1769/70		Burleydam
1774/75		Harthill
1775/76	2	Bowdon
1776/77		Tarvin
1781/82		Farndon
1789/90		Alsager
1795/96	2	Malpas
1811/12		Haslington
1811/12		Marple
1816/17		Threapwood
1817/18		Church Lawton
1821/22		Whitewell
1824/25		Stockport St Thomas
1827/28		Birkenhead
1832/33		Whitegate

FLAGON RING OR STAND

1711/12		Chester St Mary without the Walls

JUGS

1719/20		Wrenbury
1729/30		Warmingham
1734/35		Handley
1735/36	2	Rostherne (jugs/flagons)
1768/69		Tushingham
1784/85		Hargrave (jug/flagon)
1804/05		Norbury
1834/35		Tintwistle – claret jug – sold 1980

BEAKER

c.1700	Hargrave – no date mark – 1700 shown in inscription

LOVING CUP

1774/75	Tarvin – on loan to Grosvenor Museum

TANKARD

1677/78	Wybunbury – sold

LADLE

Late 18th/early 19th century	Malpas

SPOONS

?	Great Barrow – strainer spoon – missing
1691/92	Chester Cathedral – strainer spoon
c.1720	Wybunbury – probably provincial
?18th century	Chester St Mary without the Walls – mote spoon – marks illegible
?18th century	Nantwich – apostle spoon – Swiss

WINE STRAINERS

Late 18th century	Frodsham
1822/23	Nantwich

MACE

1787/88	Chester Cathedral

VERGES

16th century	Chester Cathedral – The Dean's Verge
?1591	Chester Cathedral – The Canon's Verge

BAPTISMAL BASIN

1744/45	Audlem

CANDLESTICKS

1678/79	Chester Cathedral
1809/10	Malpas

SERVICE BOOKS MOUNTS

?	Chester St Mary without the Walls – no date
18th century	Chester St Mary without the Walls
?	Chester St Mary without the Walls – no marks
?	Chester St Mary without the Walls – no marks

WAFER BOX

?	Audlem – no date – of German origin

Appendix 6
Grosvenor Museum

The following plate, once in parish churches in the diocese, was purchased by the museum and is now housed in the Ridgway Gallery. The pieces are fully described in Peter Boughton, *Catalogue of Silver in the Grosvenor Museum*, Chester, Phillimore & Co. 2000, to which readers are referred. Numbers given are the catalogue numbers.

CHESTER ST BRIDGET

- 11 Communion cup by Richard Richardson I Type 3 (Compendium 6815), 1718/19, Chester.
- 101 Silver gilt flagon by Hugh Roberts (Grimwade 2382), 1697, London. (Plate 38.)
- 102 Pair of plate patens by Hugh Roberts (Grimwade 2382), 1697, London. (Plate 39.)

CHESTER ST MARTIN

- 103 Parcel gilt communion cup by Peter, Ann and William (I) Bateman (Grimwade 2141), 1804/05, London.

CHESTER ST MICHAEL

- 1 Communion cup by William Mutton (Compendium 1), *c.*1570, Chester. (Plate 40.)
- 12 Communion cup by Richard Richardson I Type 3 (Compendium 6815), 1723/24, Chester.
- 12 Standing paten by Richard Richardson I Type 3 (Compendium 6815), 1723/24, Chester.
- 13 Plate paten by Richard Richardson I Type 3 (Compendium 6815), 1724/25, Chester.
- 98 Silver gilt standing cup/communion cup by Edward South (Jackson, p.116), 1635/36, London. (Plate 41.)
- 99 Pair of flagons by Seth Lofthouse (Grimwade 1945), 1701/02, London.

CHESTER ST OLAVE

- 100 Ewer/flagon by Humphrey Payne (Grimwade 1061), 1728/29, London.

Stoak St Lawrence

- 2 Communion cup and paten by William Mutton (Compendium 1), c.1570-78, Chester.
- 104 Waiter/paten by Richard Rugg (Grimwade 2420), 1764/65, London.
- 105 Ewer/flagon by John Dare (Grimwade 1244), 1771/72, London.

Appendix 7

List of Parishes and their Plate

Note: (S) denotes for use when visiting the sick

Chester Cathedral
Chalice		1496/97

Restoration silver
Communion cup		1662/63
Paten covers	2	1662/63
Stand patens	2	1662/63
Flagons	2	1662/63
Alms dish		1673/74
Candlesticks	2	1678/79
Alms plates	2	1737/38
Communion cup		1685/86
The Dean's verge		16th century?
The Canon's verge		1591
Mitred mace		1787/88
Strainer spoon		1691/92
Communion cup		?Swiss, *c.*1630
Chalice and cover (or ciborium)		?Dutch, *c.*1661

The Leycester Warren bequest
Communion cup		1677/78
Paten		1677/78
Alms box		1677/78
Flagon		1677/78
Communion cups	2	1838/39

Acton
Plate paten	17th century
Communion cup	1633/34
Flagon	1705/06

Appendix 7: List of Parishes and their Plate

Stand patens	2	1706/07
Communion cup		1764/65

ALDERLEY EDGE
Plate paten		16th century
Communion cup		1696/97
Communion cup (S)		c.1697
Plate paten (S)		No marks
Stand paten		1713/14
Flagon		1752/53

ALSAGER
Communion cup		1789/90
Plate paten		1789/90
Stand paten		1789/90
Flagon		1789/90

ALTRINCHAM
Base metal only

ASHTON UPON MERSEY
Plate stolen in 1840

ASTBURY
Communion cups	2	1707/08
Stand paten		1707/08
Tazza		1709/10
Paten covers	2	1712/13
Flagons	2	1716/17

ASTON
Chalice		?14th century
Plate paten		?14th century
Stand paten		1675/76

AUDLEM
Communion cup		1635/36
Stand paten (or alms plate)		1683/84
Alms dish		1683/84
Baptismal basin		1744/45
Chalice		c.1725
Wafer box		c.1725

BACKFORD
No early plate

BADDILEY
Plate paten   16th century
Communion cup   1624/25

BARNSTON – see BIRKENHEAD

BARROW – see GREAT BARROW

BARTHOMLEY
Communion cup   1669/70
Communion cup   1676/77
Paten cover   1676/77
Stand paten   1681/82
Flagons   2   1749/50

BEBINGTON
Stand paten   1704/05
Communion cup   1736/37
Communion cup   1769/70

BIDSTON
No record

BIRKENHEAD
Stand paten   1698/99
Communion cups   2   1827/28
Plate paten   1827/28
Flagon   1827/28

BLACON – see CHESTER HOLY
AND UNDIVIDED TRINITY

BOWDON
Alms dish   1705/06
Communion cups   2   1775/76
Salver patens   2   1775/76
Flagons   2   1775/76

BRERETON
Communion cup   1653/54
Flagon   1660/61

Stand paten		1660/61
Communion cup		1722/23
Stand paten		1722/23
Alms dish		1722/23

BRUERA
Communion cup		1695/96

BUGLAWTON
Communion cups	2	1839/40
Stand paten		1839/40
Alms paten		1839/40

BUNBURY
Paten		*c.*1600
Communion cup		1632/33
Stand paten		1716/17
Flagons	2	1735/36
Alms plates	2	1747/48
Communion cup		1834/35

BURLEYDAM
Communion cup		1769/70
Paten		Marks illegible
Stand paten		1769/70
Flagon		1769/70

BURTON
Communion cup		1809/10
Alms plate		1809/10
Ewer		1809/10

CALVELEY
Communion cup		1796/97

CARRINGTON
Flagon		1688/89
Stand paten		1688/89
Communion cup		1759/60

CHEADLE
Communion cup		17th century
Paten or alms dish		1666/67
Stand paten		1718/19

Flagon		1731/32
Communion cups	2	1804/05

CHELFORD
Communion cup	1652/53
Stand paten	1693/94
Alms plate	1709/10
Flagon	1759/60
Tazza	No date

CHESTER CITY CHURCHES

BISHOP'S PRIVATE CHAPEL
Communion cup (S)	Inscribed 1731

CHRIST CHURCH
Stand paten		1725/26
Communion cups	2	1821/22
Alms plate		1838/39

HOLY AND UNDIVIDED TRINITY
Communion cup		1570-75
Paten		1570-75
Stand paten		1694/95
Flagons	2	1727/28
Communion cup		1752/53

ST JOHN THE BAPTIST
Communion cup		1633/34
Paten		1664/65
Communion cup		1672/73
Alms dish		Inscribed 1683
Paten		1717/18
Communion cup (S)		1725/26
Paten cover (S)		1725/26
Flagons	2	1729/30
Alms plates	2	1735/36

ST JOHN WITHOUT THE NORTHGATE
Communion cup	1641/42
Stand paten	1716/17
Stand paten	*c.*1764
Chalice	1781

ST MARY ON THE HILL – see
ST MARY WITHOUT THE WALLS

ST BRIDGET
Flagon					1697
Plate patens		2		1697/98
Communion cup				1718/19
Communion cup				1783/84

ST MARTIN
Communion cups		2		1804/05
Stand paten				1805/06

ST MARY WITHOUT THE WALLS
Communion cup				c.1570
Paten cover				c.1570
Paten					1638/39
Paten (stand paten)			c.1683
Flagon					1712/13
Flagon ring or stand			1711/12
Communion cup				1759/60
Paten cover				1759/60
Alms dish				1822/23
Mote spoon				18th century
Service book mounts	4		18th century

ST MICHAEL
Communion cup				c.1570
Communion cup				1635/36
Flagons			2		1701/02
Communion cup				1723/24
Stand paten				1723/24
Plate paten				1724/25

ST OLAVE
Ewer/flagon				1728/29

ST PAUL
Communion cup				1804/05
Communion cup				1830/31

ST PETER
Stand paten				1708/09

Communion cup		1713/14
Flagon		1713/14
Flagon		1719/20
Alms plate		1736/37
Communion cup		1762/63

ST THOMAS OF CANTERBURY
Communion cups	2	1725/26
Stand patens	2	1725/26
Alms dish		1725/26
Flagon		1725/26
Communion cup (S)		1724/25
Paten cover (S)		c.1725

CHRISTLETON
Alms basin	1595/96
Flagon	1722/23
Communion cup	1722/23
Stand paten	1722/23
Alms dish	1763/64
Communion cup (S)	1833/34
Paten cover (S)	1833/34
Cruet	1833/34

CHURCH HULME
Stand paten	1700/01
Flagon	1719/20
Stand paten	1722/23
Communion cup	1723/24
Communion cup	1776/77
Paten cover	1776/77

CHURCH LAWTON
Communion cup	1817/18
Paten	1817/18
Flagon	1817/18
Communion cup	1835/36

CHURCH MINSHULL
Communion cup	1704/05

CODDINGTON
Stand paten	1725/26
Ewer	1727/28

Communion cup		1727/28
Paten		1727/28

CONGLETON
Communion cup		1696/97
Stand paten		1696/97
Stand paten		1699/1700
Communion cup		1709/10
Flagon		1718/19
Alms dish		No marks

COTEBROOK
Communion cup		Elizabethan
Paten		Elizabethan
Stand paten		c.1684

DARESBURY
Stand paten		1654/55
Flagon		1731/32
Stand paten		1746/47
Communion cup		1773/74

DAVENHAM
Communion cup		1570/71
Communion cup		1633/34
Stand paten		1707/08

DELAMERE
Salver		1768/69

DISLEY
Communion cup		c.1765
Cover		No marks
Dishes (patens)	2	No marks
Ewers	2	No marks

DODLESTON
Communion cup		1732/33
Stand paten		1805/06
Ewer		1796/97

EATON
Flagon		1711/12
Stand paten		Marks illegible
Communion cups	2	1748/49

ECCLESTON
Communion cup		Inscribed 1683
Paten		1736/37
Flagon/jug		1746/47
Salver		1786/87

FARNDON
Paten cover		*c.*1622
Flagon		1781/82
Communion cup		1792/93

FOREST CHAPEL
Communion cup		*c.*1720
Paten cover		*c.*1720

FRODSHAM
Communion cups	2	1763/64
Alms dish		No date letter
Flagons	2	1763/64
Stand patens	2	1766/67
Ewer		1774/75
Wine strainer		18th century

GAWSWORTH
Communion cup		No marks
Paten		No marks
Communion cup		1763/64

GOOSTREY
Stand paten		1705/06
Communion cup		1759/60
Flagon		1759/60

GRAPPENHALL
Flagon		1766/67
Communion cup		1797/98
Paten cover		1797/98
Alms dishes	2	1797/98
Communion cup (S)		1825/26
Paten cover (S)		1825/26

GREAT BARROW
Communion cup		*c.*1662
Paten cover		*c.*1662
Flagon/jug		1718/19

Great Budworth

Communion cup		No date
Paten		No date
Stand paten		1743/44
Flagons	2	1719/20
Communion cup (S)		1763/64
Paten (S)		1763/64
Salver		1766/67
Communion cups	2	1796/97

Guilden Sutton

Communion cup	1821/22

Halton

Communion cup	1731/32
Stand paten	1731/32
Flagon	1731/32

Handley

Communion cup	16th century
Jug	1734/35
Paten	Victorian

Hargrave

Beaker	*c.*1700
Paten	*c.*1700
Jug/flagon	1784/85

Harthill

Stand paten	1769-80
Communion cup	1773/74
Flagon	1774/75
Alms dish	1775/76

Haslington

Communion cup	1811/12
Paten cover	1811/12
Flagon	1811/12
Alms dish	1811/12

Hazel Grove – see Norbury

Heswall

Stand paten	1718/19
Communion cup	1739/40

Flagon		1736/37
Chalice		?Danish

HOLMES CHAPEL – see CHURCH HULME

HUNTINGTON – see also
CHESTER ST MARTIN

Communion cups	2	1804/05
Stand paten		1805/06

INCE
Communion cup		1788/89

KNUTSFORD
Communion cup		17th century
Flagon		1768/69

LITTLE BUDWORTH
Communion cup		1711/12
Paten cover		1711/12
Flagon		c.1710

LOWER PEOVER
Flagon		1685/86
Communion cup		1715/16
Stand patens	2	1715/16

LOWER WHITLEY
Communion cup		1824/25

LYMM
Communion cup		?1623/24
Communion cup		1691/92
Paten cover		1691/92
Stand paten		1691/92

MACCLESFIELD
Communion cups	2	1624/25
Paten covers	2	1624/25
Stand paten		1719/20
Flagons	2	1745/46
Alms plates	2	1758/59

MALPAS
Communion cup		1674/75

Paten cover		1674/75
Communion cup		1717/18
Paten/alms plate		1718/19
Alms plates	2	1742/43
Communion cups	2	1765/66
Paten/alms plate		1772/73
Flagons	2	1795/96
Candlesticks	2	1809/10
Ladle		*c.*1800

MARBURY
Stand paten		1632/33
Communion cup		1742/43

MARPLE
Communion cup		1629/30
Salver		1795/96
Flagon		1811/12

MARTON
Communion cup		1597/98

MIDDLEWICH
Communion cup		1608/09
Communion cup		1667/68
Stand paten		1667/68
Flagon		1732/33
Flagon		1739/40
Communion cup (S)		No marks
Paten cover (S)		No marks

MOBBERLEY
Communion cup		1571/72
Communion cup		1835/36

MOTTRAM
Stand paten		1709/10
Flagon		1748/49
Flagon		1763/64
Communion cups	2	1779/80

NANTWICH
Communion cup		1604/05
Paten cover		1604/05
Communion cup		1633/34
Flagons	2	1659/60

Sweetmeat dish (paten)		c.1640
Alms dishes	2	c.1740
Wine strainer		1822/23
Apostle spoon		18th century

NESTON
Plate/alms dish		1683/84
Communion cup		1717/18
Paten		1752/53
Communion cup		1780/81

NETHER TABLEY – see
CHESTER CATHEDRAL

NETHER WHITLEY – see
LOWER WHITLEY

NORBURY
Communion cup		1804/05
Paten cover		1804/05
Jug		1804/05

NORTHWICH
Stand paten		1764/65

OVER
Communion cup		1663/64
Flagons	2	1747/48
Stand paten		1747/48

OVERCHURCH
Communion cup		1618/19
Paten cover		1618/19

POTT SHRIGLEY
Paten cover		Inscribed 1576
Communion cup		1622/23
Communion cup		1711/12
Stand patens	2	1711/12
Flagon		1711/12

PRESTBURY
Communion cup		?1626 or 1628
Flagon		1668/69

Communion cups	2	1676/77
Stand patens	2	1770/71

RINGWAY AND HALE BARNS
Communion cup		1719/20
Stand paten		1725/26

ROSTHERNE
Jugs/flagons	2	1735/36
Paten		1735/36
Salver		1735/36
Communion cups	2	1770/71

RUNCORN
Communion cup		No marks
Flagon		1703/04
Communion cup		Inscribed 1670
Stand paten		No marks

SANDBACH
Communion cups	2	1656/57
Paten covers	2	1656/57
Alms dish		1709/10
Flagons	2	1733/34
Alms plate		*c*.1737

SHOCKLACH
Stand paten		1691/92
Communion cup		1799

SHOTWICK
Communion cup		*c*.1685

SIDDINGTON
Plate stolen in 1792

STOAK
Communion cup		No date
Paten/salver		1764/65
Ewer		1771/72

STOCKPORT ST MARY
Communion cup		1580/81
Paten cover		1580/81

Alms dish		1674/75
Stand paten		1715/16
Ewer		1716/17
Flagon		1718/19
Communion cup		1758/59
Paten cover		1758/59
Plate paten		1758/59

STOCKPORT ST PETER
Communion cup		1767/68

STOCKPORT ST THOMAS
Communion cup		1824/25
Flagon		1824/25

STRETTON
No early plate

SWETTENHAM
Communion cup		1704/05
Stand paten		1713/14

TABLEY HALL – see
CHESTER CATHEDRAL

TARPORLEY
Communion cup		1711/12
Stand paten		1711/12
Flagon		1711/12
Communion cup (S)		1724/25
Stand paten (S)		1726/27
Alms plates	2	1737/38
Chalice		No date
Paten		No date

TARVIN
Loving cup		1774/75
Communion cups	2	1775/76
Stand paten		1775/76
Stand paten		No date
Flagon		1776/77

TATTENHALL
Flagon		1761/62
Communion cup		1762/63

Salver	1767/68
Stand paten/paten cover	1767/68

THORNTON-LE-MOORS
Communion cup	*c.*1567
Paten cover	*c.*1567
Stand paten	1731/32

THREAPWOOD
Communion cup	1816/17
Paten cover	1816/17
Stand paten	1816/17
Flagon	1816/17

THURSTASTON
Communion cup	1826/27
Paten	1826/27

TILSTON
Communion cup	1666/67
Paten cover	1666/67

TUSHINGHAM
Communion cup	1768/69
Jug	1768/69

WARBURTON
No early plate

WARMINGHAM
Communion cup	1663/64
Paten	1664/65
Jug	1729/30
Stand paten	1740/41
Alms dish	1786/87

WAVERTON
Communion cup	1711/12

WEAVERHAM
Stand paten	1714/15

WHITEGATE
Communion cup	1832/33
Paten	1832/33

Ewer 1832/33
Flagon 1832/33

WHITEWELL
Communion cup 1817/18
Paten 1824/25
Alms dish 1819/20
Flagon 1821/22

WILMSLOW
No early plate

WINCLE
Communion cup 1645/46
Paten 1645/46

WISTASTON
Stand paten 1720/21
Flagon 1732/33
Communion cups 2 1791/92

WITTON – see NORTHWICH

WOODCHURCH
Communion cup No date

WRENBURY
Sweetmeat dish 17th century
Communion cup 1664/65
Flagon 1707/08
Jug 1719/20
Communion cup 1727/28

WYBUNBURY
Communion cup 1677/78
Stand paten 1702/03
Spoon c.1720
Communion cup 1728/29
Flagon 1726/27
Communion cup (S) 1830/31
Paten (S) ?1830/31

Bibliography

Ball 1905a: T. Stanley Ball, 'Tarvin Church Plate', *Chester Observer*, 5 August 1905

Ball 1905b: T. Stanley Ball, 'Shotwick Church Plate', *Chester Courant*, 30 August 1905

Ball 1907: T. Stanley Ball, *Church Plate of the City of Chester* (1907)

Beazley: F.C. Beazley, *Thurstaston in Cheshire: An Account of the Parish, Manor and Church* (1924)

Bennett: Douglas Bennett, *Collecting Irish Silver 1637-1900* (1984)

Bristow: Adrian Bristow, *Dr Johnson and Mrs Thrale's tour in North Wales* (1995)

Brocklehurst: Charles Brocklehurst, *Festival Exhibition of Ecclesiastical and Secular Plate* (1951)

Budden: C.W. Budden, *Old English Churches, their architecture, furniture, and customs as illustrated by the Wirral peninsula* (1925)

Burne: R.V.H. Burne, *Chester Cathedral* (1958)

Cartlidge: J.E. Gordon Cartlidge, *Newbold Astbury and its history: a descriptive and historical account of an ancient Cheshire church and parish* (1915)

Cheshire Sheaf, New Series (1891); 3rd Series (1937)

Chester Cathedral, 'minute of 25 November 1869', *Chapter Act book* (1841-45)

Chester Festival Silver Exhibition, *Catalogue of Silver from Chester and other areas including London and Edinburgh at the Grosvenor Museum, Chester* (1973)

Cox 1963: Canon F. Cox, *Centenary History of the Parish of Ringway* (1963)

Cox 1975: Marjorie Cox, *A History of John Deane's Grammar School* (1975)

Croston: James Croston (ed.), *The history of the County Palatine and Duchy of Lancaster*, rev. edn (1888-93)

Delieb and Roberts: Eric Delieb and Michael Roberts, *The Great Silver Manufactory* (1971)

Duffy: Eamon Duffy, *The Stripping of the Altars* (1992)

Earwaker 1880: J.P. Earwaker, *East Cheshire* (1880)

Earwaker 1890: J.P. Earwaker, *History of Sandbach* (1890)

Earwaker 1898: J.P. Earwaker, *The History of the Church and Parish of St Mary on-the-Hill, Chester* (1898)

Glynne: Sir Stephen R. Glynne, *Notes on the Churches of Cheshire*, 2nd series ed., Revd J.A. Atkinson, vol. 63 (1894)

Grimwade: Arthur G. Grimwade, *London Goldsmiths 1697-1837: Their Marks and Lives* (1976)

Hall: James Hall, *A History of the Town and Parish of Nantwich* (1883)

Heginbotham: Henry Heginbotham, *Stockport Ancient and Modern* (1882)

Holme: Randle Holme, *The Academy of Armory, or, a Storehouse of Armory and Blazon, etc* (1688)

Jackson: Ian Pickford Jackson, (ed.), *Jackson's Silver & Gold Marks of England, Scotland & Ireland* (1989)

Jackson 1905: Charles James Jackson, *English Goldsmiths and their Marks* (1905)

Jackson 1911: C.J. Jackson, *An Illustrated History of English Plate, Ecclesiastical and Secular* (1911)

Jackson 1921: Sir Charles James Jackson, *English Goldsmiths and their Marks*, 2nd edn (1921)

Jones 1906: E. Alfred Jones, *Church Plate of the Diocese of Bangor* (1906)

Jones 1981: Kevin Crisp Jones, *The Silversmiths of Birmingham and their Marks 1750-1980* (1981)

Morris: Rupert H. Morris, *Chester in the Plantagenet and Tudor Reigns* (1894)

Nightingale: J.S. Nightingale, *The Church Plate of the County of Dorset* (1889)

Oman: Charles Oman, *English Church Plate 597-1830* (1957)

Pevsner and Hubbard: Nikolaus Pevsner and Edward Hubbard, *Buildings of England. Cheshire* (1971)

PSA: Proceedings of the Society of Antiquaries

Richards: Raymond Richards, *Old Cheshire Churches*, 1947

Ridgway 1968: Maurice H. Ridgway, *Chester Goldsmiths from early times to 1726* (1968)

Ridgway 1980: M.H. Ridgway, 'The Early Plate of Chester Cathedral', *Journal of the Chester Archaeological Society*, vol. 63, pp.95-108 (1980)

Ridgway 1985: Maurice H. Ridgway, *Chester Silver 1727-1837* (1985)

Ridgway 1996: Maurice H. Ridgway, *Chester Silver 1837-1962 with special reference to the Chester Plate Duty Books 1784-1840* (1996)

Ridgway 1997: Maurice H. Ridgway, *Church Plate of the St. Asaph Diocese* (1997)

Ridgway and Priestley: Maurice H. Ridgway and Philip T. Priestley, *The Compendium of Chester Gold & Silver Marks 1570 to 1962* (2004)

RSLC: Record Society of Lancashire and Cheshire

Scott: S. Cooper Scott, *Guide to the Church of St John the Baptist in the City of Chester* (1899)

Simpson: Frank Simpson, *A History of the Church of St Peter in Chester* (1909)

Stone: Sir Leonard Stone, *Bunbury Papers*, No.6 (1955)

THSLC: Transactions of the Historic Society of Lancashire and Cheshire

Weston: John Weston, *Historical Notes and Records of the Parish Church (St Helen's), Northwich* (1908)

W.I. Scrapbook: Barrow Women's Institute, *The Book of Barrow* (1952)